HN 720

The Crisis of Welfare in East Asia

The Crisis of Welfare in East Asia

Edited by
James Lee and
Kam-wah Chan

LEXINGTON BOOK
A division of
ROWMAN & LITTLEFIELD PUBLISHERS, INC.
Lanham • Boulder • New York • Toronto • Plymouth, UK

LEXINGTON BOOKS

A division of Rowman & Littlefield Publishers, Inc.
A wholly owned subsidiary of The Rowman & Littlefield Publishing Group, Inc.
4501 Forbes Boulevard, Suite 200
Lanham, MD 20706

Estover Road
Plymouth PL6 7PY
United Kingdom

Copyright © 2007 by Lexington Books

All rights reserved. No part of this publication may be reproduced, stored in a retrieval system, or transmitted in any form or by any means, electronic, mechanical, photocopying, recording, or otherwise, without the prior permission of the publisher.

British Library Cataloguing in Publication Information Available

Library of Congress Cataloging-in-Publication Data

The crisis of welfare in East Asia / edited by James Lee and Kam-wah Chan.
   p. cm.
  Includes bibliographical references and index.
  ISBN-13: 978-0-7391-1178-9 (cloth : alk. paper)
  ISBN-10: 0-7391-1178-7 (cloth : alk. paper)
  1. East Asia—Social policy. 2. Public welfare—East Asia. I. Lee, James, 1950–
II. Chan, Kam-wah.
  HN720.5.C75 2007
  361.6'1095—dc22
                                                           2007017203

∞™ The paper used in this publication meets the minimum requirements of American National Standard for Information Sciences—Permanence of Paper for Printed Library Materials, ANSI/NISO Z39.48-1992.

To Chun-yu

Contents

List of Figures	ix
List of Tables	xi
Preface	xv
Acknowledgments	xvii

1 Deciphering Productivism and Developmentalism
  in East Asian Social Welfare 1
  James Lee

2 Emerging Issues in Developmental Welfarism in Singapore 27
  Beng Huat Chua

3 Aging Population in East Asia: Impacts on Social Protection
  and Social Policy Reforms in Japan, Korea, and Taiwan 43
  Chyong Fang Ko, Kyeung Mi Oh, and Tetsuo Ogawa

4 Change and Inertia in Housing Policy: Japanese Housing
  System during Economic Crisis 71
  Connie P. Y. Tang

5 Globalization, Regime Transformation, and Social Policy
  Development in Taiwan 101
  Wan I. Lin and Wen-Chi Grace Chou

Contents

6   The Crisis of Social Security Financing in Hong Kong   125
Raymond Man Hung Ngan

7   Age Discrimination in the Labor Market: Barriers to Active Aging in Hong Kong   147
Raymond Man Hung Ngan, Ping Kong Kam, and Jacky Chau Kiu Cheung

8   Contradictions of Welfare and the Market: The Case of Hong Kong   165
Sam Wai-kam Yu

9   Managing the SARS Crisis in Hong Kong: Reviving the Economy or Reconstructing a Healthy Society   185
Kam-wah Chan and Lai Ching Leung

10   Between Idealism and Realism: The Evolution of Full Employment Policy in China   203
Ho Lup Fung

11   The Coming Housing Crisis of China   223
Ya Peng Zhu and James Lee

12   Concluding Observations: Is There a Crisis of Welfare in East Asia?   243
Kam-wah Chan

Index   257

About the Contributors   265

List of Figures

4.1	Housing Production, Housing Consumption Flowchart	77
4.2	House Prices in Japan 1990–2004	81
4.3	Ratio of Housing to Non-Housing Loans from Japanese Government, 1990–99	85
5.1	Social Welfare Expenditures from 1986–2002 in Taiwan	110
6.1	Increase in Recurrent Social Welfare Expenditure, 1994–2004	127
6.2	Unemployment Rate, 1997–2004	129
6.3	Gini Coefficient in Hong Kong, 1971–2001	129
6.4	Consolidated Deficits, AKSAR, 1997–2007	130
6.5	Increase in CSSA Cases, 1994–2005	132
6.6	Increase in Aging Population, 1981–2031	134
6.7	Social Security Expenditures in Hong Kong, 1993–2004	136
6.8	Social Welfare Expenditures in Hong Kong, 1993–2004	136
7.1	Age Discrimination in the Labor Market	152
9.1	Age Distribution of Infected and Fatal Cases	187

List of Tables

1.1	The State of Welfare in East Asia Before and After Economic Crisis in 1997	2
1.2	Singapore Housing Indicators	13
3.1	Population Structure of Taiwan Area: 1951–2051	52
3.2	Living Arrangements of Elderly People in South Korea 1997 (%)	64
4.1	Housing Tenure in Japan, 1978–2003	75
4.2	The Sixth and Seventh Five-year Housing Construction Program for Japan, 1991–2000 ('000 units)	84
4.3	New Dwellings Started by Source of Funds in Japan, 1990–2003	86
4.4	Housing Tenure in Tokyo, 1988–1998	88
4.5	Households Living below the Minimum Housing Standards in Tokyo in Comparison with Japan, 1998	90
5.1	A Brief Description of Recent Elections in Taiwan by Different Parties	107
5.2	Major Economic Indicators and Government Spending	117

7.1	Background Characteristics by Age Range	151
7.2	Internal Consistency (Reliability Alpha)	152
7.3	Means of Perceived Discrimination Against Older Workers by Age Range	153
7.4	Means of Negative Stereotypes About Older Workers by Age Range	154
7.5	Perceived Organizational Goals by Age Range	155
7.6	Health Situation by Age Range	155
7.7	Standardized Effects of Causal Factors on Perceived Discrimination Against Older Workers	156
7.8	Means of Perceived Causes of Age Discrimination by Age Range	157
7.9	Social Constructionist Attribution by Age Range	158
7.10	Comparison of Perceived Consequences of Age Discrimination by Age Range	158
7.11	Perceived Harm of Age Discrimination to General Workers by Age Range	158
7.12	Perceived Harm of Age Discrimination to Society by Age Range	159
7.13	Perceived Harm of Age Discrimination to Older People by Age Range	159
7.14	Means of Perceived Harm of Age Discrimination to the Organization by Age Range	159
7.15	Preference for Legislation Against Age Discrimination by Age Range	160
8.1	Disregarded Earning Scheme under CSSA	174
8.2	Composition of CSSA Recipients in 2001–2002	175
9.1	Age Distribution of Infected and Fatal Cases	191

List of Tables

10.1	Urban Employment Conditions of China in Terms of Ownership Structure	215
11.1	Housing Completed in Urban and Rural Areas and Housing Situations of Urban Residents (1978–1999)	227
11.2	Comparison of the Two Housing Reform Approaches	230
11.3	Home Purchase at Different Periods in Cities	233
11.4	Housing Situation by Occupation	233
11.5	Housing Situation by Rank	234
11.6	Ratio of House Price to Household Income in Major Cities in 2004	234

Preface

On January 13, 2007, the *South China Morning*—a leading local English daily in Hong Kong—carried an interesting feature article titled "It's About Fairness, Not the Widening Wealth Gap." In it the author condemned the way social inequality in Hong Kong has been legitimized by the rich few and how the government played a role in fostering such social division. The undertone was that success or failure in Hong Kong is very much seen as a matter of an individual's ability to cope and survive. Welfare is essentially an individual's responsibility, not the state's; and the state will only come to rescue those who are proven least able to help themselves. That roughly summarizes Hong Kong's dominant approach toward welfare! The problem is this approach creates more problems than it could solve and is far from the ideal East Asian welfare model as portrayed by some academics who did brief research in the city. Hong Kong is still besieged by unemployment and rapidly deteriorating social inequalities. The essence of the news article is one among many who are increasingly critical of the way in which social welfare is structured, produced, consumed, and interpreted here.

Taking a broader view, for a long time since the 1990s, East Asia's social welfare has been depicted by Western scholars as one in which a high standard of living was achieved without burdening the state with heavy social expenditures. Much of what the West loathed about a welfare state doesn't seem to find root or sympathy here. We are sometimes called "the light welfare states." Economic growth and social welfare had strangely been made bedfellows as government championed full employment and workfare policies. The poor in East Asia, as was once widely put, if given work, would produce and thrive. The prime minister of Singapore, PM Lee, said in a speech on November 13,

2006: "Singapore has treated social welfare as a dirty word. The opposition and the Workers' Party have called for a *permanent unconditional needs-based welfare system*. I think that is an even dirtier five words." How far is it true that East Asia practices a different welfare model from the West, and how far should the West look to us as welfare innovators?

While the background of the Chinese scholars represented here is diverse, one common theme which emerges from the collection is that East Asian societies are facing a very similar set of social problems and social policy issues as the West. The well regarded East Asian welfare model doesn't seem to be alive and well as some anticipated. Even widely dubbed as ideologically the most social democratic place in East Asia, Singapore's income inequality worsened in the 2006 UN Human Development Report (with a Gini index of 42.5 percent), notwithstanding the fact Singapore is East Asia's second richest country after Japan, with a GDP of US$27,000. Focusing on work, the Singapore Manpower Ministry data revealed that among the 124,000 new jobs created in 2006, 45 percent of them went to non-Singaporeans. FDI and labor growth do not necessarily benefit the people. Hong Kong's economy went through a painful period of recovery after the Asian economic crisis and it is only since 2004 the economy slowly recovered. Even then, a recent study by a pro-government think tank, the Bauhinia Foundation, revealed the sad fact that although the economy has done better, people at the lower end of the income ladder actually do not benefit from it. In fact, working class income is still 26.8 percent below the 1997 peak, despite per capita income of 2006 having broken the 1997 record.

It is the presence of these contradictions in East Asian societies, and the urge to find an explanation for them that set the scene for this volume. South Korea and Taiwan present two extremely interesting cases of social welfare in the last decade, both beset by their turbulent political environments. Sometimes politics could provide social welfare great opportunities, such as in the case of South Korea and Singapore; equally, it could stifle its development, like the case of Taiwan and Hong Kong. While we do not espouse to provide answers to all our questions, we do consider ourselves at a vantage point to do this project better, as most contributors are brought up in this region. We also believe that by clearing up some of our misconceptions about East Asian social welfare systems, we are thus one step nearer toward avoiding any possible impending crisis.

Acknowledgments

This book germinated from a group of Chinese scholars who are concerned about the way in which East Asian social welfare has been interpreted or understood in the West. We are indebted to a research grant from the Governance in Asia Research Center (GARC) of the Faculty of Humanities and Social Sciences, City University of Hong Kong, for editorial and data collection work. We are indebted to support from Professor Julia Tao, the GARC center director. Every book has its primary intellectual mentor. James Midgley (University of California at Berkeley), his social development approach, and his many works in international social policy have provided an important theoretical foundation for this book. We are grateful to the staff of Lexington Books who provided us highly professional advice throughout the process.

1

Deciphering Productivism and Developmentalism in East Asian Social Welfare

James Lee

The last decade of the twentieth century has seen a thriving interest in the economic successes of four East Asian economies: namely, Singapore, Hong Kong, South Korea, and Taiwan. These tiger economies have been hailed as achieving successes both in sustaining a high growth economy and a low social expenditure regime (Jacobs 2000). Productivism as a model of social development, characterized by the overriding importance and emphasis on economic imperatives in all social policy arenas, has been put forth as the key variable in explaining their successes (Holliday 2000, 2005; Gough 2004). Notwithstanding the theoretical plausibility of such characterization, the 1997 Asian Financial Crisis and its aftermath has led many to question the robustness of the productivism thesis. In fact, since the economic crisis, all tiger economies have, to varying degree and extent, suffered from maladies arising from unemployment, widening urban poverty, and income inequalities. As a consequence, we find rising social expenditures on the one hand and decapacitated families losing intra-familial support on the other. Similar to many Western industrial economies, urban welfare politics have been intensified as the system fails to ameliorate economic hardship and family failures. This scenario could be partly explained by the statistics in Table 1.1.

The five East Asia high growth societies in Table 1.1 all registered a substantial increase in unemployment rate after the financial crisis. For Japan, one can argue that its unemployment situation has been more structural than incidental. The Asian crisis of 1997 merely aggravated its labor situation, but was not a root cause of it. None the less, for the four tiger states, the impact of the economic crisis was much more apparent. They all demonstrated a contraction of the economy as reflected by acute drop of GDP growth rates, with

Table 1.1. The State of Welfare in East Asia Before and After Economic Crisis in 1997

	Hong Kong	Singapore	Taiwan	S. Korea	Japan
Unemployment	3.2 (1995) 6.8 (2004)	2.0 (1995) 4.0 (2004)	1.8 (1995) 4.4 (2004)	2.1 (1995) 3.5 (2004)	3.2 (1995) 5.0 (2001)
GNP per capita (US$)	25280 (1997) 23250 (1999)	32940 (1997) 29610 (1997)	13910 (1997) 13350 (1999)	10550 (1997) 8490 (1999)	37850 (1997) 32230 (1999)
GDP growth rate	13.0 (1987) 3.2 (2003)	9.0 (1990) 1.4 (2003)	7.7 (1990) 0.8 (2003)	9.2 (1990) 3.1 (2003)	5.5 (1996) 1.39 (1999)
% increase in so. security & welfare expense (base yr. 1995)	199% (2000)	440% (2001)	235% (2000)	323% (2001)	—
Contribution rates for social security program	3% (2002) insured 0% employer	20% (2002) insured 16% (2002) employer	2.77% (2002) insured 8.13% (2002) employer	6.81% (2002) insured 8.7% (2002) employer	13.8% (2005) insured 0% employer
Human development index	0.859 (1990) 0.888 (2000)	0.815 (1995) 0.885 (2000)	0.874 (1997) —	0.818 (1995) 0.882 (2000)	0.909 (1990) 0.933 (2000)

Source: *Key Indicators 2004* Asian Development Bank.

the worst case registered in Hong Kong (from 13 percent to 3.2 percent). The consequence was a substantial reduction in per capita GNP, followed by a reduction in domestic consumption and investment. Concomitant with this, unemployment and household economic crises have led to serious blows on existing families' coping ability and hence resulted in a great demand on social welfare. Table 1.1 suggests a twofold to fourfold increase in the percentage of welfare and social security expenditures in the fifth year after the Asian Financial Crisis, with Singapore and South Korea in the lead. What is interesting is why some East Asian countries spend more than a fair share in welfare than others in the post-crisis era? Huck (2005) suggests that cultural and institutional difference account substantially for such difference. Whereas Singapore needs a much bigger boost in welfare to reassert her state capacity and legitimacy as argued by Beng Huat Chua in his chapter, Taiwan's increases have much to do with the development of democratization and the politicization of social policies in a particular socio-political juncture as suggested by chapter 5.

Against this background, this chapter, or more broadly, this edited volume, raises two fundamental sets of questions: one concerns with theories and the other concerns with problems and issues. 1) How robust is the current conception of productivism to explain social welfare development in East Asia? How true is it that East Asian societies are benefiting from a model of welfare that is different from the West in terms of social expenditure patterns and familial support? How is the concept of productivism or productivist social welfare connected to a related set of concepts, *social development* and *developmentalism*? 2) What are the major social policy issues facing East Asian governments and societies under the overarching influence of productivist thinking? Are East Asian welfare systems on a track leading toward sustainable development or if not, is it heading for some form of crisis? My purpose of the first set of questions is thus to take stock of the conceptual development of two groups of theoretical arguments which are termed *productivist* and *developmentalist*, and to distinguish their meaning in terms of social policy change. This chapter is divided into two parts. Section one begins with a re-examination of the current state of explanations on productivist and developmental social welfare, followed by a discussion on the assumptions of productivism and developmentalism. Here it is argued that one basic assumption of the productivist thesis is problematic: the subordination of social policy to economic policy and the inability of social policy to be autonomous or become one of the shaping forces of the social order (Deyo 1992; Holliday 2005). Section two will examine in detail the various issues concerned by this selected group of researchers who share one common concern: the future of welfare in East Asia. Although our selected chapters cover most East Asian countries (including China) these chapters do not aim at providing an overview of the state of social welfare in respective countries. What these chapters attempt to do is to highlight some of the more controversial social policies that carry contemporary policy significance, particularly those that we considered to be more crisis-prone.

THE EMERGENCE OF DEVELOPMENTAL SOCIAL WELFARE

The economic successes of the four tiger states in the 1970s and 1980s caught the attention of the world economy. Many scholars were intrigued by the scenario that some newly industrialized economies (NICs) in East Asia were able to achieve both high economic growth and a high living standard. Initially, academic discussions were focused on whether the emergence of state welfare services was the result of rapid industrialization, as it was posited that the logic of industrialism creates political pressure on the state to provide for welfare (Wilensky and Lebeaux, 1965). Midgley's (1986) paper "Industrialization and Welfare: The Case of the Four Little Tigers" was an important pioneer effort to link the phenomenon of industrial growth with welfare development. He concluded that there was no clear indication to suggest that social welfare services emerged as a result of industrialization. What then accounted for the growth of social welfare in East Asia? As a partial explanation, Midgley suggests that incrementalism might be the key. Interestingly, Midgley's studies unveiled an era of studies all aimed at explaining the nature of social welfare in East Asia. One strand of work begins to emerge in the 1990s focusing on the examination of the link between economic policy and social policy. Given an emphasis on growth and employment, it was observed that East Asian states deliberately used selective social policies to enhance labor productivity and to foster economic growth. Deyo (1992) argues that developmentally-supportive social policies, such as education, social welfare, and housing, were evidently used in East Asia to complement economic policy. Beyond that, it was also the argument about the "light welfare states," where East Asian economies taken as a group did reflect a uniquely low level of social expenditures. Didier Jacobs (2000) of LSE was interested in the sources of low public expenditure on social welfare in Japan, Korea, Taiwan, Hong Kong, and Singapore at the turn of the century. Six factors were analyzed based on aggregated data: the public/private mix of welfare program, the age structure, the maturity of old age pension schemes, the coverage, the relative generosity of social security, the role of enterprises and families as alternative providers. He concluded that East Asian states relied heavily upon the private sector and the family to provide a variety of mandatory welfare benefits normally provided by state welfare in the West and further suggested that demographical changes and the immaturity of pension systems largely accounted for the comparatively low social expenditures (Jacobs, 2000:14). In other words, it is too early to conclude that the "light welfare state thesis" works.

Theorization of developmental social welfare took its most significant turn in the mid-1990s when James Midgley published his seminal article: "Defining Social Development: Historical Trends and Conceptual Formulations" (Midgley, 1994) and his subsequent treatise in the following year on social development (Midgley, 1995). Central to his proposition is the argument that there is "a need to integrate economic and social policy because social expenditures in the form of social investment do not detract from but contribute positively to economic development" (Midgley and Tang, 2001:246). Social policy in this genre is thus *selective* rather than universal. It should be able to enhance human capacities, promote effective participation in the economy and contribute to the overall productivity of the economy. The developmental approach in social welfare challenges the basic neoliberal argument that social programs are essentially harmful to growth. For example, Martin Feldstein identified in the 1970s that the social security program in the United States approximately halved the personal savings rate, implying that the welfare state substantially reduces capital stock and hence the level of national income (Feldstein, 1974). To bring developmental social welfare down to the practical level, Midgley and Tang (2001) specify four major areas of social policies which are developmental in nature, namely 1) investment in human capital through vocationally-oriented education; 2) investment in employment and self-employment programs; 3) investment in social capital formation through community organizing in poor neighborhoods, 4) investment in asset development through the creation of the Individual Development Account—direct monetary incentives for individual to create capacity enhancement activities or income-generating economic opportunities (Sherraden, 1991). The purpose of these policies is to remove potential barriers for disadvantaged individuals and families from economic participation. Social policies are thus facilitative in the creation of economic opportunities and are essentially inclusive in nature. Critics of this mode of developmental social policies might point to the likely exclusion of severely deprived social groups, such as the elderly and the handicapped. However, investment-oriented developmental social welfare presupposes inclusion and the building of social capital. Investment is thus the overarching concept, not discrimination among different facets of social policies.

DEVELOPMENTALISM VERSUS PRODUCTIVISM: IDEOLOGICAL ROOTS AND PROBLEMS

Developmentalism or developmental social welfare found a new acquaintance at the turn of the new century—the idea of *productivism* or *productivist welfare capitalism*. It was soon popularized and treated as synonymous to developmentalism by some scholars (Gough 2004; Holliday 2000, 2005). Sometimes these two terms are used synonymously in describing a state of social policy that is characterized by work and growth (Wilding, Huque, and Tao, 1997). Overtly, both terms are being used to describe the importance placed by the state on the strategic use of social policies in development among East Asian states. Using Esping-Andersen's (1990) typology on welfare regime, Holliday (2000, 2005) was instrumental in the popularization of this terminology. He argues that "social policy is an extension of economic policy, and is *subordinated* to and defined by economic objectives." "In a productivist state, the perceived necessity of building a society capable of deriving growth generates some clear tasks for social policy, led by education but also taking in all other sectors" (Holliday, 2000:148). At this level, productivism and developmentalism appear to be synonymous and share a common interest on the close relationship between economic and social policies. However, a distinction emerges when one looks at the core assumptions behind the two concepts. Elaborating on productivism, Holliday (2000:710) refines the concept into three distinct levels: *facilitative, developmental-universalist* and *developmental-particularist*, the idea of subordination of social policy to economic policy becomes clear. This stands in stark contrast with developmentalism where the idea of *integration* prevails. Midgley (1997:181) suggests, "social development seeks to integrate economic and social policies." "Social development cannot take place without economic development, and economic development is meaningless if it fails to bring about significant improvements in the well-being of the population as a whole" (Midgley and Tang, 2001:245). On one level, one could argue that such distinction reflects a minor difference and a matter of degree among theorists who develop their propositions from slightly different points of departure. However, such distinction could matter much more if they reflect different ideological stands.

Ideological Roots

Developmental social welfare, according to Midgley (1997:143), has its ideological root in Veblen's views on neoclassical economists' claim that market is the only viable means of social resources allocation. Veblen favored a technocratic approach, or what Midgley termed the *institutional approach* "by which expertise could be harnessed to serve wider social interests" (Midgley, 1995:143). Following Veblen, one could draw a genealogy of modern theorists who favored institutionalism in social welfare. Richard Titmuss (1962) was instrumental in establishing the whole subject of social administration in London School of Economics, putting trust on planning and collective redistribution of social resources. At the same time, Gunnar Myrdal (1968) spearheaded the development of a unified approach in development planning in the United Nations in the 1960s, calling for a rational comprehensive approach to social development in the third world. O'brien and Penna argue that the ideological roots of the modern welfare state lies in the influence of the Enlightenment, a period where reason and science was thought to be capable of righting social errs, where "the dominance of Enlightenment narrative is a feature of the social power that is exerted through the institutions and hierarchies of science and social administration, not an indication of its truth as a historical account" (O'brien and Penna, 1988:76).

Productivism or productivist social welfare, however, is less explicit with its ideological root. On one level, Holliday's conceptualization of productivism is based on Esping-Andersen's welfare regime schema—one which places emphasis on social rights, social stratification, and the degree in which labor could be decommodified. "Social rights are viewed in terms of one's capacity to make their living standards independent of pure market forces, while social policy is supposed to address problem of stratification or inequality between classes" (Esping-Andersen, 1990:3). This appears similar to developmentalism that is also rooted in institutionalism and is by nature social democratic. On another level, however, the assumption of a high degree of *subordination* of social policies contrasts sharply with developmentalism's emphasis on integration. How then could we reconcile this discrepancy? Fitzpatrick (2004) perhaps has a more elaborated negotiation with the concept by linking productivism with productivity. He argues that increase in productivity leads to growth and hence the possibility of spending on state welfare. Henceforth, productivity is essential to the positive sum strategies of social democratic capitalism. "Productivism is the institutional, discursive and psychological process by which social goals are *subordinated* to the domain of productivity growth' (Fitzpatrick, 2004:216). Thus to realize the logic of productivism, social policy must then be subsumed under the logic and values of growth. In his latest book on new welfare theories, Fitzpatrick (2005) coins the *new productivism*, a variant of the new social democracy in which the state no longer emphasizes vertical redistribution, but horizontal redistribution in which emphasis is being placed on an increased labor participation rate, notably of women. However, Fitzpatrick (2005:23) also warns that the emphasis by productivists on paid work is potentially dangerous. Without any form of social ideal which promises the working mass "some freedom from the market" new productivism could easily be paternalism or conservatism in disguise—a society in which the duty to earn is held to override all other forms of social value and contributory activity.

A Fundamental Problem

However, the assumption of *subordination* in productivism is still problematic. This is perhaps best illustrated by Fitzpatrick's (2004) idea of *reproductive value*. He argues that there are certain core values (emotional and ecological) within the economy that are essential to the improvement of productivity but are not fully incorporated or commodified for by the state, for example, the contribution of care work within the family or the ecological value of a clean environment. When properly combined, these factors contribute to positive increase in productivity. However, one important observation made is that modern productivism undermines the sources of its own value and is ultimately self-defeating. "Reproductive value is the ultimate source of economic value yet it is the destructive effects of affluence and growth which now provide us with the reflexive skills and resources needed to preserve reproductive activity: the ethics of affluence and growth are undermined the moment we render visible the foundations upon which they rest because it is these foundations which they are gradually eroding" (Fitzpatrick, 2004:216). This is a fundamental contradiction that modern capitalism fails to resolve under the auspice of the new social democracy (Fitzpatrick, 2003).

Hence, productivism in East Asia (when it works) could not have been realized if social policy is simply subordinated to economic policy. At best, subordination could only be used to describe the early phase of developmentalism, where social welfare services are highly *residualized*. According to Richard Titmuss (1962), residualization is opposite to institutionalism, moving productivism further away from developmentalism. Examples could be cited for the situation of social welfare in the 1960s and 1970s in Hong Kong which reflected a high degree of residualization (McLaughlin, 1993). This could also be reflected by a much publicized Hong Kong welfare philosophy: "to help those who are least able to help themselves" during the 1970s (Chow, 1986). Social policies during this period had been minimalist and largely subordinated to growth. However, social welfare development from the 1970s to the 1990s had been marked by a clear development of emerging institutionalism. Spurred by political uncertainties about 1997 and the development of democracy and grassroots politics, the last three decades of the century had witnessed a tremendous growth of social policies, particularly in the area of welfare, education, and health services (Scott, 1989). Nonetheless, the real essence of developmentalism lies in *integration*. Taking into account the wide varieties of cultural and historical configurations of various East Asian societies, integration is about merging selected social policy arenas to foster development and meeting social needs simultaneously. Development leads to growth and vice versa. Social policies are thus embedded in economic policies. As such, social policies are to some extent both dependent and autonomous. Take employment and health policies as examples, East Asian societies are well known for their reluctance and caution in providing comprehensive employment protection and national health insurance coverage. Social investment in employment and health has always been associated with periods of economic buoyancy rather than crises. However, in a recent comparative social policy study, Kwon (2005) argues that, as a result of democratic development and inclusive politics, Taiwan and South Korea have succeeded in a major transformation of social policies in employment and health protection compared to Hong Kong and Singapore in the post-Asian Financial Crisis period. As such, certain social policies are capable of being integrative with broad economic change on the one hand while also remaining relatively autonomous and self-evolving on the other.

THE USE AND ABUSE OF PRODUCTIVISM: MANAGERIALISM AND THE POLITICS OF THE SOCIAL

While making a fine distinction between productivism and developmentalism contributes to understanding the dynamics of East Asian social welfare, it is apparently not the end of the story. Two important points came out of this brief discussion: first, any successful application of productivism/developmentalism must entail a careful integration of the economic and the social, and be thoroughly supported by a suitably-designed and widely supported institutional framework in implementation. In other words, we cannot simply say that a certain social policy is in rhythm with economic policy and hence they are integrated. Integration must be supported by a change in institutions, or more correctly a change in the rule of games favoring integration. Second, developmentalism takes on a holistic view of social development and therefore at any historical juncture, its development must be understood with the political and social context. As such productivism could not be understood by detaching from the polity within which it operates. These two assumptions of productivism thus provide insight into explaining why productivism works in some but not all of East Asia, if we take a time-space specific of history. However, the one variable that has not been dealt with hitherto, but will to some extent be implicated by different chapters in this book concerns *the politics of using productivism*. Since the early 1980s, Western public policy was represented by a transition from the old or traditional governance approach characterized by a state-centric mode of production of social services to a new mode of public management (NPM) which is characterized by efficiency, effectiveness, and the heightened use of the market (Clarke and Newman, 1997; Peters, 2000). Concomitant with this was the invention of a new set of governing values characterized by accountability, openness, transparency, predictability, and participation. This new mode of state management carried far and wide impact on Asian and Pacific states since the early 1990s as most government scrambled to emulate what has become the new rule of game in modern governance. Many public services had gone through major reforms or re-engineering exercises during the period, taking on new values such as management-by-objectives, accountability, and the whole notion of "doing more with less." Social services and social policies were streamlined to meet budget caps often disguised as the need for community resource mobilization with an emphasis on revitalizing family values. Rose (1999) suggests that all these purported to a reconstruction of the "social" through a new set of government technologies aiming at creating a new identity of the "self"—the attempt to individualize social needs through enabling personal entrepreneurship or productivity. In advanced liberal democracies, it is argued, that the social is fragmented into a multitude of markets where consumers (formerly welfare dependents) purchase what they need from quasi-markets, within which different providers compete: state-funded operations, NGOs, and private for profit agencies. For example, the adoption of a one-line budget system for NGOs since 2000 has effectively reshaped social service provisions in Hong Kong to the effect that the power and role of social work professionals has been subdued as contractualization has provided service providers a clear boundary of what they could and couldn't do. Within this context, unfortunately the application of productivism in East Asian states immediately fell prey to the rhetoric of neoliberalism. The emphasis on economic integration with social policy provides the best shield for policy makers who seek to equate productivism with marketization or privatization. This is especially so for the period after the Asian Financial Crisis. To provide immediate alleviation to the failing economy, East Asian states had no choice but resort to all methods of downsizing in the public arena. Cheung and Scott (2003) argues that recent economic and political crises in Asia have engendered adaptations by various governments, to the extent that building and retaining state capacity outweighs many social objectives. Seen in this light, the implementation of productivism has come to bear new meanings in East Asia. In social welfare, it means the emphasis on workfare, self-reliance, entrepreneurship building, and family mutual-aid. In housing, it means homeownership, private renting, and lesser dependence on public housing subsidies. In health, it means fee-charging, prioritization of illnesses, and private health insurance. All East Asian societies try to combine these social policies in various formats and manifestations, fitting different histories of institutions and structures; but nonetheless the common spirit underpinning social policies is consonant with what Rose (2003) aptly coined "the end of the social."

THE TROUBLE WITH COLLECTIVE RESPONSIBILITY

Without prejudicing contemporary productivism we have also discovered one important loophole in the application of the concept of welfare state and welfare regime to East Asian societies. To clearly discern its complexity we need first to revisit the connection between economics and social policy, as well as the very nature of welfare capitalism. One of the rubrics of Western welfare states is the primacy of collective responsibility. In nineteenth century Britain, welfare was characterized by voluntary provision, with mutual and friendly societies delivering a whole range of benefits and services. Local authorities and private hospitals, coupled with a national system of panel doctors, were financed through health insurance contribution that was set by the state. Even in medieval Britain, many hospitals were church-run; and for a long time, parishes had a responsibility to the poor. In the early 1900s, even old age pension for the 1970s or more had to be means-tested. In 1911, Lloyd George, the chancellor of the exchequer, helped pass legislations for sickness and invalidism, but such was not supported by the taxation system. By and large, nineteenth century Britain was happy with a mixed economy of social welfare where the state, the individual, and the church all played a part (Marshall, 1964). It was not until after the Second World War, when mass destruction and a high level of unemployment provided a contingency that warranted mass welfare intervention by the state. On the theoretical side, there was always lukewarm support for collective goods as classical economists suggested that there was no strict economic case for transferring income from the rich to the poor since there was no way to prove that the marginal utility of different classes of people could be compared (Galbraith, 1987). It was only until the publication by Pigou in 1920 of *The Economics of Welfare*, that the rudiments of a welfare state justification began to take shape. Pigou (1999) argues that so long as the total production is not reduced by welfare expenditures, the sum total of satisfaction of the society will be enhanced by the transfer of spendable resources from the rich to the poor. His views gave a partial theoretical justification, for the first time, about the rationale behind the redistribution of income from the rich to the poor. The assumption of Pigou's model is of course full employment. But this was a tricky question which economists failed to answer adequately and therefore the British welfare state didn't really take shape until much later. It had much to do with the great American economic depression of 1929. The problem facing economists then was why aggregate demand could fade away suddenly after the 1929 Wall Street stock market crash? This had germinated a worldwide search by economists for a solution to restimulate demand and revitalize the world economy.

 The climax of this search was none compared to the production of the most important work of economics by John Maynard Keynes in 1936—*The General Theory of Employment, Interest, and Money*. The essence of his argument is simple. He argues that modern economy does not find its equilibrium at full employment; instead it always finds itself in disequilibrium and hence unemployment. Therefore, the government can and should always take steps to overcome it, particularly during prolonged economic depression. Keynes's idea was seriously taken up by the United States in the New Deal years of President Roosevelt. In an open letter to the president in *The New York Times* on December 31, 1933, though not seriously taken by the public then, Keynes told the new U.S. Administration that he "places overwhelming emphasis on the increase of national purchasing power resulting from government expenditure, which is financed by loans" (Galbraith, 1987:227). Keynes's (1936) idea essentially was about how the level of output and employment could be determined. His argument was that as output, employment, and income increase, consumption from additional increments of income decreases, hence resulting in a decline in the marginal propensity to consume. The promise by classical economists that this unconsumed part of the income would then be automatically invested does not exist. No longer could governments wait for self-correcting forces to provide a remedy. Low interest rates could not be depended upon to stimulate investment, which incidentally is self-evident to many naked eyes during the last few years with the American economy, when Greenspan economics was all about keeping interest rates low but without much success. In order to bring the economy back to equilibrium even when full employment could not be achieved, the government must take steps to raise the level of investment expenditure—government borrowing and spending for public purposes. Keynes' idea was extremely influential in constructing post-war welfare states in both Europe and the United States. However, the world economy changed dramatically after the Second World War. A booming post-war economy in the United States had led to a sustained process of price inflation. The pendulum of economics had shifted from one of stimulating demand to one of cooling off the runaway economy. It was then realized that one of the major drawbacks of Keynesian thoughts was that it really was meant just for a depressed economy. It was much less effective in working with adversities arising from an inflationary economy and rising interest rates. The Keynesian model had its best years from the 1940s to the 1960s in post-war reconstruction but not so from the 1970s onwards. Since then the nature and extent of collective welfare have been seriously called into question. The oil crisis in the 1970s exacerbated the latent problem of inflation and rapid state expansion. State intervention in welfare was severely criticized by a new breed of economists having a unique view on the flow of money and inflation with modern economies (Friedman, 1962). They questioned the very role of the state and its departure from personal freedom under the ambit of a heavily taxed-based welfare system. The controversy was thus about the very foundation of the welfare state—the collective provision of social welfare. Do collective goods such as social security necessarily require an insurance system to make provision? In the following section we will demonstrate how Singaporeans give a negative answer to both questions. More important, we argue that the Singaporean model provides us with new insights into understanding the idea of real asset and investment in developmental social welfare.

A CASE OF INTEGRATION: HOME OWNERSHIP AND MANAGED CONSUMPTION IN SINGAPORE

While it remains polemical whether a compulsory saving scheme like the Central Provident Fund (CPF) for all working populations by the state is intrinsically good, it is clearly evident Singaporean citizens enjoy being homeowners from as early as the mid-1960s. Homeownership rate reached 82 percent in 1999 (see table 1.2) and has since been slightly reduced because some wealthier public housing homeowners have shifted to the private sector when they managed to capitalize their HDB housing assets. The government carefully monitored the rate of CPF contributions in its early years and made progressive increases in contribution rates since 1968. Contribution rates were carefully determined to reflect income level, household consumption and price level.

Table 1.2. Singapore Housing Indicators

Year	Total HDB Public Flats	Home Ownership (HDB) Rate (%)
60	—	29
70	—	59
90	—	81
93	655,487	81
96	—	82
97	—	82
98	790,898	82
99	823,760	82
00	846,649	82
01	863,552	82
02	866,071	83
03	874,183	82

Source: Singapore Annual Report 1999 *and* Year Book of Statistics 2004

It is apparent that Singapore does not want to face inflation when workers have surplus purchasing power. Clearly the state helps pave the way for a managed lifelong consumption pattern where it seeks, whenever possible, to manage consumption behavior through state social programs. Hence CPF, which is essentially a national personal savings institution, is being used as a macroeconomic tool to promote economic well-being. Clearly one can argue that for such a system to work, it requires a high degree of social control, administrative efficiency and effectiveness, and most important of all, a broad-based social consensus that can provide the government with a high level of legitimacy. Singaporean government has apparently hard-earned this level of legitimacy through successive demonstration of effective administration. Western welfare states have evolved a sophisticated system of collective welfare through the principle of pooled risk. The swinging changes as a result of popular politics and the pandering to various interest groups do create difficulties and intractable problems of welfare dependency. As a result, the state encourages more individuals to be dependent, thus incurring serious public debts and economic drawbacks. Another consequence is that the state shares all the financial risks while the most disadvantaged social groups are still susceptible to social risks after years of welfare state implementation. The choice regarding the risks and how to share them out will matter. In the final analysis, individuals must be made accountable for the choice of their risks. Theoretically, this is the most crucial aspect of the Singaporean model. For it to work, it requires a restructuring of the state, market and family nexus. In Singapore, the concern is not so much about the degree of social goods one can obtain outside the market, but rather how the market, and the state can ensure families to get what they want, even though it requires a high degree of commodification.

Collective Provisions of Individualized Welfare

The Singaporean system is clearly built on a workfare system rather than a welfare system. It is an extreme form of productivism. Unlike Western welfare states where collective welfare is provided collectively, Singapore shuns the *pooled risk system* of social insurance and seeks to provide individualized welfare. Chua (2000) coined this *state-client relationship* where the state acts as the agent for its people in terms of providing them with welfare services. CPF is individualized saving and HDB is practically a public developer. Through capital formation, CPF provides funding for housing investment to the government. At the same time, the profitability of real estate development provides households with a future stream of secured income through asset appreciation of HDB flats. It then enables citizens to harbor rising home equities, ultimately enhancing collective social security welfare for the Singaporeans. Pushed to the limit, Singapore could be coined the world's first *property-based welfare system* since the major part of citizens' welfare spins around the long-term capitalization of a family's property value. The following quotation from the former prime minister, Mr. Goh Chok Tong serves to illustrate this notion best (Goh, 1994:14–15):

> We have been rewarding Singaporeans for many years. The biggest prizes are the 600,000 HDB flats which 90 percent of Singaporeans own. Now HDB is buying back three-room flats and reselling them at a discount to help the poorer Singaporeans to own their flats. Actually, our HDB residents have done very well. For example, one in three HDB homes has air-conditioners. One in five has personal computers. These are not essential items like telephones or refrigerators. Yet their ownership rate has increased by three times from 1987. It is the single biggest asset for most people, and its value reflects the fundamentals of the economy.

The state also recognizes that, with growing affluence, people tend to have more aspirations than simply housing needs. They need to invest (Sherraden et al., 1995). It is the belief of the Singapore government that aspiration is an important national asset for development and must therefore be properly managed. In the case of housing, it means that Singaporeans aspire to own a house because it can provide an important future stream of income to augment the possibility of CPF not being a sufficient guarantee of income security for old age. However, since the early 1990s, HDB flats have appreciated two to threefold in value. Many Singaporeans sought to capitalize their first HDB flat and upgrade for a larger flat by way of their second opportunity to purchase. While the state does not encourage speculation on public flats, the expectation of asset appreciation is deeply embedded in the presence of a mature secondhand market. To some extent, high aspirations for improved housing as well as a steady growth in the economy tend to fuel housing speculations, as was the case of Hong Kong before 1997. Indeed in his memoir, Lee Kuan Yew (2000) did regret not to have used effective policy measures in the earlier days to thwart excessive housing demands when the property market became too buoyant in the mid-1990s.

> Once worker got used to a higher take home pay, I knew they would resist any increase in their CPF contribution that would reduce their spendable money. So, almost yearly I increase the rate of CPF contributions, but such that there was still a net increase in take home pay. It was painless for the workers to keep inflation down (Lee Kuan Yew, 2000:97).

See for a moment the simple logic of the Singapore model: (a) housing in a high growth urban economy is a highly profitable economic activity; (b) government steps in to monopolize its supply and demand; (c) it then shares capital gains with citizens through regulating and monitoring of a closed market; (d) citizens are compelled by law to save and contribute to national capital formation through CPF; to do this they need first to have a secure paying job, and then their family investment will be more or less predetermined by a property-oriented consumption pattern—one that is steered mainly by mortgage repayment and finding sufficient income to foot the housing bill; (e) with a bit of a fortune, which includes a stable housing market as well as a not so unstable world economy, they are then compensated by a positive return to their housing investment which was built with their own savings and pray that the government will be able to maintain long-term house price stability.

The Question of Sustainability, Workfare, and Social Exclusion

The functioning of the Singaporean system depends on a number of important factors. First, it greatly depends on the competence of the government to maintain housing values. Politically, a successful housing program adds to the legitimacy of the ruling People's Action Party, but the downside is that a property slump, particularly one affected by an exogenous factor like the Asian Financial Crisis, would be disastrous both for the government and its people. The evaporation of 90 percent housing equities of 90 percent of Singaporeans would be unthinkable and a social minefield. To keep afloat, the HDB is now demolishing the 2–3 room flats for redevelopment in order to create artificial scarcity and demand. HDB is also using the buy-back policy to buy back smaller flats in order to create artificial housing scarcity. These flats are demolished, some of them prematurely, to make way for the development of new and larger flats. In addition, HDB is engaged constantly in long-term upgrading programs for older housing stock in order to keep housing values from depreciating. House price stability is a major part of housing politics. When a society has reached 100 percent home ownership, the irony is that the state becomes a victim of its own success. In the face of economic globalization and the inevitable liberalization of the Singapore economy, long-term stability of Singapore's public housing market could be unattainable. Second, the Singaporean housing system favors those who work. For people who are outside the formal labor system, particularly low-income foreign workers, public homeownership is beyond their means. They remain in either the public rental sector or very rundown low end private renting. They do not have a CPF account or if they do, there aren't sufficient savings to cover basic living.

The Singaporean case has brought us to a deeper understanding of the possibility/impossibility of productivism. Integration within the context of productivism takes on at least two levels of meaning: one refers to investment-oriented social policies such as those spelled out by Midgley and Tang (2003) and the other refers to system integration such as what has been discussed here in the case of Singaporean housing and social security. If integration rather than subordination is a key dimension in the identification of productivism, then perhaps one could be tempted to ask whether the three key dimensions (rights-decommodification, social stratification, and the state-market-family nexus) of the "welfare state regime" approach are sufficiently robust to explain Singapore.

Deconstructing Decommodification

Singapore's case certainly prompts questions on social rights and decommodification—a situation when a person can maintain basic livelihood without reliance on the market. Chua (2000) suggests that the concept of "limited rights" is the case of Singapore. As the housing program covers almost the entire population, the dependency of citizens on the state becomes more and more absolute. The role of homeowners as consumers of public housing becomes increasingly vulnerable as they are subject to rules and regulations tied to other social policies, such as a pro-family priority criteria in allocation and the imposition of a racial quota in every living block. Most important, being clients of the state also erodes citizens' ability to exercise their electoral power. In Chua's (2000) words: "it renders them captive and largely impotent in the face of the state's threats of withholding continual provisions because to confront the threat would be to seriously jeopardize their material interests." Esping-Andersen (1990) suggests that when workers are completely market dependent, it is difficult to mobilize them for solidaristic action. This explains why labor movements have remained largely docile in Singapore. Such is also echoed by the recommodification of public housing to the extent that it doesn't weaken the authority of the employers and hence a social policy system that continues to receive the support of employers and capitalists.

In terms of social stratification, the Singaporean model of home ownership has been explicit in its pursuit of middle class values, seeking to achieve a society that is self-reliant, responsible, and privatized. The constant process of destigmatization and upgrading of public housing estates and the introduction of eco-design and modern facilities have been instrumental in successfully forming the imagery of middle class living. In Singapore, homeowners as a consumption class have been the preferred citizenry, except for the very few who could afford the high-end, low rise, single family home.

The most revolutionary aspect of the Singaporean system is perhaps about the market-state-family nexus. The monopolization of housing and the dependence of real estate as the major source of wealth accumulation to some extent reduce this triangular nexus to a bipolar nexus composing of merely the state and the family. The market has been completely merged with the state or to put it more bluntly—the state is the market and vice versa. The CPF-housing configuration has helped to keep up labor demand in the construction industry, the government machinery, the real estate agencies, and the housing management profession. The key question here, if seen from a welfare regime perspective, is whether Singaporean housing is sufficiently decommodified to provide opportunities for welfare outside the market. The Singaporean answer, however, is to suggest otherwise. Commodification, rather than decommodification, of housing is perhaps the key to its success.

The Singaporean model also highlights the upper limit to the whole notion of asset-based social policy as exemplified by social policy theorists (Sherraden, 1991; Sherradden, Nair, Vasoo, and Ngiam, 1995). While they propose the asset approach for the low-income groups, Singapore applies it to the middle class. It is a known fact in many welfare capitalisms that property ownership is central to middle class value. Becoming a stakeholder through home ownership has been one of the major forces of middle class formation, not to mention its various effects on income and consumption patterns (Saunders, 1990; Lee, 1999). The Singaporean housing model calls for a re-examination of fixed real assets as a fundamental component of *a managed lifelong consumption* of social resources. Other than social investment in human resources, asset investment in housing is still categorically the most neglected aspect of social policy.

Returning to the beginning question concerning the robustness of the concept of productivism and its link with developmentalism, this chapter has suggested a more rigorous look at the concept of integration. Nonetheless, through explaining the Singapore case as an extreme case of developmentalism, two criticisms are raised on the general application of the productivist approach to East Asia: 1) the nature of collective provisions of social welfare, and 2) the primacy of linking housing and social security as a major social policy instrument. Theoretically, this chapter is far from suggesting a new dimension for regime classification. Nonetheless, the Singapore case does call for a more rigorous understanding of the nature of social welfare and how it is found, enhanced and understood in East Asia.

IDEOLOGICAL HEGEMONY, WELFARE CRISIS, AND INDIVIDUAL JURISDICTION

When this edited volume was conceived we had only a modest aim. We wanted to find out how the Asian Financial Crisis had impacted various countries and how both states and societies responded to the crisis through respective social policies. However, two things happened in the interim. One is that during this period there was a plethora of post–AFC crisis studies, some systematic, others comparative, but most focused on the resilience of the East Asian welfare systems and the prospect of an East Asian model (Tang, 2000; Ramesh and Asher, 2000; Holliday and Wilding, 2003; Tang and Wong, 2003). Surprisingly few took on a more self-critical approach toward their current state of welfare. The zest for claiming an East Asian identity might perhaps be one of the reasons behind this incessant endeavor to be different from the West. Second, interestingly, except Japan, welfare studies in East Asia have tended to follow a scholarship of explaining successes rather than failures (Wad, 1999). Few have attempted really to unshroud the so-called "Asian myth." Our collection of chapters in this volume is generally more pessimistic in outlook and is more concerned with problems of structure and sustainability rather than how an individual country excels. Nonetheless, a number of common issues do recur in our collection and it is worth sketching them here as a starter.

Taken not as an intrinsic principle of social development, productivism/developmentalism has always served an instrumental purpose in Asia. The developmental state is not here as the people's choice. It is instituted for two purposes—one about creating work and employment, the other about maintaining ruling legitimacy. Productivism, whether or not it is institutionally appropriate, must be in tune with these two objectives from the beginning. Such affinity between politics and social policy is clearly apparent in some of our chapters, notably Beng Huat Chua's chapter on Singapore's housing system (which is briefly discussed in this chapter to illustrate the idea of integration) and also in Lin and Chou's chapter on Taiwan. Quoting Chua (2001)—"home ownership has helped discipline the workforce because the monthly mortgage repayments can be met only through regular employment in the formal sector of the economy" (p. 7). In addition, housing policy has "given government the room to use the sale of flats as a vehicle to carry out other social policies . . . the most obvious are the slew of government's pro-family policy" (p. 8). Reading Singaporean history, one would easily find that the priority of investing in public housing was seen as a political choice—something the PAP has little choice not to do well (Rodan, 1989). Similar situations could be located in Taiwan recent political change. Lin and Chou's chapter succinctly points out the importance of using social policies by Chen's first popularly elected government. In fact, Chen's political ideology had been much influenced by UK's Third Way philosophy in its early conception. It was more about emphasis on social investment in education, vocational training, and lifelong learning to meet the challenges from globalization. To launch a new breed of politics in the new political era, a repackaging of social policy to incorporate the concept of entrepreneurship, individual responsibilities, and stakeholding became the central concern of the Democratic Progress Party (DPP). Beyond that, the new regime also sought to woo particular sector of the electorate—providing low interest loan to young workers who couldn't afford private housing. This and many other minor improvements in social policy provisions, according to Lin and Chou's chapter, had a clear political agenda—using social policies to attain political goals.

If there is one common welfare issue that besets East Asian societies it is definitely about the *aging society*. Nowhere is population aging more rapidly and the potential consequences and responses more diverse than in East Asia. In China it is said, "the speed of population ageing versus the speed of economic development are now the two key variables in population debate." Demography has already warned us that the compound problem of ageing and its associated issues of pension and health care is going to be the key issue of East Asian welfare. By 2003, the average percentage of elderly people over sixty reached 18–20 percent, with Japan topping the lists (34 percent) and Hong Kong coming second (21 percent). If we project the figures to 2023, the figures are quite alarming. Some East Asian countries are increasing their aged population more rapidly than others as a result of cultural and policy bias, notably Japan (46 percent) and China's (29 percent) one child policy. Hong Kong (36 percent), Taiwan (32 percent) and Singapore (30 percent) are all running quite close. Do-nothing is not an option for East Asian governments. The pervasive themes now are about demographic change, the role of the family, and the issue of overloading in pension policy and welfare services. Three chapters have been devoted to the problem of an aging East Asia in this volume. Ko, Oh, and Ogawa's chapter lays out the aging social policy issues in Japan, Taiwan, and South Korea. This trio is interesting not simply because they have the highest growth rate in elderly population. What they represent are societies whose pension policies were much more institutionalized and yet are confronting problems at different stages of maturity. Japan has the most advanced pension system covering the entire population. However, they are facing problems of public distrust, income inequality, and insufficient problems for low-income families. To alleviate the pension crisis, Ko, Oh, and Ogawa show that the Japanese government is now resorting to prolong the retirement age from sixty-five to sixty-seven. In addition, part of the Japanese pension system, particularly the middle-income households, need to be privatized to make way for more competition. In the case of South Korea and Taiwan, the role of politics and democratization in recent years has been central to the development of National Health Insurance in Taiwan and the National Pension Plan in South Korea. Ngan's chapter on the minimalist approach in social security in Hong Kong touches on one of the more extreme cases of productivism in East Asia. Politically, Hong Kong has never meant to achieve a consensus in the role of state to provide for income security for its citizens. The going doctrine was again the emphasis on residualism, workfare, and a public assistance that is punitive in nature. The whole ethos of social policy is to provide disincentives for welfare dependence and to promote personal entrepreneurism, falling squarely into the use of the "self" as suggested by Rose (1999) and others in describing governing technologies of advanced liberalism. However, the chapter by Ngan et al. reveals a highly contradictory case of social policy for the elderly. Within a value framework of workfare, many elderly people shun public assistance and resort to continue their work lives in old age. However, Ngan's research suggests that the labor market in Hong Kong is highly discriminatory toward the aged. Elderly people at work are paid poorly. At a time of economic crisis, elderly people are more likely to be unemployed and hence must fall back to the public assistance system. Similar labor and employment issues arise in China during the entire period of economic reform. From a historical perspective, Fung's chapter highlights that even in a socialist regime like China, labor security is not what the West usually conceived. Whereas the Chinese espoused universal job security, the reform process has actually created more job displacement than creation, hence, creating hardship for many workers who had grown dependent on the universal workfare system.

Vastly different from Western social policy, public housing takes on an extremely important dimension in East Asian social policy. Housing investment, be it public or private, produces an important economic impact on domestic capital formation and individual wealth, largely through the buying, owning, and selling of properties. As a consequence, many East Asian governments are deeply engaged in both housing provisions and services. At least three chapters in this volume look at this dimension seriously. Other than Beng Huat Chua's chapter on Singapore, Tang's chapter on Japan provides important evidence to support our claim about the importance of the housing dimension. Tang argues that, Japan, having been through one of the strongest expansion eras of home building and homeownership, has sadly found herself deeply entrenched in a non-reviving economy built on property booms. Since the Japanese economy has been so deeply involved in borrowing and lending businesses related to real estate, the Koizumi government finds the housing market so insurmountable that it is almost impossible to bring it back up to the pre-1990 level. Zhu and Lee's chapter, on the other hand, describes a picture of property boom in China, largely the result of an overt neoliberal developmental policy. While two decades of housing reform has provided China with new urban centers and a complete facelift of major cities, unfortunately, the creation of the new housing market has brought along with it the issues of housing affordability and urban segregation. House prices in many cities are now far beyond the working class's reach and consequently many people are still trapped in substandard housings. This is one kind of contradiction resulted directly from overexposure to neoliberal urban development. Western industrial economies have suffered tremendously from the aftermath of neoliberalism and uneven development, social segregation, and excessive competition for urban resources.

Contradiction also takes on another form in the operation of a productivist welfare system. Yu's chapter cites two interesting examples of contradiction found in the Hong Kong welfare state: one concerns the public assistance, the other relates to health care. While the government consciously tries to minimize the negative impact of social welfare, such as dependency on the Comprehensive Social Security Assistance scheme (CSSA), the opposite tends to happen. The effectiveness of productivism was seriously doubted. Even during acute social crisis, such as the SARS epidemic in 2003, the effectiveness of productivism was again called into question. Chan and Leung's chapter on the Hong Kong SARS experience is an interesting example to show how an overeager and overproduced health care system has made serious blunders during the fight against the epidemic.

Perhaps what we try to put forth and argue here in this volume is two-prong: one concerns ideological orientation, and the other the practice of government, or governance, to be more in vogue. The failure of the welfare state and the decline of old social democracy in Western industrial economies have prompted a strong desire for academics and politicians alike to look for solutions in the East. The economic successes of Japan in the 1960s and 1970s, and subsequently the four tiger economies (Hong Kong, Singapore, Taiwan, and South Korea) have heightened the search for miracles, not simply in the economic domain, but also in the social. Even Esping-Andersen (2002) is keen to locate a third alternative to the choice between a service economy based on low unemployment and high levels of income inequality or one based upon high unemployment and high replacement ratio. That sets the stage for the East Asian welfare model project that to us is far from complete. As outlined in the Singaporean case of integration, a good use of institutional innovation proves vital, but whether or not it is sustainable is still being time-tested. The experience of Singapore must always be judged from a social laboratory perspective, where perhaps it is the only government on earth that enjoys the highest level of state capacity (and also the degree of sanitation possible in any polity) into making things happen, given its size and scale. Nonetheless, what we consider here most important and dangerous is the ideological hollowness of many of the works on East Asian social welfare successfully shrouded by a veil weaved of culture, pragmatism, and familial mutual help. In their struggle for an identity in the global market, many East Asian countries took to believe their miraculous power in solving their own social problems. Many explanations of success thus flow directly from such mindsets. This we consider an ideological crisis about social welfare — we believe in something that doesn't exist, or even if it exists, not in the way it is being understood.

The other concerns the practice of social policies in East Asia. This requires more substantial discussions in the subject matter of social policy. The chapters in this volume represent only snapshots of the way social policy programs are constructed in East Asia. Certainly we do not claim any form of representation. Nonetheless, two elements came out succinctly from our brief introduction, first the pervasive subordination of social policy to economic imperative in the name of productivism; second, a continual sign that our cultural veil does not provide us immunity against the perils of welfare capitalism. A crisis of welfare is highly feasible and is just around the corner. If this edited volume is of any practical value it is intended to be flagging a warning sign.

REFERENCES

Central Provident Fund Board. (1997–2003). *Annual Report*. Singapore: Ministry of Information.

Cheung, A., and Scott, I. (2003). *Governance and Public Sector Reform in Asia: Paradigm Shifts or Business as Usual?* London: Routledge, Curzon.

Chua, B. H. (1997). *Political Legitimacy and Housing: Stakeholding in Singapore*. London: Routledge.

———. (2000). "Public Housing Residents as Clients of the State." *Housing Studies*, vol. 15(1), pp. 45–60.

———. (2001). "Housing Provisions & Management of Aspirations." Paper presented at the International Conference on Housing and Social Change, City University of Hong Kong, April 16, 18, 2001.

Clark, J. and Newman, J. (1997). *The Managerial State: Power, Politics, and Ideology in the Remaking of Social Welfare*. London: Sage.

Deyo, F. C. (1992). "The Political Economy of Social Policy Formation: East Asia's Newly Industrialized Countries," in Appelbaum, R. P. and Hendersen, J. (eds.)

States and Development in the Asian Pacific Rim. Newbury Park, CA: Sage, pp. 289–306.
Ermisch, J. and Ogawa, N. (1994). *The Family, the Market, and the State in Ageing.* Oxford: Clarendon Press Societies.
Esping-Andersen, G. (1990). *Three Worlds of Welfare Capitalism.* Oxford: Polity Press.
——. (1999). *Social Foundations of Postindustrial Economies.* Oxford: Oxford University Press.
——. (2002). *Why We Need a New Welfare State?* Oxford: Oxford University Press.
Feldstein, M. (1974). "Social Security, Induced Retirement, and Aggregate Capital Accumulation." *Journal of Political Economy*, vol. 83, 447–75.
Fitzpatrick, T. (2003). *After the New Social Democracy.* Manchester: Manchester University Press.
——. (2004). "A Post-productivist Future for Social Democracy?" *Social Policy and Society*, vol. 3(3), pp. 213–22.
——. (2005). *New Theories of Welfare.* London: Palgrave.
Friedman, M. (1962). *Capitalism and Freedom.* Chicago, IL: Chicago Press.
Galbraith, K. (1987). *Economic Perspective: A Critical History.* Boston: Houghton-Mifflin.
Gilbert, N. (2004). *Transformation of the Welfare State: The Silent Surrender of Public Responsibility.* Oxford: Oxford University Press.
Goh, Chok Tong. (1994). "National Day Rally, 1994." Singapore: Ministry of Information and the Arts.
Goodman, R., White, G., and Kwon, H. (1998). *The East Asian Welfare Model: Welfare Orientalism and the State.* London: Routledge.
Gough, I. (2000). "Welfare Regimes in East Asia and Europe." Paper presented to the Annual World Bank Conference on Development Economics Europe, 2000, Paris, June 27, 2000.
——. (2004). "East Asia: The Limits of Productivist Regime," in Gough, I. and Wood, G. (eds.) *Insecurity and Welfare Regimes in Asia, Africa, and Latin America: Social Policy in Development Context.* Cambridge: Cambridge University Press, pp. 169–201.
Holliday, I. (2000). "Productivist Welfare Capitalism: Social Policy in East Asia." *Political Studies*, 48, pp. 706–23.
——. (2005). "East Asian Social Policy in the Wake of the Financial Crisis: Farewell to Productivism?" *Policy and Politics*, 33(1), pp. 145–62.
Holliday, I. and Wilding, P. (2003). *Welfare Capitalism in East Asia: Social Policies in the Tiger Economies.* London: Palgrave.
Jacobs, D. (2000). "Low Public Expenditures on Social Welfare: Do East Asian Countries Have a Secret?" *International Journal of Social Welfare*, vol. 9(1).
Keynes, M. (1936). *The General Theory of Employment, Interest, and Money.* New York: Harcourt, Brace, and World.
Kwon, H. J. (2005). "Transforming the Developmental Welfare State in East Asia." *Development and Change*, vol. 36(3), pp. 477–97.
Lee, J. (1999). *Home Ownership and Social Change in Hong Kong.* London: Ashgate.

Lee Kuan Yew. (2000). *From Third World to First: The Singapore Story: 1965–2000*. New York: Harper and Collins.

Low, L. and Aw, T. C. (1997). *Housing a Healthy, Educated, and Wealthy Nation through the CPF*. Singapore: Times Academic Press.

Marshall, T. H. (1964). *Class, Citizenship, and Social Development*. New York: Anchor Books.

McLaughlin, E. (1993). "Hong Kong: A Residual Welfare Regime," in Cochrane and Clarke (eds.) *Comparing Welfare States: Britain in International Context*. London: Sage, pp. 105–40.

Midgley, J. (1986). "Industralization and Welfare: The Case of the Four Little Tigers." *Social Policy and Administration*, 20(3), pp. 225–38.

———. (1995). *Social Development*. London: Sage.

———. (1997). *Social Welfare in Global Context*. Thousand Oak: Sage.

Midgley, J. and Tang, K. L. (2001). "Social Policy, Economic Growth and Developmental Welfare." *International Journal of Social Welfare*, vol. 10, pp. 244–52.

———. (2003). "East Asia Welfare: Theoretical Perspectives." *Social Development Issues* 25(3), pp. 6–26.

Mills, J. (1990). *The State of Welfare: Welfare State in Britain since 1974*. Singapore: Ministry of Information and the Arts, 1997, 1998, 1999.

Myrdal, G. (1968). *Asian Drama: An Inquiry into the Poverty of Nations*. New York: Penguin Books.

O'Brien, M. and Penna, S. (1998). *Theorizing Welfare: Enlightenment and Modern Society*. London: Sage.

Peters, G. (2000). "Governance and Comparative Politics." in Pierre J. (ed.) (2000) *Debating Governance*. Oxford: OUP.

Pigou, A. (1999). *The Economics of Welfare*. Hampshire: Macmillan.

Phang, Sock Yong. (2004). "House Prices and Aggregate Consumption: Do They Move Together? Evidence from Singapore," *Journal of Housing Economics*, vol.13(2).

Ramesh, M. and Asher, M. G. (2000). *Social Welfare in Southeast Asia*. New York: St. Martin's Press.

Rodan, G. (1989). *The Political Economy of Singapore's Industrialization: National State and International Capital*. London: Macmillan.

Rose, N. (1999). *Powers of Freedom: Reframing Political Thought*. Cambridge, UK: Cambridge University Press.

Saunders, P. (1990). *A Nation of Home Owners*. London: Pious.

Scott, I. (1989). *Political Change and the Crisis of Legitimacy in Hong Kong*. Oxford: Oxford University Press.

Sherraden, M. (1991). *Assets and the Poor: A New American Welfare Policy*. Mermonk, NY: Sharpe.

Sherradden, M., Nair, S., Vasoo, S., and Ngiam, T. L. (1995). "Social Policy Based on Assets: The Impact of Singapore's Central Provident Fund." *Asian Journal of Political Sciences*, vol. 3(2), pp. 112–33.

Singapore Statistics Department. **(YEAR??)**. *Singapore Yearbook of Statistics 2000–2003*. Singapore: Singapore Statistics Department.

Tang, K. L. (1999). "Planning for the Unknown: Social Policy Making in Hong Kong, 1990–1997." *International Journal of Sociology and Social Policy*, vol. 19(1/2) pp. 27–56.

———. (2000). *Social Welfare Development in East Asia*. London: Palgrave.

Tang, K. L. and Wong, C. K. (2003). *Poverty Monitoring and Alleviation in East Asia*. New York: Nova Science.

Titmuss, R. (1962). *Income Distribution and Social Change*. London: Allen and Unwin.

Tremewan, C. (1998). "Welfare and Governance: Public Housing under Singapore's Party-State," in Goodman, R., White, G., and Kwon, H., (eds.) *The East Asian Welfare Model: Welfare Orientalism and the State*. London: Routledge.

Wilding, P., Huque, S., and Tao, J. (1997). *Social Policy in Hong Kong*. Cheltenham, UK: Elgar.

Wilensky, H., and Lebeaux, X.?? (1965). *Industrial Society and Social Welfare*. New York: Free Press.

2

Emerging Issues in Developmental Welfarism in Singapore

Beng Huat Chua

Singapore, an ex-British colony, gained political independence in a circuitous manner in 1965, after two years as a member of Malaysia. The colonial entrepôt economy left Singapore, on the eve of political independence, without any significant industrialization and hence to utilize adequately the rapidly increasing local-born population. Industrialization became the consuming preoccupation and synonymous with national development and nation building. Upon independence, it immediately embarked on export-oriented industrialization, by then the trial and tested path taken by South Korea, Taiwan, and Hong Kong and before that, Japan. Since then, the developmental trajectory of Singapore has shared broad similarities with the three East Asian newly industrialized economies.

In the area of social welfare, the policies of what has come to be called the four Asian "tiger" economies are remarkably similar in ideological orientation. Holliday and Wilding have succinctly identified five interlocking characteristics: primacy of political purpose; economic growth and full employment as the main engines of welfare; welfarism being shunned; the family being accorded a key welfare function; and the role of the state being strong but limited (2003:161–3). In practice, welfare in terms of "hand-outs" is eschewed. State financial support is provided to improve the employability of the recipients. For example, education expenditure is an obvious form of human capital investment aimed at transforming the individual into a productive resource. In Singapore, even transport infrastructure is conceived in productivist terms: traffic congestion impedes punctuality at work and slows down the circulation of everything, thus extracting a production cost. Within the broad similarities in ideological orientation there are, of course, significant differences in actual policies. Comparisons in the areas of health care, education, housing, and social security in the four economies are now readily available (Holliday and Wilding, 2003; Ramesh, 2004; Tang and Tremewan,, 2000). Singapore's productivist orientation in general and social welfare policies in particular are rooted in the island-nation's political history. To understand the current issues and difficulties in social welfare delivery in Singapore, it is necessary to first review the developmental effects of the social policies.

LEGITIMACY OF PAP DOMINANT STATE

The political trajectory of how the People's Action Party (PAP) transforms Singapore into a single-party dominant regime for the past four decades, since it first won parliamentary majority in 1954, is by now a well-worn tale. The Party's rapid political ascendancy was enabled by the popular anti-colonial mobilization, engendered largely by left-wing political leaders within the party who had widespread support among economically poor masses. Once in power, the "moderate" English-educated leaders in the Party enacted a series of repressive legislation that clipped the power of independent trade unions and radical student and community organizations. Within the Party, this English-educated group outmaneuvered its left-wing counterpart, resulting in the break away of the latter to form a new political party, the Barisan Socialis, in 1963. Significantly, even with many of its leaders in detention without trial, the Barisan Socialis still managed to capture more than 30 percent of the popular vote in the 1963 general election. However, its political leadership made a strategic mistake of boycotting, in 1968, the general election. Consequently, PAP won in all constituencies. Its absolute political and parliamentary dominance was hence established and institutionalized. The resultant single-party dominant regime is often called "authoritarian" (Mauzy and Milne, 2002:128–142) and/or "illiberal state" (Bell et al., 1995). The PAP government seldom contests these criticisms because it sees itself as marching to a different tune from that of the liberal "West," preferring some version of "communitarianism" as the "Asian" way.[1] This situation is unlikely to change in the immediate and medium term.[2]

The PAP has molded the absolute political power of the single-party dominant state structure into a very efficient instrument of economic development. The government has a free hand in passing legislation, managing national budgets, wielding instruments of coercion, and formulating public policies without any effective political opposition. Opposition political parties and periodic general elections are seen as mere "inconveniences" and "hindrances" to the proper functioning of laws and policies that, the government claims, are formulated in the interest of the "greater good" of all. The PAP thus claims that it is the embodiment of and works for the common good.[3]

Four decades of rapid economic growth, delivering general improvements in the material life of the entire population, albeit unevenly, has provided the "evidence" of the PAP government's claim. It has become the ideological core for a corporatist strategy to incorporate identifiable non-state interest groups and some civil society organizations into working for the general good. The economic success has engendered a significant degree of ideological consensus between the PAP and the electoral ground. This can be gleaned from wide public resonance and support among the citizens for its antiliberalism. The ability to act ostensibly for the economic common good has given the PAP regime a surplus rather than deficit of political legitimacy among the electorates enabling it to defend itself against both local and foreign criticisms but also to gain grudging appreciation among foreign critics.[4]

HOUSING POLICY AS ANCHOR DEVELOPMENTAL POLICY

Industrialization began with the first fully-elected PAP government in 1959. It instituted two new statutory boards in 1960: the Economic Development Board (EDB) and the Housing and Development Board (HDB). The EDB immediately undertook to develop a large tract of industrial estate on land recovered from swamp, prior to any committed investments from any industry. It then proceeded to "sell" it to foreign, multinational corporations. Early skepticism of critics quickly turned into admiration and accolades of success, as new "pioneer" industries began to pour into the once empty space.[5] The success of the industrialization program has been aptly summarized by the following features: "sound infrastructure, compliant work force, generous tax incentives, allowance of 100 percent ownership in most sectors of the economy, negligible restrictions on the repatriation of capital, duty-free importation of machinery and equipment and a reputation for offering one of the highest returns on manufacturing investment in the region" (Rahim, 2001: 208).[6]

The rapid success was historically determined. The developmental policies dovetailed with what we now call the "new international division of labor": multinational industries from developed economies in search of cheap production platforms in order to escape high labor costs at home. It also benefited greatly from the fact that the very large pools of labor in the People's Republic of China (PRC), India, Indonesia, and other parts of mainland Southeast Asia were, for ideological reasons, locked away from foreign capital investments. Should the tiger economies have entered the export-oriented industrialization after the economic opening of the PRC to foreign capital in 1978, they would have faced an uphill task, as witnessed by other developing nations in the late twentieth century. In any case, by the early 1990s, the per capita income of Singaporeans was already at "developed" country level. "Success" had by then become part of the constellation of elements that constitute the elusive Singaporean "identity."

The immediate task of the HDB was to construct minimal but permanent housing for a growing population that had been largely neglected by the British colonial administration.[7] Beginning modestly with one-room rental flats, where residents had to share common kitchen and toilet facilities, it quickly moved to constructing modest three-room flats for "sale"—on a ninety-nine-year leasehold basis—in 1964, three short years after its building program began. The initial sluggish sales program was given a tremendous shot in the arm when, in 1968, Singaporean households were permitted to use their Central Provident Fund (CPF) savings to finance their monthly mortgage on the public housing flats.

The CPF, an individualized compulsory monthly social security savings program, provides an effective financial mechanism or circuit that facilitates the expansion of homeownership while the HDB acts as both the vendor and mortgage lender to any household which is eligible to purchase a public housing flat. Members of the household, individually or collectively, can utilize their CPF savings to pay the monthly mortgage. The transfer of funds is conducted administratively between the CPF and the HDB. The entire process is conducted in a closed circuit of transactions—the working population save in CPF, the government borrows from the CPF for infrastructure development including loans and grants to the HDB, the HDB sells the public housing, which is paid by the households monthly through deductions from their CPF—without involving any conventional banking and financial instruments. Once this mode of mortgage payment is instituted, immediately, the ratio of those who applied to purchase the ninety-nine-year lease went up rapidly. By the early 1990s, more than 85 percent of the resident population lived in HDB flats and an equal percentage of these "own" a ninety-nine-year lease on their flats.

Furthermore, "resale" policies of public housing flats, in which significant capital gains were made by families who sold their flats, encouraged households to upgrade their accommodation. This generated an inflated arena of consumption that was a major contribution to the expansion of the domestic economy. Economists at the National University of Singapore noted that the ease with which the buying and selling of public housing flats can be conducted with CPF money had led to a general overconsumption of housing in Singapore (CPF Study Group, 1986). The government, for political reasons, continued to encourage "upgrading" of housing consumption until after the 1997 Asian Financial Crisis, when it acted to limit the amount of CPF that can be drawn for housing purposes.[8] Details of the public housing system are now easily available in the literature, what is important here is to emphasize the centrality of the national housing program in the economic development of Singapore.[9]

Improvement of the housing conditions of the general population has accomplished a number of development objectives simultaneously. Nationally, the ubiquitous planned, high-rise housing estates constitute part of the national capital formation. They are literally concrete monuments to the progressively accumulated wealth of the nation. Homeownership has helped discipline the workforce because the monthly mortgage payments can be met only through regular employment in the formal sector of the economy. It has, therefore, contributed to transforming the population, whose attitudes toward labor were formed by unemployment and underemployment, into regular wage labor; transforming the population into a proletariat essential to capitalist development.[10] Improved housing conditions provide permanent shelter; improve sanitation, public health, and individual well being; reduce absenteeism at work; and increase productivity of labor. In all these productive functions, housing could be regarded as "human capital" investment rather than simply welfare expenditure. Finally, with about 90 percent of the population living in public housing estates, public housing living bears no social stigma. All residents are served by the same services—schools, public transport, and shopping—in the estates. The routines of the residents, regardless of income or classes, are approximately the same. Public housing estates thus reduce the visibility of income inequalities, hence potential class frictions.

In accordance with its anti-welfare ideology, the opportunity to purchase subsidized public housing flats is not legally a welfare entitlement by virtue of citizenship. This is evident from the fact that public housing allocation is not means tested but is distributed entirely through the household's ability to pay. Citizenship merely provides the "privilege" to gain the subsidy on the flat purchased. The transaction between the HDB and the household is strictly a business transaction between a willing vendor and a willing buyer. If the conditions of transaction are not agreeable, each party can walk away from the deal. This has given the government the room to use the sale of flats as a vehicle to carry out other social policies. The most obvious are the slew of government's pro-family policies: Until the late 1990s, only households could purchase a flat and singles were excluded. Singles were later allowed to buy three-room resale flats as families began to upgrade to bigger and newer flats. Young families that opt to live close to their parents are given priority on the waiting list as well as a much larger cash subsidy for the purchase of the flat.

When demand for flats was at its highest in the mid-1980s, this could reduce waiting time by almost two years, from five to three years. The pro-family policies are motivated by the government's desire to reduce dependency on public institutions in matters such as child and elderly care in accordance with the idea that family is the first-line care institution.[11]

The contribution of the public housing program to the economic and social development is without precedent anywhere in the world, where failures of national housing policies are the norm. The manner in which other social policies and social benefits are piggy-backed on the successful housing program is something quite remarkable. While improved housing conditions undoubtedly improve the material life of the population, the state as provider of housing also extracts its political returns. However, this virtuous circle of benefits for the population and the government was somewhat bent, if not exactly broken after the 1997 Asian Financial Crisis by a conjunction of several social and political developments, particularly the increasing maturity of the capitalist economy domestically bringing with it structural unemployment, globalization, skills upgrading of industrial productions, and the declining birthrate of a largely middle class society.

BREAKING THE VIRTUOUS CIRCLE
OF PUBLIC HOUSING OWNERSHIP

The housing program that has, until the late 1990s, delivered so much positive consequences to economic and social developments is not without systemic risks. One weakness in the system is the fact that it is a pay-as-you-go system. The viability of homeownership at the household level is, therefore, dependent on the continual employment for the leaseholder for the length of the mortgage. If employment is disrupted, the monthly contribution to the CPF would stop, and once the accumulated sum is depleted, the leaseholder will be in arrears of monthly mortgage payment. This possibility was kept at bay at both the national economic level and that of leaseholders' financial and psychological concerns during the four decades of rapid industrial development (1960s to the early 1990s) of the late developing economy of Singapore. During these decades, rapid development of labor-intensive economies and other necessary physical infrastructure developments provided an abundance of employment opportunities for successive generations of Singaporeans entering the workforce. Unemployment was not a social concern, as Singapore moved from an economy with high unemployment to one that was chronically short of labor, importing labor from the neighboring regions.

However, while there is still a labor shortage at the overall demand level, from domestic maids to chief executive officers of multinational enterprises—

one in four people on the island is a foreigner—there is simultaneously the beginning of structural unemployment among Singapore citizens. This should not be a surprising development because it is a part of the inherent logic of the capitalist economy of a nation. As the national capitalist economy moves out of labor intensive industries due to rising labor costs and intensified competition from low-wage labor markets in the region, segments of the Singaporean population, especially the older and lesser educated, become increasingly marginalized in the domestic labor market. A mismatch of skills of these marginalized workers and the skills demand of an increasingly technology driven industrialized economy begins to emerge and continues to widen. Without the appropriate new skills, older and lesser skill workers are increasingly cast off and become progressively unable to regain their income levels, even if they were able to find re-employment. If and/or when unemployment becomes a structural feature of the economy, then the virtuous circle of financial accumulation at household level through public housing homeownership is immediately threatened.

Empirically, the Asian Financial Crisis in 1997 marked the first shock to the employment situation in Singapore: a record number of 29,000 workers were retrenched. This was followed by sustained global economic downturn until 2003, when the economy began to recover strongly. The sustained downturn, of course, had a depressing effect on housing prices, including those of public housing. Uncertainty of sustained long-term employment asserted a discouraging effect in property investments, causing generalized sluggish real estate market. In the public housing sector, the queue for new flats disappeared. Many households on the waiting list declined to buy when offered, often penalized by the HDB with forfeiture of the down payment for the flat. This reflected a general lack of consumer confidence among potential homeowners and thus reluctance to commit to a long-term mortgage.

The consequence was, in the late 1990s, a surplus of 10,000 completed units of housing remained unsold. This has caused the HDB to discontinue its registration system for public housing flats and to adopt the practice of the private sector, in other words, to pre-sell every block of housing and commence construction when 70 percent or more of the block has been sold, within a fixed period of time. If there are not enough buyers within the specified period, construction will not proceed and the intention to build is withdrawn. Those who have placed their bookings will have to reapply and the entire process will be repeated. This has understandably caused dissatisfaction among potential buyers, especially first time public housing homeowners. Despite dissatisfaction of buyers and potential political cost to the incumbent government, the HDB is unlikely to change its mode of operation back to the registration system.

In the resale market, the depressed housing market is exacerbated by the fact that the HDB has effectively achieved 100 percent homeownership among those who are eligible for public housing, except newly conjugated families. It is important to clarify, here, that the level of homeownership in the public housing sector is determined by rules of eligibility set by the public housing authority, thus by the government. If the rules change, the number of eligible homeowners at any point in time also changes. For example, if the eligible age of an individual to purchase a public housing flat is reduced to twenty-eight years old, instead of the current thirty-five, then the number of those eligible would increase significantly, the existing relative percentage of homeowners would shrink from its 100 percent. Within existing eligibility rules, the close to 100 percent homeownership rate has effectively reduced demand for resale housing to a trickle; as every eligible household already owns its flat, there is little incentive to move up or down the consumption scale, particularly in view of future economic and employment uncertainties. Furthermore, new entrants to the housing market have greater tendency to purchase smaller flats; and consequently, smaller flats have proportionally greater gains in resale values against larger flats.

The decline in housing demand for both new and resale public housing flats is further aggravated by an aging population, with a falling birthrate and marriage rate. In the long run this could potentially create a housing surplus that will further depress prices of existing housing units. The HDB has been cognizant of this potential problem since the late 1980s, realizing that to continue building housing units for the newly married would inevitably lead to a surplus of housing that results from those left behind by their parents. Hence, the HDB had radically reduced its building program since the early 1990s. The fact that it had 10,000 completed units unsold, at the end of the 1990s, only served to emphasize the seriousness of the problem.

The slowing down and depression of housing prices in the resale market have resulted in many households facing the problem of negative equity, especially those who bought their flats immediately before the 1997 financial crisis, when prices were at their inflated highest. This has created severe financial hardship for two groups of homeowners: those whose breadwinners have been retrenched and those who are facing retirement. In both cases, the negative return on their investments in public housing flats has jeopardized the homeowners' ability to face their economic future, especially for those who are looking forward to capital gains from selling the flats to finance their retirement years.

From a market point of view, of course, downturns and upswings in property prices within a capitalist economy are to be expected and households are supposed to make their own calculations and decisions in purchasing and consuming their housing needs. However, the peculiarity of the Singapore situation is that public housing homeownership has been very highly promoted by the government for reasons other than shelter. The rising prices of public housing flats which potentially translate into private capital gains for the homeowners also deliver to the government a very high level of political goodwill and legitimacy among the citizen-consumers of housing that is provided by the state. Indeed, the high level of homeownership is a direct result of the government's promotion of public housing homeownership as an "asset." The declining value of this "asset" that, for the unemployed family, looks increasingly like a "burden," may yet translate itself into a political problem and legitimacy cost for the incumbent government.

On the other hand, it could be said that the homeowners might be thankful that in spite of unemployment, they still have a secure roof over their heads, especially since the HDB does its utmost to help the homeowners who are displaced from the labor force to restructure their mortgages rather than to seek repossession of their flats. Only a state agency is able to maintain such restructuring processes and costs when faced with a multitude of households in arrears. Such financial costs are borne by the state as political necessity. However, such ad hoc accommodation of mortgage arrears and falling prices would require a more systematic set of solutions in the future as the demography continues to move toward an aging population and the economy continues to shift toward technological intensification.

The government has already taken steps toward management of housing consumption. To prevent overconsumption, it has introduced restraints by increasing the quantum of cash down-payment for purchasing public housing from zero to 10 percent in line with the private sector. Previously, the 10 percent down payment could be paid by using the CPF. It has also lowered the total quantum of CPF available to finance mortgages whereas the entire mortgage could be paid in full from CPF in the past, currently only 50 percent of price of the property can be paid with the CPF, the remaining mortgage interest costs have to be paid in cash. These measures, obviously, do not lift the currently depressed housing market. Indeed, it is likely to add to its depression in the immediate term. However, their effect in the long term is to introduce sobriety into public housing consumption and investment.

OTHER EMERGING WELFARE MEASURES

Structural unemployment has very quickly become a reality in Singapore in the beginning of the twenty-first century. Following the marketization of the People's Republic of China (PRC) with the opening up to foreign capital in labor intensive industries, almost all low-wage industrial jobs worldwide have migrated to the PRC, along with that a very significant number of middle-management employment opportunities. After forty years of rapid economic development, Singapore has become a high-wage location, with an average annual wage of more than US$20,000, compared to less than US$1,000 in PRC and even less in places like Vietnam. The worst affected are, obviously, the older, uneducated, and unskilled middle-age workers, who were neglected by the colonial administration and missed out on the mass education opportunity provided by the independent government. Behind them are the middle-age, middle management workers who are retrenched as a consequence of global competition for jobs and outsourcing of lower level managerial work to places like India, where there is a massive supply of highly educated labor at significantly lower wages.

Obviously, unemployment has become a structural problem in Singapore. Unemployment is the source of a multiplicity of social problems and issues, including family financial difficulties, such as daily necessities, health care, and more specifically, education needs of children. Accordingly, social welfare provisions have increased significantly. In the 2005 annual national budget, a Community Care (ComCare) Endowment fund of S$500 million is allocated for social welfare expenditures; this is likely to generate more than $50 million a year for expenditure. The total endowment is likely to be increased to $1 billion over the years, with corresponding greater sums available to finance welfare programs.[12] Significantly, this increase in social welfare funding is independent of health care and education subsidies and is therefore completely targeted at social security of individuals and families.

Consistent with its long-standing position that cash-handouts are detrimental to work ethics of the population, there have not been any changes in the PAP government's ideological position on welfare, in spite of the increase in targeted funds. It continues to maintain a three-point principle: fostering self-reliant individuals, family as the first line of support, and "many helping hands." The last is the easiest to comprehend. The government has consistently maintained a philanthropy mode of social welfare in which the better-offs contribute to charity to help the needy in the society, thus the "many helping hands." This mode has been relatively successful, with contribution amounting to several hundreds of millions to charity each year. This mode has enabled the government to displace the idea that social welfare of the needy is the sole responsibility of the state, instead of just contributing its share as a constitutive part of the helping hands, and avoid the idea that citizens are "entitled" to state welfare provisions.

The emphasis on family as the first line of support is consistent with the government's pro-family policies, which it often insists as ideologically consistent with Asian communitarian values. The government argues that to avoid weakening the family as a bedrock social institution that is fundamental to the well-being of individuals in society, the state should not assume the responsibilities of the family by substituting itself for the family for the care of the family members. With this ideological formulation, the state will provide funds for the family as a unit in order to help itself. For example, one component of ComCare, code name ComCare Grow, is aimed at helping children of low-income families in their education efforts.

It is argued that investment in the children has potentially the greatest economic and social returns. ComCare Grow programs provide financial assistance to children from disadvantaged families for education purposes, thereby improving their employability in the long run and breaking the poverty cycle. The programs help children gain access to development programs very early, from preschool or kindergarten. They provide financial assistance throughout the student's school years. For children who are "at-risk" of falling out of the social safety net, financial assistance and counseling for the children and their parents will begin from preschool age. Obviously, the family is expected to develop the "right" attitudes in order to foster the educational achievements of its children, upon whom the future social and economic stability of the entire family depends.

The emphasis on "self-reliance" for individuals sees financial assistance as a temporary stopgap practice for those who are unemployed. It ties provision of welfare benefits as a step toward self-reliance in gainful employment. Consequently, social assistance is close to work assistance programs, namely assistance in job-placement and new skills training. The National Trades Union Congress and the Ministry of Manpower have developed several agencies and programs in both areas to help retrenched and displaced workers (Wong, 2005).[13]

One of the innovative programs to develop employment opportunities for the lowly educated, middle-age workers deserves particular mention. Singapore has been very dependent on foreign labor for the so-called 3-D jobs — dirty, dangerous, and degrading. They are employed in the cleaning of housing estates and food centers throughout the island. Foreign workers are able to do these jobs at low wages because of the low self-maintenance cost while they are contracted to work in Singapore, as their local accommodation cost is borne by the employer and their families at home live with far lower cost and standard of living. On the other hand, an unemployed Singaporean has to maintain his own family in the high cost environment of Singapore. Consequently, unemployed Singaporeans are unable to take up such low paying jobs. The solution is to "redesign" such jobs by enlarging its scope of work and mechanizing many of the job processes. Mechanization reduces labor intensiveness and increases productivity, making it possible to improve the wages for the job and enabling unemployed Singaporeans to take up such employment. The Ministry of Environment has successfully placed more than one thousand workers since the scheme was initiated a couple of years ago. It is envisaged that such job redesign programs will be expanded into different areas of work.

Of course, as the economy matures and the population ages, not every unemployed person and his family can be made self-reliant through the various schemes. The chronically needy and poor, especially the aged-single and the physically disabled, are part of the society. Long-term assistance for these individuals is unavoidable as part of the responsibilities of the state. Means-tested public assistance will still need to be provided by state agencies and voluntary welfare organizations.

In accord with the "many helping hands" policy, most of the expanded welfare programs will be decentralized and managed by different community organizations, ranging from the Community Development Councils, which are chaired by elected government members of parliament (MP) who are appointed as "mayors" of constellations of new towns of public housing estates, to the National Center of Social Services (NCSS), which is the coordinating body of most of the voluntary welfare organizations in the country, to individual stand-alone voluntary welfare organizations which have very specific constituencies of clients. The Ministry of Community Development, Youth, and Sports may in fact provide a very substantial part of the annual operating and development budget for these voluntary organizations but still prefer not to take full responsibilities for their daily operation. It is the government's argument, if not conviction, that the cold bureaucracy of state welfare agencies is inferior to organizations that help the needy in society who need not only financial assistance but also the warm care and concern of the personal touch.

It should be apparent that as a consequence of the changing economic and social, particularly the demographic, conditions in Singapore, state expenditures in terms of providing social security to individual citizens and families has increased significantly. Politically, this is unavoidable, regardless of the explicitly espoused "anti-welfare" stance of the incumbent PAP government. Apart from the fact that without social assistance the unemployed workers and chronically needy might resort to anti-social activities, including crime, the incumbent government is also interested in getting re-elected to parliamentary power. Its legitimacy to govern is thus dependent on its ability to provide sufficient financial assistance to those who have fallen out of the social safety net. In this, the single-party dominant state of the PAP regime is not different from other governments. Indeed, it may be argued that the pressure on the PAP is even greater because its ability to keep all opposition parties out of government is crucially dependent on its "performance" in securing the economic well-being of the people as citizens and electorate.

In the last few years, the social policies of Singapore have been under scrutiny as a component member of the Asian newly industrialized economies of Korea, Hong Kong, and Taiwan, the so-called "tiger" economies, with the aim of developing conceptually an East Asian model or "regime" of the welfare state (Tang, 2000; Holliday and Wilding, 2003). Two general findings are common in these efforts: the East Asian states spend very little on social security and all social policies and attendant expenditure are aimed at improving the developmental and global competitive positions of the countries. Hence, they are called developmentalist welfare states.

Taking the Singapore case that social policies, including social security expenditures are predominantly geared toward development of human resources so as to improve productivity and competitiveness of the domestic labor force is not to be doubted. Even at the deepest point of economic downturn, direct financial handout is eschewed and financial assistance is provided through various schemes which aim eventually to reposition the unemployed for better employment, if not for the worker himself then through the future of their children. In this sense, the new social security programs introduced in the 2005 Singapore national budget are developmentalist.

However, the generalization that the East Asian economies are miserly in social security expenditures is less definitive. Indeed, Ramesh (2004) has argued that the small expenditures in certain social policies in these economies have to be explained contextually; for example, the low expenditure in social medicine in Singapore is largely because hitherto it has had a rather young population and health is not a significant social issue. The contextual argument suggests that the actual level of expenditure in any social policy area is a function of the changing condition of the society and not overdetermined by an ideological stance toward something called the "welfare state." The by now conventionally understood European welfare state must itself be subjected to historical analysis; its ideological underpinning in the context of the emerging Cold War politics in the immediate post-World War II days, and the fluctuations in expenditures in different social policy areas, in different countries, since the idea of the welfare state is initiated, mapped out. The idea that a "welfare state" is one in which social expenditure is consistently maintained at a very high level is more mythical than real.

The level of social policy expenditure in a country is partly a function of the stage of its capitalist development. The logic of capitalism throws up economic inequalities, unemployment, and other forms of economic redundancies that require contextual solutions from the incumbent government of the country in question. What is important to note is that there are no in-principle-once-and-for-all solutions to these issues that are intrinsic to the logic of capitalism.

By the early twenty-first century, after forty years of sustained rapid industrialization and economic development, Singapore has reached a stage in its capitalist development where structural unemployment is no longer avoidable. The social and financial problems associated with structural unemployment are conjuncturally compounded by the onset of the demographic transition to an aging population, with seriously declining birthrate as the increasingly middle class population eschews the perceived financial burdens of large families. Under such conditions, like all economically successful capitalist societies, Singapore cannot avoid expansion of social welfare provision, when the problems associated with unemployment emerge as its economy matures. However, the modes of provision of social security are unlikely to be the same as those of other countries. And perhaps, having seen and learned from the difficulties of the prevailing welfare regimes in Western Europe, the modes of provisions are understandably very different from these countries.

NOTES

1. The ideological foundation of Singapore is "pragmatism," however, to the extent that the effects of pragmatism includes possible extreme self-interest in exclusively materialist terms, it is insufficient as the "moral" basis of society, hence, over the past two decades, the PAP government has been experimenting with different "national" ideologies, including the present preference for "communitarianism;" for details of this ideological trajectory, see Chua (1995).

2. As a result of this entrenched hegemony, many PAP leaders are wont to believe that the history of independent Singapore is synonymous with the history of the PAP party and leadership; for example, the two-volume autobiography of Lee Kuan Yew (1998, 2000), who was prime minister for the first thirty-one years, is titled, *The Singapore Story*. For more critical political analysis of the ascendancy and hegemony of the PAP, see Rodan (1989), Chua (1995), and Tremewan (1994).

3. Khong (1995) has listed the PAP government's incorporation of the various non-state sectors into its ideological embrace through the idea of the "collective" good, thereby enhancing the government's political legitimacy to rule.

4. Among academic writings, see Khong (1995), Case (1995), Mauzy and Milne (2002).

5. Mauzy and Milne (2002: 9) suggest that the Jurong project, once called "Goh Keng Swee's Folly" after the first minister of finance and generally recognized as the "architect" of Singapore's early economic development program, had been praised as a "Herculean achievement" by Mr. Goh Chok Tong, the prime minister who succeeded Lee Kuan Yew.

6. For a comprehensive view of the activities of the EDB, see Schein (1996).

7. The colonial administration in Singapore, through the Public Works Department and the Singapore Improvement Trust, had built more housing and infrastructure compared to other British colonial territories elsewhere in the world.

8. The CPF has progressively become a primary instrument of social policy beyond housing. It is now used to finance part of the household's medical care, education needs and ultimately, retirement. The literature on CPF is extensive, for a sampling see, Asher (1994) and Low and Aw (1997).

9. For a sampling of the literature on the housing program, see Wong and Yeh (1985); Castells, Goh and Kwok (1990), and Chua (1997).

10. For a critical view of the relations between public housing and working class Singaporeans see Tremewan, who refers to the public housing estates as "working class barracks" (1994: 47–53).

11. Pro-family social policies are extensive in Singapore, including very substantial tax breaks for children, especially the third and fourth child, children bearing the costs of hospitalization of their parents through the use of the children's CPF medisave funds, and finally, the law that allows parents to sue children for old age maintenance.

12. Details of ComCare and its programs are given during parliamentary session on March 11, 2005 by the Minister of State for Community Development, Youth, and Sports, Mrs. Yu-Foo Yee Shoon.

13. For details of the role of the National Trades Union Congress in job-retraining and job-placement programs see Wong (2005).

REFERENCES

Asher, Mukul. (1994). *Social Security in Malaysia and Singapore: Practices, Issues, and Reform Directions*. Kuala Lumpur: Institute of Strategic and International Studies.

Bell, Daniel. (1995). *Towards Illiberal Democracy in Pacific Asia*. New York: St. Martins Press.

Castells, Manuel, Goh L., and R.W. L. Kwok. (1990). *The Shek Kip Mei Syndrome: Economic Development and Housing in Hong Kong and Singapore*. London: Pion.

Central Provident Study Group. (1986). "Report of the CPF Study Group." *The Singapore Economic Review*, 31(1).

Chua, Beng Huat. (1995). *Communitarian Ideology and Democracy in Singapore*. London: Routledge.

———. (1997). *Political Legitimacy and Housing: Stakeholding in Singapore*. London: Routledge.

Holliday, Ian, and Paul Wilding. (2003). *Welfare Capitalism in East Asia: Social Policies in the Tiger Economies*. Basingstoke: Palgrave Macmillan.

Khong, Cho-Oon. (1995). "Singapore: Political Legitimacy through Managing Conformity," in Muthiah Alagappa (ed.) *Political Legitimacy in Southeast Asia: The Quest for Moral Authority*. Stanford, CA: Stanford University Press, pp. 108–35.

Lee, Kuan Yew. (1988, 2000). *The Singapore Story: Lee Kuan Yew's Memoirs*. Singapore: Times Editions.
Low, Linda and T. C. Aw. (1997). *Housing a Healthy, Educated and Wealthy Nation Through CPF*. Singapore: Times Academic Press.
Mauzy, Diane K. and R. S. Milne. (2002). *Singapore Politics Under the People's Action Party*. London: Routledge.
Rodan, Garry. (1989). *The Political Economy of Singapore's Industrialization*. London: Macmillan.
Schein, Edgar H. (1996). *Strategic Pragmatism: The Culture of Singapore's Economic Development Board*. Cambridge, MA: MIT Press.
Tremewan, M. (1999). *The Political Economy of Social Control in Singapore*. Hampshire, UK: Macmillan.
Wong, Aline A. K. and Stephen Yeh. **[(YEAR??).]** *Housing a Nation: 25 Years of Public Housing in Singapore*. Singapore: Housing and Development Board.

3

Aging Population in East Asia

Impacts on Social Protection and
Social Policy Reforms in Japan, Korea, and Taiwan

Chyong-Fang Ko, Kyeung Mi Oh, and Tetsuo Ogawa

Aging population is an important trend experienced by most industrial countries East and West. One of the major challenges we are confronting today is what is commonly referred to as an "aging society." With average life expectancy increasing steadily, the question of the role of this increasingly important sector of the population (over sixty-five) and the economic implications of the changing demographic structure is at the forefront of policy debates. It appears that the implications of aging in East Asian societies are pervasive and the effects have been regarded pessimistic in recent decades due to their unstable economic situations and Asian Financial Crisis. Among various East Asian societies, Japan, Korea, and Taiwan people are now living longer and healthier. It is widely understood that population aging means health and long-term care costs are likely to rise, and the central challenge is whether these expenditures are cost-effective and meet with the most pressing requirements in the region. Caregiving for frail, elderly people is often fragmented due to underdevelopment in social policies, and sometimes it may be unnecessarily costly to users. As demographic trends point to a particularly rapid increase in the number of elderly people, it is important for each government to develop adequate policies and financial arrangements for caregiving. The Organization for Economic Cooperation and Development also states that "spending for pension, health and long-term care must be increased for elderly people" (OECD, 1998). Strategic frameworks need to be in place at the national level and to build-up support for elderly people in the region (Hoskins, 2002: 13). This chapter examines important demographic aspects of this significant social phenomenon and its likely impact on social policies in Japan, Korea, and Taiwan. After the introduction, we will outline policy responses addressing aging issues in the region, and then discuss the principles for ongoing reforms and programs. The third part will discuss the policy imperatives for social policy changes and reform prospects for the future.

THE PRACTICE OF INCOME PROTECTION

The initial research question of this chapter is to what extent the Japanese, Taiwanese, and Korean welfare systems for elderly people could be compared to each other in terms of policy responses to the elderly issue. In the following section we will focus on social protection systems and practices of these three major East Asian countries.

Japan

A set of policy principles has been developed to guide reforms in Japan. Since the early 1990s, the Japanese government has begun to emphasize policy reforms in pension, health, social care, and employment policy in order to respond to the aging issue. It is important to point out that long-term policies on aging require a broad view of Japanese economy in order to understand the government's capacity to generate resources, and the effect of long-term demographics and its associated demands on the economy (OECD, 1998). In reality, Japanese government seeks to coordinate social welfare with economic policy in order to sustain a basic level of social protection expenditures and to avoid excessive financial burdens of aging (OECD, 1998; Ogawa, 2000).[1] However, the current economic situation is stagnant even though Japan has tried various strategies to recover its economy. In general, issues of Japanese aging society are mainly concerned with social solidarity, intergenerational conflicts, and generational equity. A central feature of Japan's demographics is a long-run decline in fertility (Ogawa, 2003). The implication of this dramatic fall in fertility is that, fewer young workers are expected to enter the economy. As a result, there is a decline in labor forces. The government is also concerned with the increase of social expenditures. There is the need to tackle aging issues by a series of social policy reforms (Ministry of Health, Labour and Welfare [MHLW], 2000). It has focused mainly on two initial questions: 1) to what extent should welfare benefits be trimmed? 2) How to finance the rise of social security expenditure?

Pension Schemes

The Japanese pension schemes have three pillars.[2] As Japan's population ages, its payments from the current pay-as-you-go (PAYG) pension system will increase considerably (Barr, 2001). This means that social responsibility for the National Pension Scheme (NPS) and the amount of contributions will also increase. The relationship between pension payments and wage level is significant. It emerges that while pension payments are roughly on par with western European countries, national pension contributions are lower (MHLW, 2000). While the total costs of National Pension Scheme contributions in Japan are approaching European levels, the rapid aging of Japan will increase contributions, and the payment/contribution ratio will decline rapidly (MHLW, 2000; Barr, 2001). Consequently, the social shares of funding pension payments increase across generations from the current generation receiving pensions at the high end to future generations receiving at the low end. One of the major issues in coming years is the need to find solutions for sustaining the current balance of payment and funding.

Retirement Policy

Japanese elderly people have higher labor force participation rates than that in other OECD countries, which can be explained by two factors: a high commitment to work and an inadequate retirement system. Statistics in 2000 shows a high proportion of elderly men in employment of 61 percent for those aged fifty-five to fifty-nine, 71.6 percent for those aged sixty to sixty-four, and 58.6 percent for those aged sixty-five to sixty-nine. With regard to women, the employment rates are 56.1 percent of those aged fifty-five to fifty-nine, 39.8 percent of those aged sixty to sixty-four and 32.1 percent of those aged sixty-five to sixty-nine. However, the labor participation rate of those aged sixty-five and above is on the decline. The relation between the working age population (those aged fifteen to sixty-four) and elderly population (those aged sixty-five and over) is regarded as one factor that determines the dynamics of a country. In 2000, it is projected that the ratio of the young population (aged between zero and nineteen) continues to fall, while the ratio of the working age population (those aged between twenty and sixty-four) remains relatively high (National Institute of Population and Social Security Research [NIPSSR], 2000). Kono (1994: 159) argues that "the old age dependency ratio is particularly relevant in as much as this indicator roughly quantifies the weight of social costs that the current working age population has to bear in order to support social security and medical expenses for elderly people." An increase in the old-age dependency ratio will result in an increase of social costs shared by the working age population. For example, when the old-age dependency ratio is 25.1 percent, there will be only two persons of working age to support one aged person under the current PAYG system. Therefore, there are considerations about raising the retirement age from sixty to sixty-five and delaying pensionable age. The aim of these policy changes is to encourage elderly people to remain independent rather than relying on the present social care system.

Financial Burden

Japan's aging population will have enormous impacts on pension, health, and long-term care spending in the future. The central challenge is whether these rising expenditures are cost-effective and able to meet the pressing requirements in the society. The Japanese government has emphasized the achievement of economic growth rather than increasing social protection expenditures. Although spending on social protection is relatively low compared with that of western Europe, the government still needs to cope with tremendous costs of social protection caused by population aging in the coming decades. As a consequence of recent low fertility rates, Japan will have to devote an increasing share of output to support a large number of elderly populations. In Japan caregiving for frail, elderly people was often described as fragmented due to its underdevelopments in social policies, and sometimes it was unnecessarily costly to users. One of the issues with which Japan is faced is insufficient formal care provision for elderly people. While a breakdown of social security payments shows that medical treatment costs are roughly comparable to the United States and western European countries, welfare expenditures for elderly people are still low in Japan (MHLW, 2000).

Korea

One of the important concerns of elderly Koreans is the lack of the pension income and hence financial independence. There are five types of income maintenance programs currently in place: 1) public pensions, 2) public assistance programs 3) senior discount programs, 4) employment programs and 5) retirement benefit programs.

Public Pension

The public pension programs that are designed to operate as contributory social insurance schemes include: the National Pension (NP), the Government Employee Pension (GEP), the Military Servicemen Pension (MSP), and the Private School Teachers Pension (PSTP). Except for 6.2 percent of Korean workers who are covered by three occupational-specific pensions (GEP, MSP and PSTP), the majority of workers are covered by the National Pension (NP). Therefore, among those income maintenance programs, the national pension program is the most concerned area for the elderly population's income maintenance. However, preferential treatment of certain groups with respect to pension rights (U.S. Department of Health and Human Services, Social Security Administration, 1994; Palley and Usui, 1995) has also been observed in South Korea. For instance, while the three occupational-specific pensions (GEP, MSP, and PSTP) were introduced in the early 1960s and in the middle of the 1970s, the National Pension only began later in 1988. As a result, most of the elderly Koreans currently aged sixty and over were not eligible for the benefits of an old-age pension that requires at least twenty years of contributions and being sixty years old. In other words, almost all elderly Koreans are not covered by this old-age pension until 2008. Only 2.8 percent in 1998 of elderly Koreans aged sixty-five and over were recipients of the old public pension (Chung, 1998).

The general lack of pension income is considered a big problem as mandatory retirement age has been set at fifty-five to sixty years. Consequently, the lack of the old-age pension and the early exit from the labor force leaves long and "non-earning years" for the general elderly population. The NP was initially introduced in 1988 for firms with more than ten employees; the self-employed in rural areas joined the NP in 1999; and the urban self-employed were also covered by the NP in 1999. After twenty years in operation, it is anticipated that this pension will face a serious fiscal problem. In fact, GEP and PSTP have already presented serious fiscal instability, including the MSP that has already faced fiscal deficit a long time ago. At present, the proportion of elderly Koreans aged sixty and over is about 10 percent and is expected to increase up to 20 percent twenty years later and 33 percent fifty years later. In other words, among the general population, one out of three will be a pensioner (Poston and Kim, 1999; Kim, 2001).

Accordingly, for long-term sustainability of the pension scheme, several reform measures were discussed but the measures were strongly objected by unions. For example, the labor unions of the government employees and schoolteachers strongly objected to reforming the GEP through collective action. According to Kwon (2001), the reform measures represent a decrease in the replacement ratio as well as a gradual increase in the age of eligibility for old-age pension payments. As a first step, the replacement ratio, which is the ratio of the benefit amount to earnings before retirement, has recently been decreased from 70 percent to 60 percent, with forty years of contributions. It was stipulated that the pension schemes should be revised every five years based on analysis of the fiscal status of the pension fund.

Public Assistance Programs

Elderly Koreans are eligible for two kinds of public assistance programs: the Livelihood Protection Program (LPP) and Respect-Elder Pension (REP). The Livelihood Protection Program was designed to guarantee a minimum standard of living for all populations by a means test regardless of age which covers five categories of benefits for elderly people: 1) livelihood, 2) medical, 3) housing, 4) self-reliance, and 5) funeral assistance. Koreans aged sixty-five and over took up 21.2 percent of recipients of LPP benefits and represent 8 percent of all the elderly population. The REP was introduced to solve the problem not covered by the NP. Notwithstanding its good intention, the effect of the program on the recipients' quality of lives is minimal (Choi, Kim, and Koh, 2001). The main reason is that only about 20 percent of elderly people are eligible for this program and the amount of benefit is not sufficient to support old people's independent living.

Senior Discount Program and Employment Programs

This is a universal program provided to all elderly people aged sixty-five and over and is financed by the local government. The program provides elderly people with discounts on public transport and on admission to public facilities. Additionally it also provides elderly people with a transportation allowance. Income insecurity of elderly people has augmented the desire of elderly people to get paid work. However it is extremely difficult for elderly people to have access to paid work since unemployment is high in South Korea (Kwon, 2001). According to Hwang et al. (2001), the primary reason of old people to work is "money," and the reason for quitting is the job being "too tough." There are five kinds of income-generating programs that provide elderly people with an opportunity to earn income by making good use of their free time: Elderly Employment Center (OPEC); Elderly Workshop (EW); Elderly Workers Bank; Elderly Workers Job Selection; Elderly Worker Employment Quota. Albeit the intention for these programs sounds good, the function of them seems disappointingly negligible (Hwang et al., 2001).

Retirement Benefit Program

This program is for workers in all work places by the provision of the Labor Standard Act. This benefit is paid as a lump sum when the worker leaves the workplace because of having reached mandatory retirement age or for other reasons. At present, the program is the main income source for most retirees in Korea because they are not covered by the National Pension.

HEALTH AND WELFARE SERVICES

Korea

Health Insurance

Health care in South Korea is delivered primarily by independent medial practitioners and private sector organizations that operate more than 91 percent of all hospitals and clinics (Ministry of Health and Welfare [MHW], 2000a). Private hospitals and clinics are predominantly located in urban areas, largely unregulated, and operate within a competitive market. Their activity is underwritten through the state health insurance scheme. The government basically finances medical, paramedical and nursing education. While the private market approach has raised the volume and quality of services, the level and growth of government health expenditures have been problematic for several South Korean governments. In fact, the health insurance fund has been in deficit since 1996. Financial stability of health insurance depends on the behavior of both health care providers and consumers (Kwon, 2001). For instance, from 1994 to 1998, the medical expenditure of elderly people grew by 176 percent, but the proportion of elderly people to the total population grew only by 16 percent (National Health Insurance Corporation [NHIC], 1999).

Home Care

Home health care was introduced since 1991 and operates from the primary care centers under the Community Health Care Act. In 1993 the *Association of Korean Registered Nurses* initiated home health care from four hospitals. Moreover, the government provided a model hospital-based home health service from four tertiary hospitals during 1994–1996, and experimented with a similar scheme with 45 secondary hospitals during 1997–1999. The primary care center-based services emphasises health promotion and disease prevention among low-income groups. Meanwhile, Hospital-based services are available to patients of all ages, whereas the largest patient group consists of elderly people, including those with terminal conditions such as cancer and functional disabilities. The majority of South Koreans are unaware of community-based services, and home health services remain largely marginal.

Elderly Health Examination

There is always an uneasy strain between universal and targeted provision. The former has been driven by the increasing expectations and rising affluence of the population and the rising political "leverage" of health issues, while the latter much more by moral, humanitarian, and collective concerns for the welfare of the most deprived (Oh and Warnes, 2001). Welfare programs targeted at the disadvantaged and lowest income groups were initiated in 1984 with means-tested forms of income support, defined in South Korea as "Livelihood Protection." These extended into food or "nutritional supplement" programs operating from the primary care centers. These laid the foundation for the establishment in 1983 of the "elderly health examination service" which provides free health examinations, health education, early diagnosis, and refined management of multiple chronic diseases among elderly people. The quality of this service has subsequently greatly improved but, due to budget constrains, access continues to be limited to those who are eligible for Livelihood Protection. Services are also exclusively available in urban areas. Home care supports those who have difficulties with daily living. It was established in 1987 and expanded greatly from 1995 (MHW, 2000b). Elderly people who are registered in the Livelihood Protection scheme are eligible for free home care. Other elderly people are only able to access fee-for-service home care. As the majority of home care recipients are eligible for Livelihood Protection, it is evident that those in need are not willing to pay for home care services (Oh and Warnes, 2001).

Day Care and Respite Care

Day care centers for elderly people provide bathing facilities, rehabilitation, social activities, and meals service for those who somehow don't manage to be cared for by their families. The number of centers has been growing and reached 107 in 2002 (Choi, Kim, and Koh, 2001). Like other services for elderly people, access to this service is limited to a small minority of the poor. Respite care aims to support informal family caregivers by enabling them to take a respite from the long-term care of a disabled elderly person. The duration is confined to 45 days for each respite, and not more than three months' care is granted to an individual during a year.

Residential and Nursing Home Care

Lasting adherence to the belief that the family supports and cares for elderly parents has impeded the development of institutionalized care. The main types are residential homes, nursing homes, specialized hospitals for elderly people with chronic illness, and municipal and provincial dementia hospitals. As in northern European countries, residential homes are for elderly people who suffer from multiple disorders and need assistance with functional limitations, while nursing homes are primarily for those who suffer from dementia, paralysis, or severe functional disabilities. There is little evidence on how well this distinction is maintained, that is, whether there are good assessment and admission procedures in place. Specialized hospitals are for people who have severe (and often multiple) chronic diseases and need continuing medical treatment and relatively intensive nursing care. Access to free institutional care is limited to the poorest elderly people. There are too few residential places for physically and mentally disabled elderly people, and significant proportions of the available places are luxurious and only serve the rich. Among those aged sixty-five years and over, only 0.3 percent are residents in institutions, compared to 6 percent in Japan, 5.7 percent in the United States and 5.1 percent in the United Kingdom (OECD, 1998). Recently, most Western countries are prioritizing the development of home-based services rather than residential services in order to reduce the total cost of "elderly care."

By the revision of the Older Persons Welfare Act of 1993, the establishment of independent homes in a competitive market for residential care was permitted in order to encourage private sector investment. Diverse individuals and companies had expressed interest in establishing residential homes, but the legislation prohibits the sale of a care home and this has somewhat hindered investment. Only non-profit organizations and large commercial companies that seek to improve their image were interested in the expansion of provision.

Until recently, most Koreans accepted the responsibility to take care of their parents as an expression of their familial responsibility. They were less likely to admit the parent to a mental hospital, not until 1989 when it had begun to be covered by the national health insurance (Sung, 1996). Lately, however, the population's understanding of dementia, and its attitude toward the care of elderly people with dementia, has changed and the demand for services has substantially increased. The adoption of both Western models of health care and of a rationalist view of mental illness have since engendered a more positive view that patients would be treated and cared for better by professional medicine.

Taiwan

The Impact of Party Politics and Aging on Social Policy

The demographic shift toward an aged population is not as extensive in Taiwan as it is in Japan, Europe, or North America. In Taiwan, people over sixty-five represent a mere 8.8 percent of the total population, while the old-age dependency rate is 12.5 percent and youth dependency rate 29.6 percent (table 3.1). Although the proportion of the elderly is not significant compared to the total population, it is increasing rapidly. In 1951, the elderly population in Taiwan was less than 3 percent, but by 1993 Taiwanese society had aged considerably. This trend is continuing, such that it is estimated that the elderly proportion of the population will increase up to two-fold (reaching 14 percent) by 2019 (Council for Economic Planning and Development, 2002). The same change occurred in France over one hundred and fifteen years,

Table 3.1. Population Structure of Taiwan Area: 1951–2051

Year	1951	1961	1971	1981	1991	2001	2011*	2021*	2031*	2041*	2051*
Total population (in thousands)	7,869	11,149	14,995	18,136	20,557	22,339	23,547	24,314	24,400	23,517	21,907
(%)	(100)	(100)	(100)	(100)	(100)	(100)	(100)	(100)	(100)	(100)	(100)
Age 0–14	3,312	5,112	5,805	5,731	5,412	4,649	4,038	3,745	3,446	3,064	2,844
(%)	(42.09)	(45.85)	(38.71)	(31.6)	(26.33)	(20.81)	(17.15)	(15.4)	(14.13)	(13.03)	(12.98)
Age 15–64	4,364	5,759	8,736	11,605	13,804	15,725	17,050	16,714	15,437	14,143	12,545
(%)	(55.46)	(51.65)	(58.26)	(63.99)	(67.15)	(70.39)	(72.41)	(68.74)	(63.27)	(60.14)	(57.27)
Age 65 and over	193	278	454	799	1,341	1,965	2,459	3,855	5,516	6,309	6,518
(%)	(2.45)	(2.49)	(3.03)	(4.41)	(6.52)	(8.8)	(10.44)	(15.85)	(22.61)	(26.83)	(29.75)
Young age dependency rate	75.89	88.77	66.44	49.38	39.21	29.6	23.68	22.41	22.33	21.67	22.67
Old age dependency rate	4.42	4.82	5.2	6.89	9.71	12.5	14.42	23.06	35.73	44.61	51.96
Total fertility rate	7.04	5.585	3.705	2.455	1.72	1.43	1.45	1.6	1.6	1.6	1.6
Life expectancy at birth											
male	53.1	62.62	67.19	69.74	71.83	72.86	75.25	77.64	78.09	78.55	79
female	57.32	67	72	74.6	77.15	78.74	81.68	84.62	85.08	85.54	86

Note: * = Estimated figures.

Source: *Population Projections for Taiwan area, Republic of China 2002–2051*. Council for Economic Planning and Development (Manpower Planning Department), Executive Yuan. 2002.

between 1865 and 1980; in Britain it took forty-five years, while in Japan it took twenty-six years (Kinsella and Taeuber, 1992). According to the medium series population estimate made in 2002 by the Council for Economic Planning and Development (Manpower Planning Department), Executive Yuan, in the year 2021 the old age dependency rate will be higher than that of the youth dependency rate, with the former rising up to 15.85 percent and the latter declining to 15.40 percent. By that time, on average, there will be one aged dependent per every 4.3 working persons and one young dependent per every 4.5 working persons; that is to say, every 2.2 working persons will be responsible for a dependent. Due to the proportionately small aged population and the high cohabitation rate of elderly people with their married children, the government did not establish any old-age security scheme over the past few decades, and established only a few social assistance or welfare stipend schemes. Nevertheless, with the rapid increase of the aged population and changing social values, the government did implement a Living Allowance for the Elderly in 2002.[3]

The National Pension System was designed to insure the economic well-being of the aged, but it did not originate with pressure from the aging population itself. Rather, it resulted from local elections. Before 2000, when the Nationalist Party (KMT) was in power, the government aimed to assist the elderly people in need under a complete set of welfare measures rather than a simple cash payment. In order to win elections, the candidates of the Democratic Progress Party (DPP) presented the idea of establishing Taiwan as a welfare state; hence, an Old Age Allowance scheme was proposed in 1992 that would give every senior citizen NT$3,000–5,000 monthly. Facing political threats from the DPP, the KMT government responded by creating a series of welfare programs. In 1993, the Elderly Living Allowance for the Median and Low Income Family was established, and one year later (March 1994), a special committee was organized to design a national pension system. By March 1995, the *National Heath Insurance System* was put into practice. Since then, welfare issues have become major topics of debate in political campaigns at all levels. Unfortunately, a severe earthquake struck on September 21, 1999, forcing the government to prioritize disaster relief and temporarily set aside preparations for the National Pension System.

In 2000, the DPP candidate, Chen Shui-bian, won the presidential campaign and resumed the establishment of the National Pension System to meet his campaign promises and implement the DPP's political ideas. The Legislative Yuan adopted a new labor retirement act in 2005. The act mandates the establishment of a personal account system for pensions. Savings in the account accumulate according to years of work, and account holders do not lose a penny when they change jobs. Their right to change jobs is protected and their retirement benefits guaranteed. However, the success or failure of this system depends on how the government manages the retirement fund and whether retirement fund agents are capable of satisfactory risk management. Some employers resist the new scheme and are changing their pay system for employees. One popular change is to lower the basic payment and raise the cash reward. Other employers are increasing their outsourcing or hiring part-time workers. Some medium-sized and small businesses consider laying off their employees and then rehiring them.

Change in Social Values and the Increase of Welfare Demand

It is true that rapid population aging is partially the result of the extension of life expectancy, but it has more to do also with the speedy decline of the birthrate. In 1951, the total fertility rate in Taiwan was 7.04, which means, on average, every woman had 7.04 live births during her lifetime. The life expectancy was 53 years for males and 57 years for females. In 2001, the total fertility rate dropped to 1.43, while the life expectancy was 73 for men and 79 for women. The extension of life expectancy reflects the development of socioeconomic conditions and the improvement of health care and medical standards. The decline in the birthrate reflects changes in social values, the improvement of women's education levels, increases in female participation in the labor force, and a widespread preference for nuclear families. Traditional Chinese society envisaged a division of labor between men and women, with the elderly taken care of by their children, the middle-aged employed, and the young brought up by collective effort of the family. Family, according to this tradition, is not only a unit of production, but also the place of individual growth, emotional reliance, and geriatric care. In this system, it is the children's responsibility to look after their elderly parents. But due to changes in industrial structures, young people now tend to migrate to big cities for jobs, thus reducing the possibility that they will consider living with their parents, let alone take care of them. With increases in female employment and changes in social values, moreover, married young couples often prefer to live separately from their parents or parents-in-law; and at the same time, the elderly parents choose not to live with their married children. The *Survey Summary of Senior Citizen Condition in Taiwan-Fuchen Area* showed that about 68 percent of the elderly people co-resided with their children, 24 percent lived alone or with spouses only, 6 percent lived in welfare institutions, and 2 percent lived together with relatives or other people (Ministry of the Interior, 2000). Facing historically low birthrates and the dissolution of traditional values, future challenges to geriatric care are contingent not only on the willingness of adult children to take care of their elderly parents, but whether there will be enough children for the elderly to depend upon.

The rapid increase in the aged population will result in greater demands for social welfare, especially with regard to health services, long-term care, and economic well-being. Taiwan has implemented a National Health Insurance System since March 1995; consequently, expenditures on medication are no longer a major financial burden for elderly people as it is shared by the insured and the government, whose expenditures on preventive health care has increased rapidly for the past few years. Long-term care has unfortunately, not been covered by the National Health Insurance. The government was planning to promote a long-term care insurance scheme to supplement the insufficient family care ten years ago, but it has been canceled due to the stagnation of the global economy and the financial difficulties of the government. Nevertheless, the original plan was replaced by Investigation for Insurance and Financial Scheme for Long-term Care (Wei, 2002), and, hopefully, there will be a modified long-term care service for the elderly in the near future. Currently, the implementation of the National Pension System is a top priority.

SOCIAL POLICY REFORMS AND FUTURE DIRECTIONS

Japan

The Need to Change Social Policies for Elderly People

Social policies for elderly people involve a number of social service programs, e.g. pension, labor policy, health care, long-term care, and housing policy. The combination of these policies influences the welfare of elderly people. In reality, the expenditure on public pension takes up nearly half of the expenditure, and that one third is on health insurance (NIPSSR, 2002). Japan's aging process and structural changes are likely to raise a wide range of issues concerning resource allocation and policy changes (OECD, 1989). The Ministry of Health, Labor, and Welfare [MHLW] (2000) assumes that the increasing needs of elderly care are central to national development. Also, an increase in the elderly population will generate demand for age-related services and health care industries in Japan. Public social spending is very sensitive to the age distribution of the population. In particular, the combination of rising health care and pension outlays is projected to increase total social expenditures significantly in Japan (OECD, 1989).

Generational Equity and Social Solidarity

Under the Japanese pension program of the PAYG approach, the young generation receives less benefits than their total contributions that they have made before their retirement. This indicates that there may be an inequity of the ratio of contribution/benefits over generations. In order to avoid such issues, some argue that the pension system should be transformed from the PAYG to a funded system. However, the system itself is not the solution to equalizing the ratio of contribution/benefits over the generations. Moreover, there is an issue of generational equity—equity of the ratio of contributions/benefits, and equity between the pension amounts which elderly recipients receive and the amount the working population contributes at a certain period. Social solidarity could not be developed unless there is a system to institutionalize the redistribution of wealth. It is important for Japan to improve the quality of life of the poorest and most vulnerable segments of the population by social policy making and the solutions to protect elderly people from vulnerability of old age.

Japan's Pensions Reform

As mentioned earlier, Japan faces a rapidly aging society and a shrinking labor force of unparalleled proportions. The government estimates that by the year 2050, 32.3 percent of Japanese people will be over the age of sixty-five, more than double today's percentage of just over 18 percent (NIPSSR 2001). This shift in workforce distribution will put considerable pressure on Japan's pension system. In the next fifteen years, it is estimated Japan will not have enough workers paying into the system to support benefits. In 1997, there were 4.4 workers supporting each retiree receiving benefits, but by 2020 there will just be 2 workers, and by 2050 only 1.5. In March 2000, the Japanese Diet passed key pension and social security reform legislation aimed at easing the strains on the system (MHLW, 2000). Under the new laws, the age at which Japanese elderly is to begin receiving pension payments will be raised from sixty to sixty-five. Unfortunately, a gap remains between the age at which pension payments will begin and the mandatory retirement age of sixty, which persist at many firms. Although the law states that firms have the duty to continue hiring workers between the ages of sixty and sixty-five, this will make workers of such age increasingly insecure. Therefore, this provision will not be phased in until 2018 in order to avoid adverse effects on those workers who are nearing retirement.

Both Japan's National Pension and Employees' Pension Insurance are facing financial difficulties to accumulate enough funds for pension payments.

At the moment, there are various pension reform proposals regarding pension payments *both* by cutting back benefits and raising premiums. This has been affected by a rapid aging of the Japanese population, low rate of economic growth, and low public interest rates. There is a proposed solution to delay pension benefits from sixty to sixty-five. An issue surrounding the national pension is that there is a large number of the population who have not participated in the mandatory scheme. There is also another issue of the high dropout rate in premium repayment amongst pension subscribers. The subscription rate was 73 percent in 2000. Younger generations are expected to have a higher dropout rate. In addition, there are many issues over corporation pension schemes. It has been difficult for private companies to continue defined-benefit (DB) corporation pension schemes as a result of economic recession.

Besides, there are many changes of employment patterns from a long-life employment in a single company to one of multiple employers. It is true that women may have more diverse employment patterns than men because of their various roles in the private and public spheres. At the moment, it is necessary for people to contribute to the national pension scheme for twenty-five years to receive a full benefit. However, due to the fragmented nature of women's careers, it is likely for them not to be able to satisfy the minimum duration and hence contribution requirement. In addition, there is the issue of missing periods of pension contribution for Japanese people working outside Japan in other countries. At the moment, Japan has agreements only with Germany and the UK.

There have been various attempts to cut net pension benefits, including reductions in the gross replacement ratio, higher taxation, increase in retirement age, and finally a shift to privately financed schemes.[4] Maintaining high benefits at lower contribution rates would require an increase in government transfers to the social security system. Through pension reforms, the government plans to strengthen the pension system by raising contributions from all parties (the government, employers, and employees) while also cutting pension payments to retirees. First, the government raised its share of the pension burden from one-third to one-half, beginning in 2002. Pension contribution rate will rise to 26.7 percent in 2025 from their current 17.35 percent with employers and employees sharing the burden. Finally, there will be a 20 percent reduction in the overall lifetime pension benefit under the public pension system, which will be gradually implemented over twenty years. Such increased contributions and reduced benefits are crucial to keep the pension system afloat.[5]

In June 2001 Defined Benefit Corporate Pension Law was enacted. The benefits for both the employee's pension and the national pension will be reduced by about 1 percent from April 2003 as a result of the application, for the first time in four years, of a price sliding scale, by which changes in consumer prices are reflected in pension benefits. In principle, this sliding scale was established so that pension benefits do not decline in value in times of inflation. In the face of declining birthrate and an aging population, however, the currently active working population are declining while the number of beneficiaries is increasing. As the fiscal situation of pension is expected to further deteriorate, the decision has been made to apply the sliding scale from April 2003. According to the MHLW, the number of births in Japan in 2001 was 1,170,665, a decline of nearly 20,000 compared with that in 2000. Total fertility rate, which shows the number of children that a woman can expect to have in her lifetime, reached a record low of 1.33. One of the main causes was the large drop in the birthrate among women in their late twenties. The total fertility rate has already dropped below the level of 1.34 forecast by the MHLW for 2001 in its future population estimates, issued in January 2002. The Ministry also forecasts (in the future population estimates) that the percentage of the total population occupied by persons aged sixty-five or over will rise from 17.4 percent (22.04 million people) in 2000 to 28.7 percent (34.73 million people) in 2025 and 35.7 percent (35.86 million persons) in 2050. Therefore, for a public pension system that adopts a PAYG scheme, the declining birthrate and aging of the population represent a real threat to the system.

Child Rearing and Pension

In principle the revenue for public pensions comes from the insurance premium paid by the people, although one-third of the basic pension benefits are covered by taxes. In the previous pension system reform in 1999, the government decided to raise it to one half and implemented it in 2004. As a basis of discussion for the 2004 reform, the MHLW has indicated a new formula of fixing the insurance premiums paid by the active working population so that they do not rise above a certain level. The aim here is to eliminate the concern among younger people that their burden would be increasing. The Ministry proposes that the employee's pension insurance fee of 13.58 percent of annual salary (50 percent employer and 50 percent employee) increased up to 20 percent from 2022. In this way, the concern of the working population that their burden is going to increase without limit will be eased. At present, the model pension will enable a Japanese family to receive in their old age about 59 percent of their annual salary (Replacement Rate). Under the new system, this figure would decrease to 52 percent.

In the pension system reform in 2004, there was strong measure to counter the declining birthrate. The MHLW suggests measures to provide support for child-raising. Under the present system, people who take childcare leave are exempted from paying insurance fees for a maximum of one year, and their pension does not decrease in the future as a result. In the case of a person quitting work for the sake of child-raising and having reduced income, however, the pension amount does decrease. Therefore, an increasing number of women are of the opinion that quitting work to have children is just not worth it. Bearing in mind the circumstances that have led to the declining birthrate, the ministry proposes in its basis for discussions to study a mechanism which in case a person quits work for child-raising, her pension would be guaranteed for a certain period. However, the ministry also points out that the issue of the declining birthrate should be discussed in the context of a revision of the employment environment, for example, whether people will lose their jobs if they take leave for child-raising.

Consumption Tax Increase?

In preparation for the pension system reform in 2004, the argument has begun to emerge from business circles that the consumption tax rate (currently 5 percent) should be raised to ensure sufficient revenue source. Mr Hiroshi Okuda, the Japan Business Federation chairman, has proposed the so-called Okuda vision, suggesting that the consumption tax rate should be raised by 1 percent every year from Fiscal Year 2004 onwards and fixed at 16 percent. The revenue will be used to cover social security expenditures, including pensions. The Japan Chamber of Commerce and Industry, Chairperson Mr. Nobuo Yamaguchi and the Japan Association of Corporate Executives, Chairperson Mr. Yotaro Kobayashi, appeared to agree with the Okuda vision. Since they share the burden equally among employees, business circles were strongly opposed to making the insurance fee burden any heavier. Raising the national treasury burden from one-third to one-half will require a revenue source of 2.7 trillion yen. Since this sum is equivalent to 1 percent consumption tax, politicians are concerned with its impact on the Japanese economy.

Japan's Health Care Reforms

The finance of health care is extremely complicated in Japan. Health care services are financed via a public mandatory health insurance system, which is composed of two types of schemes: 1) occupation-based and 2) regional-based. The former is called the *Health Insurance*. Employers and employees of firms of a certain size form a health insurance society and thus these are called the *society-managed health insurance*. There are nearly 1,800 societies.

For those who work at smaller firms, the government provides a collective health insurance, which is called the *government-managed health insurance*. In addition, special professions such as civil servants, day laborers and seamen form separate nationwide professional associations. These occupation-based health insurances cover employees and their dependents. For those who are not covered by the society-managed health insurance, there is the *National Health Insurance* on a regional-based health insurance for which municipalities play as insurers. The National Health Insurance (NHI) is composed of mostly self-employed people, farmers, workers of smaller firms and their families. As a result, these health insurances provide almost a universal coverage for all populations.

Thanks to the universality of the national health insurance scheme, there is no distinction between public and private hospitals from patients' points of view. Furthermore, any patient is free in selecting any health care service providers through the wide coverage of the national health services. It is also guaranteed that patients' access will face equal price and equal coverage of services in any place within Japan. According to relevant laws, the coverage of health insurance and the prices of health services are standardized and equal price health care services is guaranteed.

As a result of Japan's population aging, the public health insurance is facing an enormous financial crisis. Some claim that the Japanese health care services for elderly people must be overhauled so as to solve the issues. The share of the health care costs for elderly people in total medical costs has increased tremendously over the recent decade (OECD, 2001). As explained before, there are several health insurance programs in Japan, but the National Health Insurance (NHI) has the largest number of subscribers. In order to eliminate the burden of the health care costs for elderly people among different insurance schemes, there was a new system introduced in 1983 to separate the health care costs for those aged seventy and over in all schemes from that of those aged sixty-nine and under. While total medical expenses in Japan reach about 30 trillion yen, 11 trillion yen is used for elderly people aged seventy or over. At first, from April 1, 2003, there was a change of copayment by salaried workers to raise the current 20 percent to 30 percent of their medical costs. Especially requests for health care reform have become strong among health insurance unions. At the moment, medical expenses are the contributions from which about 70 percent of revenue collected from the working population. In principle, their companies have paid the half. In recent years, the burden of the working population has become heavier. Last year a bill was passed and a law will be enacted to raise copayment of salaried workers' medical expenses up to 30 percent of the costs. With regard to elderly persons' medical insurance system, the MHLW changed the coverage of insurance from that those for elderly people aged seventy and over, to that for those aged seventy-five and over, but it is planned that half of the costs should be paid by public money from 2007.

The future plan of the health care system for elderly people is regarded as one of the major reforms that the MHLW has drafted in recent years. The draft plan states that the present health care system for elderly people and retirees of salaried workers be abolished and there be a new introduction of two tier systems according to patient age. The system is divided by two categories, of sixty-five–seventy-four years old and of seventy-five years old and over, and a new setup of premium rates. Once three ruling parties (LDP, Conservative Party, and *Komei* Party) agree to the proposal, the draft plan will be sent to be decided on at the cabinet meeting. With the tentative plan of health care system reform which the MHLW released at the end of last year as mentioned above, Proposal A is based upon that cost sharing of elderly people and the working population is put into and the differences of the premiums will be adjusted according to the management of age or incomes. Proposal B is that separation of elder health care is made from the current system. However, the proposal of new principles seems to be the amalgamation of the above two. The MHLW proposes to introduce a burden-adjustment system into young elderly people (sixty-five–seventy-five), but a conclusion has not been made yet whether it establishes a new and separate health care insurance for old elderly people aged seventy-five and over, which introduce a new organization to manage the national health insurance. On the other hand, the MHLW tentative plan is being considered to reorganize and integrate management bodies in all prefectures, but there is a strong criticism on the plan.

Japan's Long-Term Care Reform

In long-term care policy there is a demand for system reform due to changing social environment, such as the aging society and the increasing number of women who shun the carer role for work. In addition, as the diffusion of long-term care service users continues, it has become neccesary to raise the quality of the services. Meanwhile, with the launch of the Long-Term Care Insurance System (LTCIS) and enactment of the Social Welfare Law in 2000, the Japanese welfare sysem begins to provide more choices for its users and "contracts" have begun to take shape between the service providers and the users. As a result, the number of long-term care service users increased dramatically. In addition, the delay of some service providers in taking appropriate measures for regional gaps is also presenting a serious supply issue. Long-term care services are seriously lacking in some regions, and many elderly people are still queuing up for long-term care facilities. Even after the new Long-Term Care Insurance Law (Japanese Law 123, 1997) and the Social Welfare Law, the government still strictly maintains the interpretation of the Constitution of Japan that welfare is essentially "charitable and philanthropic" activities, and that public funds cannot be provided to private company employees. It has been argued that the current welfare system must be best reformed in the direction of securing equal competitive conditions among providers, so that users can have fairer choices.

Korea

The changing situation of the elderly people in terms of support and care services has not been caused simply by the aging population. It is also a reflection of changing social norms on aging. For example, the "silent promise" that older generations will have substantial assets and therefore be less dependent on the social security system. The development of health and welfare services in South Korea has to date been strongly influenced by the structure and divisions between the welfare and medical professions. The dominant influence of physicians has contributed to a low priority for social rehabilitation and the management of chronic illnesses of the elderly. Although care services for frail and sick elderly people have a relatively short history in South Korea compared to Western countries or Japan, its development is rapid since the 1960s. Most services are available only to the minority of elderly people who are either eligible for the "Livelihood Protection" program and have very low incomes or are very rich. The needs of the majority of a frail elderly population are largely neglected. As Kwon (1997: 481) suggests, the underlying logic of Korea's social policy is for "the vulnerable population that has been left out rather than protected, and the working of the system are divisive rather than an enhancement of the solidarity of society."

Other limitations of the current health and social care system in Korea include the widespread public ignorance and misunderstanding about care services, and shortages of human resources in many areas. Most care services depend heavily on volunteer staff. There are, nevertheless, changes in the positive direction in terms of government policies. The current administration has shown greater commitment toward health and welfare issues, particularly for elderly people. Although public expenditure and fiscal concerns may be paramount, the government is now actively developing a long-term care policy which should result in improving residential and nursing home care provision, positively echoing what OECD suggests: "the traditional pattern of elderly care will need to be supplemented by a larger government role" (OECD, 2001: 15).

Another important concern for the aging population is income maintenance. As a consequence of the preferential treatment of certain groups (e.g. government employees, military personnel and school teachers) almost all elderly Koreans are not covered by the public pension until 2008. The general lack of pension income has come to mean that elderly people with low income will be substantially increased in the circumstances where the widespread mandatory retirement age has been set at fifty-five to sixty. Thus, the current problem of the income maintenance program is about the long "non-earning years' for the elderly. To alleviate this problem, the Respect-Elder Pension (REP) was thus introduced, though its effect is still small. In order to resolve the financial difficulties of those who are in the transitional period of the welfare development, the eligibility for this program should be extended. With the current problem of the income maintenance for those not covered by the public pension, Koreans are facing another problem of long-living elderly people in the coming years (Kim, 2001). According to Kwon (2001), to achieve long-term sustainability of the pension scheme, several reform measures are imperative. A decrease in the replacement ratio was the first step in the reform and a gradual shift in the eligibility age for old-age pension payments from sixty to sixty-five and an increase in the contribution rate become imperative.

Welfare Policy for Elderly People

In Korean society, aging issues in the form of income maintenance, diseases, and premature retirement began to emerge as a key social policy concern only around the 1970s. Government response was initially fragmented. Since the enactment of the Older Persons Welfare Act in 1981, the primary approach toward elderly was not simply about income maintenance and health care, but also concerns informal family care, care for single elderly, and general emotional support elderly people. The Government confirmed the traditional role of familial values (Choi, Kim, and Koh, 2001). Table 3.2 certainly reflects this reality as 56.2 percent of elderly people cohabit with their children. This emphasis on family care was further confirmed in the Amended Older Persons Welfare Act of 1989. However, since the early 1990s, the development of long-term care became a significant policy challenge and its definition was extended to home, community, and institutional-based health and social care. In 1991, the International Year of Elderly Persons, a Long-term Plan was established in preparation for the challenge of the twenty-first century aging society. Since the implementation of the Amended Older Persons Welfare Act of 1997, welfare services for the elderly became much more diverse.

Table 3.2. Living Arrangements of Elderly People in South Korea 1997 (%)

Co-resident with Children[1]	Living Alone	Living with Spouse Only	Other[2]	Total
56.2	19.4	22.9	1.5	100.0

Notes:
The sample size was 1,888 people aged 65 years and over.
1. Own or child's home.
2. Co-resident with a relative or friend or in a residential care or sheltered home.

Source: Korea Institute for Health and Social Affairs (1997). *Research on the State of the National Birth Rate and Family Health*. Seoul, Korea: KIHASA.

In January 1999, the government established a development agenda that calls for "Mid- to Long-term Development Directions for Elderly Health and Welfare in Preparation of an Aging Society in the Twenty-first Century." Its main goal was to improve independence, participation, care self-fulfilment, and dignity of elderly people through strengthening income security, securing healthy living, and generally promoting an active elderly culture. However, the 1999 Act failed to focus the ideals of long-term care. To improve, the Policy Planning Committee for Long-term Care for elderly people was established in 2000, marking a further step toward a mature institutional framework for long-term elderly care.

Civic Responses

Since the early 1980s, the independent sector (operated by the individuals, voluntary, and religious organizations) has played a great role for the welfare for elderly Koreans. These social services agencies have expanded since the enactment of the Older Persons Welfare Act in 1981. Since the 1990s, welfare services by the public sector that provide more professional services have also gradually expanded and as a result state financial assistance for the voluntary sector has been significantly reduced. Simultaneously, for-profit organizations, which provide services for elderly people in the middle and upper group, have at the same time been increasing but its provisions are less well-developed due to various constraints of registration. For instance, various for-profit organizations have been interested in establishing a care home but the legislation forbids the sale of a care home to elderly people to prevent speculations and hence discouraged private investment in this area. In order to meet the growing needs of elderly populations of various socioeconomic groups, the right mix of statutory welfare services and for-profit welfare organizations has become a controversial policy issue (Choi, Kim, and Koh, 2001). In the meantime, various voluntary associations for elderly welfare have been established, for example, the

Korean Senior Citizens' Association was established in 1969 which has 1.7 million members in 243 districts, 269 senior schools, 250 volunteer groups, and over 40,000 senior club houses by 2000. The Korean Council on Elderly Welfare Institutions, the Korean Council of Community Care Service Facilities, and the Korean Council on Elderly Welfare Centers, are all fine examples of voluntary organizations aiming at influencing policy development for the elderly welfare (Choi, Kim, and Koh, 2001).

Taiwan

Pension Payment for Professionals

Until 2002, there was not a universal pension scheme for senior citizens in Taiwan. The earliest one was the Labor Insurance Scheme, initiated in 1950. Both the employees and the employers were responsible for the premium, and the insured receive basic medication aids, welfare stipends, death compensation, and comfort measures. In general, retirees did not receive a life-long pension, but were offered a lump-sum cash payment based on position and work seniority. The Government Employees' and School Staffs' Insurance (initiated in 1958) and the Private School Staffs' Insurance (initiated in 1980) make similar arrangements except that recipients of such schemes can choose either a lump-sum cash payment or a life-long pension.[6]

The best-designed pension scheme is for veterans. It is a legacy of the large number of military personnel coming from Mainland China since 1949. Most of them were single and had no relatives in Taiwan, and it was impossible for them to return to the Mainland. The government established a special commission in 1954 to provide assistance on retirement settlements and/or career arrangements for the veterans and their families. It was subsequently renamed the Veterans Affairs Commission of Executive Yuan in 1966. In addition to its original mission, the Veterans Affairs Commission also provides medication, home care, geriatric care, and dependent allowance for the veterans. Other schemes following these include The Terms of Military Personnel Insurance 1970, The Terms of Service for Officers and Soldiers in the Army, Navy and the Air Force 1998, and The Measures of Settlement for the Military Personnel Transferring to Civilian Services 1999. Occupational pension schemes like these have been functioning as Taiwan's early social security system. Nevertheless, persons who are unemployed, as well as housewives doing home chores, are not covered by any governmental schemes. However, the DPP government established a senior welfare stipend scheme—the Living Allowance for the Aged, in 2002. Senior citizens who receive neither an occupational pension allowance, nor any other governmental subsidy, and whose personal property is not worth more than NT$5 million dollars, or whose annual income is less than NT$50,000, are eligible to receive an NT$3,000 monthly allowance. Moreover, senior citizens who are physically or mentally disabled, or who are living under the poverty line, are entitled to receive a disability subsidy or a poverty allowance.

National Pension System

Although Taiwan has begun to establish a national pension system, beginning in 1994 when the KMT was in power, the massive budgetary requirements for the program have elicited continuing debate as to whether the scheme should act as merely an aid for elderly living or constitute a major part of the social insurance system. The National Pension System Draft was finally established in June 2002. The DPP government proposed this scheme to be operated as a social insurance scheme that all citizens between twenty-five and sixty-four, permanently living in Taiwan are required to join, unless they've already received occupational insurance. Persons aged sixty-five and over are free from contributing but will receive a NT$3,000 pension each month. In addition, the National Pension System also provides disabled allowances and funeral expenses for the recipients. The premium is fixed so that all participants pay a NT$750 monthly premium, where 20 percent (NT$150) is paid by the government, and 80 percent (NT$600) is paid by the individual. For those who are in poverty, the government subsidizes 40 to 100 percent of the total premium, depending on the assessment of individual financial situations. With this pension system, the size of both the pension and the premium will be adjusted according to changes in population structure as well as in the consumer price index. So far, the draft is not adopted by the Legislative Yuan.

CONCLUSION

With the steady increase of longevity, the continual decline of fertility, and the prevalence of the nuclear family system, the need of geriatric care has become controversial, which is triggering intense policy debates now and then in Japan, Korea, and Taiwan, where the elderly were traditionally taken care of by their adult children. For public policymaking, a question to ask is: What should the government's role in promoting the well-being of the elderly be? In East Asian societies, the role of government is unique in tackling the challenges of an aging population as a result of rapid economic, political, and social demographic changes. All welfare measures demand funding and, typically, the higher the standard of a country's welfare is, the higher the tax rate.

Although the merit of welfare state has been questioned by various scholars, (Rökpe 1960; 1963; Greene, 1998; Wu, 2000) one of the common claims of social policy making in East Asian societies is that the role of government to provide social welfare is limited. However, from our descriptions of the three East Asian countries above, such a claim does not really hold. There are indications that they do plan for their long-term care provision. They might differ in pace and philosophy, but the common intention to provide better welfare for the elderly is clear. The question remains whether an appropriate institutional approach has been adopted and whether there are hidden crises in the long run. It is highly plausible that governments are providing problem-solving interim measures rather than taking a transformative view aiming at long-term sustainability of respective welfare system? With globalization and the fluidity of international capital and freer population movements across national borders, social welfare in East Asia is definitely facing unprecedented challenges needing new institutional solutions. Shedding welfare load to the community and the family in the name of raising social capital sounds bold and innovative, but thus far has met with little success in the West. This means that East Asian countries need to explore new institutional arrangement capable of maximizing state-society synergy in the realm of social welfare. In addition, the interdependence between enterprises and the state has grown more complex in Japan, Korea, and Taiwan. On the one hand, governments seek to provide investment-friendly environments (for example, tax abatement) to attract enterprises to provide employment and increase investment. On the other hand, social legislations requiring enterprises to implement pension schemes would somehow result in undermining investment incentives. To achieve a balance of such conflicting interests thus becomes one of the major public policy challenges. Of the three East Asian states under study, we have seen that although long-term elderly care was neglected at the beginning, nonetheless, each country has endeavored to devise more economically and culturally viable care programs to overcome the shortcomings of a productivist welfare regime—one which tends to overemphasize work, self-sufficiency, and growth to the neglect of social needs. In addition, it is also observed that there is a tendency for East Asian governments to measure from time to time their developmental objectives and its state capacity with changing social conditions. South Korea and Taiwan are two outstanding examples to indicate the determination of their governments to further develop their welfare system along the universalistic line after the 1997 economic crisis, reflecting thus two interesting features of East Asian welfare systems: resilience and adaptation to international and domestic changes.

NOTES

1. Please also see England, R. S. (2002), the study of the macro-economic impact of population aging, and his discussions of three models (IMF, OECD and EC), and their impacts of aging (OECD, 1998).

2. The multi-pillar pension system is widely adopted as *the first-tier pension* as intended primarily to provide poverty relief; though normally set up as a public PAYG system, it can take other forms, including finance through general taxation. *The second tier* provides consumption smoothing; it can be publicly or privately managed, funded or PAYG, and integrated into or separate from the first tier. *The third tier* is private, funded, and voluntary (Barr, 2001).

3. This policy will be abolished when the National Pension System commences operations.

4. PAYG schemes include the case of pensions that are normally funded, but where funds are mainly invested in government bonds. If population ages, net investment of these funds becomes negative, at least, part of debt needs to be paid off.

5. Sweden introduced a "national defined-contribution" scheme in 1998. The state pension is financed by a social insurance contribution of 18.5 percent of earnings, of which 16 percent goes into the public scheme. A person's pension is based on his or her notional lump sum at retirement and on projections about life expectancy and future output growth. There is a safety-net pension for people with low lifetime earnings, and periods spent caring for children carry pension rights. The remaining 2.5 percent of a person's contribution goes into a funded scheme—either a private account or a government-managed savings fund. The individual can choose to retire earlier or later, with the pension being actuarially adjusted.

6. Abolished in 1995 and combined into Government Employees' and School Staffs' Insurance.

REFERENCES

Barr, N. (2001). *The Welfare State as a Piggy Bank: Information, Risk, Uncertainty, and the Role of the State*. Oxford: Oxford University Press.

Choi, S. J., Kim, D. I., and Koh, Y. K. (2001). S*ocial Response to Aging Society (Republic of Korea): A National Paper for the Second World Assembly on Aging*. Seoul, Korea: The Korean Gerontological Society and The Korean National Council of Elderly Welfare Organizations.

Chung, K. (1998). "International Trends and the Socio-economic Meaning of Population Aging" *Health and Social Welfare Policy Forum 26*, Seoul, Korea: Korean Institute for Health and Social Affairs.

Council for Economic Planning and Development. (2002). *Population Projections for Taiwan Area, Republic of China 2002–2051*. Taipei, Taiwan (R.O.C.): Council for Economic Planning and Development, Executive Yuan.

England, R. S. (2002). *The Macro Economic Impact of Global Aging: A New Era of Economic Frailty?* Washington, DC: Center of Strategic and International Studies.

Greene, L. M. (1998). *The National Tax Rebate: A New America with Less Government*. Washington, DC: Regnery Publishing, Inc.

Hoskins, D. (2002). "Thinking About Aging Issues." *International Social Security Review*, 55(1), pp. 13–20.

Hwang, J. S., Choi, S. J., Kim, T. H., Rhee, K. O., Yoo, S. H., and Byun, J. K. (2001). "The Way of Enhancement of Employment for Elderly Population. *Journal of the Korean Gerontological Society*, 21(1), pp. 93–118.

Kim, D. (2001). "Social Responses to Aging Problems and Survival Strategies in the Coming Age of New Longevity. *Journal of the Korea Gerontological Society*, 21(1), pp. 167–81.

Kinsella, K., and Taeuber, C. M. (1992). *An Aging World II*. Washington, DC: U.S. Department of Commerce, Economic and Statistics Administration, Bureau of the Census.

Kono, S. (1994). "Demographic Aspects of Population Aging in Japan, Part 1." In *Aging in Japan*. Tokyo: The Japan Aging Research Centre (JARC).

Kwon, H. J. (1997). Beyond European Welfare State Regimes: Comparative Perspectives on East Asian Welfare Systems. *Journal of Social Policy*, 26(4), pp. 467–484.

Kwon, S. (2001). "Economic Crisis and Social Policy Reform in Korea." *International Journal of Social Welfare*, 10, pp. 97–106.

Ministry of Health, Labor, and Welfare (MHLW). (2000). *White Paper*. Tokyo: Government Paper.

Ministry of Health and Welfare (MHW). (2000a). *Guidance on National Subsidiary Tasks for Elderly Health and Social Welfare 2000*. Seoul, Korea: MHW.

———. (2000b). *The Status of Health Care*. Seoul, Korea: MHW.

Ministry of the Interior. (2000). *Survey Summary of Senior Citizen Condition in Taiwan-Fuchien Area*. Taipei, Taiwan: Department of Statistics, Ministry of the Interior.

National Health Insurance Corporation (NHIC). (1999). *Health Insurance Statistics*. Seoul, Korea.

National Institute of Population and Social Security Research (NIPSSR). (2000). *Social Security Expenditures*. Tokyo, Japan: NIPSSR.

———. (2001). *Social Security Expenditures*. Tokyo, Japan: NIPSSR.

Ogawa, N. (2003). "Japan's Changing Fertility Mechanisms and Its Policy Responses. *Journal of Population Research*, 20(1), pp. 89–106.

Ogawa, T. (2000). "Japanese Women and Elder Care: Changing Roles?" *Asian Women*, 11, pp. 135–167.

Oh, K. M., and Warnes, A. (2001). "Care Services for Frail Elderly People in South Korea." *Aging and Society*, 21, pp. 701–720.

Organization for Economic Cooperation and Development (OECD). (1989). *Working Paper No. 61: Aging Populations: Economic Effects and Implications for Public Finance*. Paris: OECD.

———. (1997a). *OECD Economic Outlook*. Paris: OECD.

———. (1997b). *Aging in OECD Countries: A Critical Policy Challenge*. Paris: OECD.

———. (1998). *Maintaining Prosperity in an Aging Society*. Paris: OECD.

———. (2001). *Economic Survey of Korea*. Paris: OECD.

Palley, H. A. and Usui, C. (1995). "Social Policies for the Elderly in the Republic of Korea and Japan: A Comparative Perspective." *Social Policy and Administration*, 29(3), pp. 241–57.

Poston, Jr., D. L. and Kim, H. K. (1999). Research on Elderly Population Prospects of South Korea and North Korea. *Journal of the Korea Gerontological Society*, 19(3), pp. 181–87.

Röpke, W. (1960). *A Humane Economy*. South Bend, IN: Gateway Editions.

———. (1963). *Economics of the Free Society*. Chicago: Henry Regnery.

Sung, K. T. (1996). "Comparison of Motivations for Parent Care Between Koreans and Americans: A Cross-cultural Approach. *Korea Journal of Population and Development*, 25(1), pp. 83–99.

U.S. Department of Health and Human Services, Social Security Administration. (1994). *Social Security Programs Throughout the World 1993*. Washington, DC: U.S. Government Printing Office.

Wei, S.-S. (2002). "How to Design a Long-term Care System." *United Daily*, May 18, p.6.

Wu, H.-L. (2000). "Uncover the Myth of 'Social Welfare.'" *Trade Magazine*, 58, August 16,

4

Change and Inertia in Housing Policy

Japanese Housing System during Economic Crisis

Connie P. Y. Tang

In the 1990s, Japan experienced a series of economic and political crises. At the second quarter of 1991, the Japanese economy plunged into recession that in the beginning was seen as an ordinary recession after the *Heisei* economic boom.[1] The 1993 Lower House election marked the end of the thirty-eight years of electoral dominance by the Liberal Democratic Party (LDP). The Japanese political scene of the mid- to late-1990s was characterized by a group of new parties that "were split and recombined at the speed and unpredictability of amoebae but totally without policy or socioeconomic logic" (Pempel, 1998:1). Such chaotic political landscape only became more stabilized when the LDP regained parliamentary control in 1996. Realizing the severity and depth of its economic crisis, the Japanese government began to carry out a series of reforms in 1997 in order to revitalize the economy. Unfortunately, one by one, these economic packages failed. In 2004, housing and land prices had been in decline for thirteen consecutive years and showed no signs of recovery. Economic and political turmoil, coupled with a negative equity environment, have found a new meaning to housing consumption. Within this context, the main aim of this chapter is to look at how the Japanese housing system reacts to these changes. I will first provide a brief sketch of the Japanese housing system and then outline what I consider the contemporary housing crisis in Japan. This will then be followed by a discussion of the effectiveness of policy responses to revitalize the housing market. Finally, I will examine the impact of changes in the Japanese housing system, with a view to highlighting its role in Japan's contemporary social and economic development.

THE EMERGENCE OF THE JAPANESE HOUSING SYSTEM

It has become a recognized fact that Japan has its own meaning of welfare, distinguished by an emphasis on family as a safety net to limit poverty and dependency (Takahashi, 1997; Goodman, 1998). Public welfare, including housing provision, is limited to the disabled, the elderly, children of lone mothers, and the deserving poor. However, a closer examination of the Japanese housing policy reveals that there is an imbalance in housing allocations among different groups, largely favoring those who are deemed important to the growth of the economy—the working families. Indeed, the development of the Japanese housing system, like welfare development, has been driven primarily by the needs of economic growth, bearing great similarities to many East Asian economies (see Deyo, 1992, pp. 289–90; Holliday, 2000, p. 709; Agus, Doling, and Lee, 2002, p.13). From the outset, housing is seen as an emergency program directly related to the needs of the state. It was made clear at the time of the first government involvement in housing provision during the First World War that it was aimed at providing housing to ensure an adequate labor in war-related industries. During the war, military industry boom led to rapid urbanization, which in turn engendered housing shortages in urban areas. In response, the government enacted two legislations—the Land Lease Law and House Lease Law—in order to protect the rights of leaseholders and tenants in private rental housing. The Ministry of Finance (MOF) also provided low-interest loans to public bodies and public enterprises to build rental housing. Government involvement in housing was greatly expanded after the 1923 Great Kanto Earthquake. The government founded the first public housing agency called *Dōjunkai* to supply dwellings for the victims. It also aimed at introducing the concept of Western-style fireproof housing and began the construction of four-story reinforced-concrete buildings for the first time in Japan. With the outbreak of war between China and Japan in 1937, war-related industries sprang up, leading to governmental intervention again to provide housing for workers employed in war industries. Tight controls on building materials and supplies resulted in an acute shortage of dwellings in industrial areas. To increase supply, the government established a housing corporation, the Housing Management Foundation, in May 1941 into which the *Dōjunkai* was consolidated. The new corporation aimed at building 300,000 housing units for wartime laborers in five years, but ended up constructing only 160,000 wooden housing units by the end of 1945. The corporation suspended its work at the end of the war and was dissolved afterwards. After the Second World War, in order to meet the most immediate and pressing needs, 300,000 simple frame makeshift houses were constructed in November 1945 to provide shelters for people during the winter. On the other hand, to secure a labor force for industrial recovery, substantial funds were made available to colliery companies to construct housing for the laborers in the coal mines. Thus, in the immediate post-war period, housing policy of the central government continued to be a quick rehabilitation of damaged areas and loan facilities toward construction of housing for workers engaged in some vital industries. Both were short-term aims for housing, and the general public had to use their depleted resources to build or repair their homes.

Housing policy ceased to serve as a national emergency relief and became a long-term policy when the Ministry of Construction (MOC—subsequently the Ministry of Land, Infrastructure, and Transport [MLIT]) was set up in July 1948. The MOC was the sole government body in charge of the overall administration of the housing affairs. Its main task was to allocate funds from the general account to publicly funded housing. It also witnessed the establishment of the Government Housing Loan Corporation (GHLC) and later the Urban Development Corporation (UDC). However, rather than providing livelihood assistance to families in distressed circumstances, housing policy under the jurisdiction of the MOC became a part of the public works program that aimed to support and encourage homeownership. The essence of the housing policy was to promote the supply of large quantity of private housing through the GHLC. The government-run GHLC, established in June 1950, was practically the monopoly mortgage provider in Japan during the early post-war years. It provided long-term low-interest loans to individuals, private constructors, and public corporations (including the UDC) to construct or purchase private houses. The size of the subsidized loans was linked to the floor space of the home and the region in which the house was located. The maximum loan was limited to about 60 percent of the purchase price; thus substantial down payment was required from personal or private sources. By the end of March 2000, GHLC had financed a total of 17.95 million houses, approximately 32 percent of the total housing stock that were built after the war (GHLC, 2000:121). Generally, GHLC lending favored owner-occupied housing over rental housing, for example, in 1998, over 80 percent of the GHLC loans were allocated to construction and purchase of owner-occupied housing. Thus, the GHLC was used as an instrument to promote homeownership to meet the housing needs of the middle-class families.

The Japanese government's priority toward private homeownership was further confirmed by its limited provision of public rental housing. Under the 1951 Publicly Operated Housing Act, local governments and local supply corporations were assigned to provide public housing to low-income groups at low rent. Through the five-year Housing Construction Plan, which was designed by the MOC and approved by the Diet, local government bodies were given targets for the number of public housing units to be built within the planned period. Before the 1996 amendment of the Publicly Operated Housing Act, there were two categories of public housing, or "publicly-operated housing" in Japanese terms. The central government subsidized 50 percent of total construction cost in Category I and 66 percent in Category II through the MOC. Category II houses were for the people with incomes lesser than those on Category I, such as female-headed households, the disabled, and welfare recipients. Initially, 80 percent of Japanese households were eligible for public housing in Category I, but actions were started in 1959 to discourage people from moving into public housing. The 1959 amendment to the Act established an obligation for those households whose income exceeded the income criteria to make an effort to move out. Then, the 1969 amendment made it possible for local and prefectural governments to request those households to vacate their units. Gradually, the income criteria for public housing was brought down. In the 1970s, only the lowest 33 percent of households were allowed to apply for Category I houses. Then, the fiscal deficits at both central and local governments after the 1973 oil crisis translated into gradual contraction in the provision of public housing. The global grants allocation to publicly-operated housing program was cut by more than double during 1974–1987. In 1974, the budget for public housing was 2.15 billion yen,[2] 81.5 percent of the housing budget, dropped to 2.03 billion yen, 35.2 percent in 1987 (Jain, 1989, table 5.5; Hayakawa, 1990: p. 680–1). Accordingly, the ratio of public housing declined from 5.3 percent in 1978 to 4.6 percent in 2003 (see table 4.1). Thus, it is clear that, rather than treating public housing as universal goods, beginning from the early 1960s, the Japanese government has regarded it as welfare housing (Hirayama, 2000, p.123).

In addition to its active role in promoting homeownership and its selective intervention in providing public housing, the Japanese government, during the years of high economic growth (1955–1973), used housing policy as a reward to working families who contributed to the phenomenal growth of the economy. Rapid economic growth (an annual average of 9.17 percent between 1955 and 1971) has led to large-scale internal migration to the three largest metropolitan regions: Nagoya, Osaka and Tokyo. To retain the workforce in the large cities, the Japan Housing Corporation (JHC) was established in 1955 with the aim to provide housing to middle-income households working in large cities such as Fukuoka, Nagoya, Tokyo, or Yokohama. The JHC relied for nearly half its financial support on local and national government funds. Another half of income was from private financing institutions such as insurance firms and trust banks. The government's actual involvement took the form of an annual subsidy to help the JHC meet interest payments due on loans from local governments and private companies. Between 1955 and 1974, the JHC was responsible for building nearly 921,000

Table 4.1. Housing Tenure in Japan, 1978–2003

	1978		1988		1998		2003	
	('000)	%	('000)	%	('000)	%	('000)	%
Owned houses	19,428	60.4	22,948	61.3	26,468	60.3	28,657	61.2
Rented houses								
Private rented houses	8,409	26.1	9,666	25.8	12,050	27.4	12,613	26.9
Public rented houses (owned by local governments)	1,726	5.3	1,978	5.3	2,087	4.8	2,160	4.6
Public rented houses (owned by UDC*)	716	2.2	821	2.2	864	2.0	918	2.0
Company houses	1,839	5.7	1,550	4.1	1,729	3.9	1,471	3.1
Subtotal	12,689	39.4	14,015	37.5	16,730	38.1	17,161	36.6
TOTAL	**32,189**	**100.0**	**37,413**	**100.0**	**43,922**	**100.0**	**46,836**	**100.0**

* They were HUDC houses between 1981 to September 1999, before that, they were JHC houses. Starting from October 1999, they are named as UDC houses.

Sources: Ito (1994) Table 93; Hirayama (2001) Table 1, Statistics Bureau (2005a) Table 3.

dwellings (McGuire, 1981, table 13.4). Almost two-thirds of its dwellings were for rent and exclusively of *danchi* housing, which was high- (six-story or above) and medium-rise (three- or four-story) apartment blocks along railway lines in the suburbs and in adjacent prefectures for the middle-income employees of enterprises in major urban areas. The ultimate goal during this period was to secure the working class in the cities for the continuity of economic growth. In October 1981, the JHC was amalgamated with the New Town Development Corporation into the Housing and Urban Development Corporation (HUDC) and began to undertake urban redevelopment and new town development in major cities. Later, the HUDC was reorganized again into the UDC in October 1999. By the end of September 1999, the HUDC had supplied a total of 1.5 million housing units, of which 790,000 (55 percent) were rental housing (UDC, 2000, p. 19) that represented only 2 percent of the total national stock of housing (table 4.1). Despite its very minor housing production, the UDC has made an important contribution in the Japanese housing industry. It introduced floor plans designed for rationalization of household spaces such as separating bedrooms from the dining room, combining the kitchen and dining room (the so-called dining-kitchen room), and guaranteeing four-hour sunlight. Its development of housing complexes with parks, assembly halls, and other social facilities later became the model of urban housing built by private developers. Thus, the Japanese government, through the UDC's introduction of new building technologies and housing standards to the private sector, indirectly upgraded the quality of the housing stock. Once again, this confirmed the minimal role of the government in housing production. The institutional housing system had been gradually forming in the post-war period; it was selective rather than universal in that it mainly focused on rewarding particular social groups according to their contribution to economic growth. Many poor families have been excluded from the housing system and they have to compete with other disadvantaged households, such as single mothers, elderly, and disabled or sick persons, for the very limited public rental housing. Nevertheless, the Japanese government had successfully solved the massive housing shortage problem in less than twenty-five years after the American Occupation (1945–1951). By 1973, the number of houses exceeded the number of households for the first time in all prefectures. Indeed, Japan's rate of housing production in 1972 (over 1.88 million units) was among the highest in the world (McGuire, 1981:214). How was the housing shortage problem tackled?

THE JAPANESE HOUSING SYSTEM

Figure 4.1 provides the broad outline of the Japanese housing system between 1955–2000. The most useful way of viewing this system is to focus on the role of government and the GHLC as intermediaries. These two agents shift resources from the capital market, or more precisely mobilize household savings, into the housing system. It is well known that the household saving ratio in Japan greatly exceeds many industrialized countries. The reasons are well-documented (Horioka, 1993; Campbell and Watanabe, 1997; Nakagawa, 1999). However, one should not overlook the active role of Japanese government to create an environment that was conducive toward household savings.

Since the beginning of the Meiji era (1868–1912), the savings promotion movement has become a feature of Japanese economic policy. The major characteristic of the movement in this period until the Second World War was that the government regarded savings as an important funding source for military development and new industries. In the months following the end of the war, savings were considered as a means to rehabilitate the Japanese economy and to cool off inflation. Sponsored by the government, some 65,500 national savings associations were in operation in 1944, comprising 59 million members (Garon, 1997:153). Such institutional arrangement had successfully boosted the household saving ratio to an extraordinary 43.8 percent in that

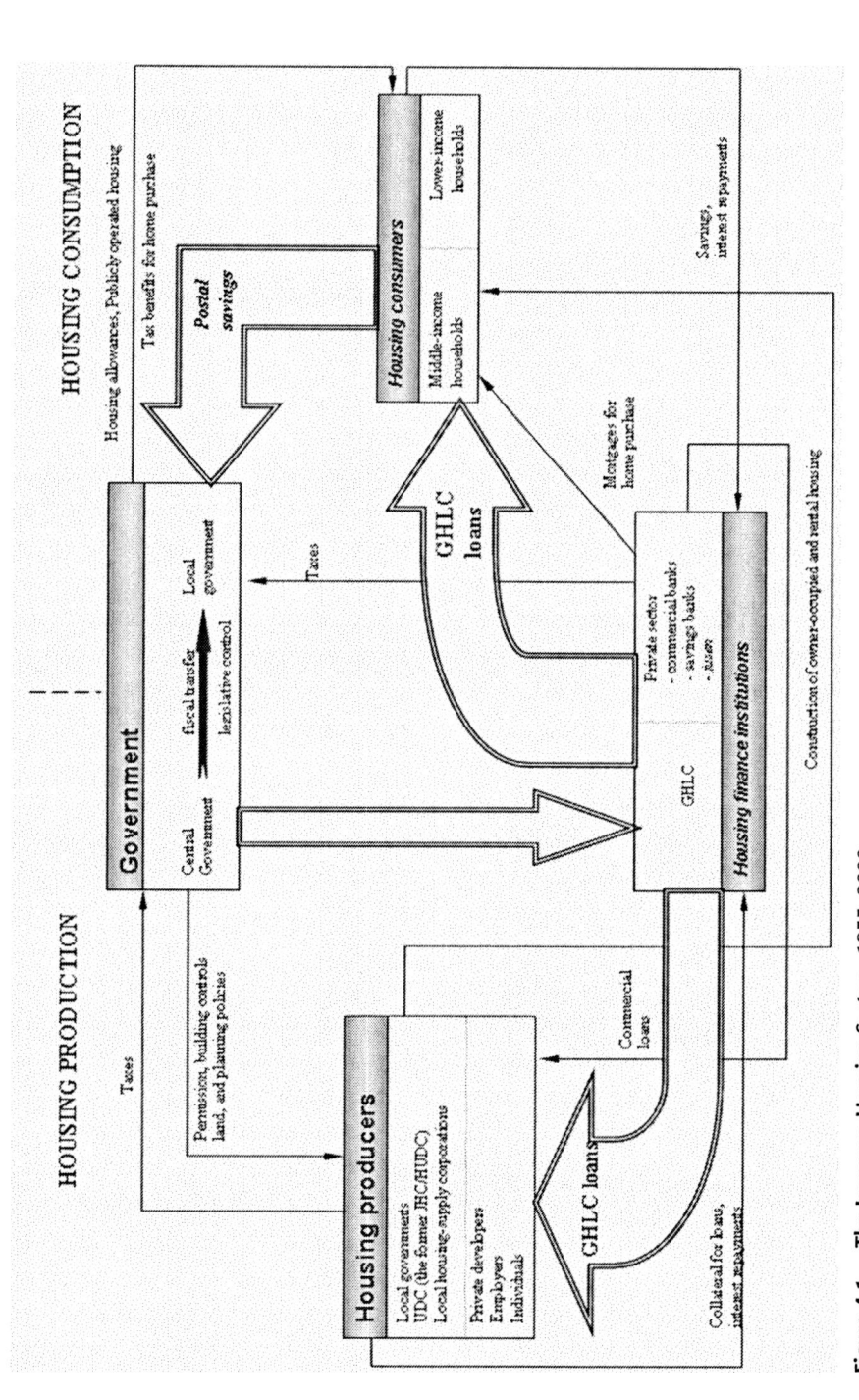

Figure 4.1. The Japanese Housing System, 1955–2000

year (Horioka, 1993: table 10.7). Although savings campaigns were suspended during the Occupation Period, once it ended in April 1952 the Japanese government immediately set up an official agency for the central organization of the savings institutions. The large amount of savings was collected through 18,941 (as at March 2005) "designated post offices" under the postal savings system. Although closely linked to the local community, the postal system was operated by the Ministry of Posts and Telecommunication (MPT). In 1963, special tax benefits under the *Maruyu* system (abolished in April 1988) were introduced to provide strong incentives to households to encourage deposits and savings in the postal system.[3] Currently, it houses a quarter of all domestic deposits in Japan (*The Japan Times*, May 3, 2005). Postal savings are mostly long-term deposits of seven years or more. Through the Trust Fund Bureau, they are lent to a variety of government agencies under the Fiscal Investment and Loan Programme (FILP), sometimes referred to as "the second budget" of the Japanese government.[4] Before the reform in April 2001, the postal savings system was the core deposits of the FILP.[5] In the early years, its funds were diverted to economic recovery through the stimulation of coal mining, electricity generation, and the iron and steel industries. Since 1955, housing has become one of the recipients of FILP funds that grew rapidly since 1962. It increased from 2.3 percent in 1955 to 20.4 percent in 1972 (Jain, 1989, table 5.5). In absolute terms, the size of FILP funds to housing (1,231.71 billion yen) was more than seven times the amount allocated from the general account of the main budget (165.6 billion yen). The major recipient of the FILP fund in the field of housing is the GHLC (see figure 4.1). The amount of the loan and the number of houses built with these loans each year are determined by the amount of the FILP funds. The GHLC then provides loans to private and public housing agents at a lower rate of interest than the rate of interest on the funds drawn from the FILP and receives a government grant covering the interest-rate differential.

Such "indirect housing financing" system, by channeling a large amount of household deposits and savings to finance the operation of the Japanese housing system, is unique. First, it helps to firmly establish the objective of the Japanese housing policy—the expansion of homeownership. Instead of constructing owner-occupied housing, the government focuses on the provision of low-interest loans to help households to buy houses from private development while subsidized public housing is left strictly for the very poor. Second, the interest rate charged by the GHLC is always kept below market level to make homeownership affordable. The provision of GHLC loans acts as a lever to stimulate housing investment to the degree necessary for economic development. Finally, while there is a very low level of direct government involvement in the provision of housing services, there remains a very high level of "hidden" government subsidies in housing consumption. Indeed, the overriding influence on the demand on housing through such hidden subsidies throughout the 1960s and the 1970s was one of the reasons why the Bank of Japan (BoJ) needed to maintain a generally low interest rate regime (Kirwan, 1987:353). The Japanese government also introduced various tax benefits for owner-occupation. These included the 1978 tax deductions for housing loans, the 1984 measure to reduce tax on gift-money for house acquisition and the 1986 tax relief for home purchase. All these indirect measures have successfully boosted the massive private housing construction to meet housing needs throughout the last half-century.

In short, the Japanese housing system relies very heavily on private sector in housing production. And in housing consumption, the government has adopted a system of support for homeowners that relies on self-help and individual effort. Even with such minimal direct government involvement, the system carries an important impact on the well-being of people in Japan. The ratio of homeownership has been maintained at a relatively high level, moving upwards from 59.2 percent in 1973 to 62.4 percent in 1983, the highest in postwar years. Although it started to decline in the mid-1980s, it still remained high at around 60 percent in 2003 (table 4.1). The living conditions of the Japanese are also improving with the average space per person in 2003 at 19.7 square meters (Statistics Bureau, 2005a: table 5), a 76 percent increase from 1973. However, the heavy reliance on private initiatives to promote homeownership has transformed houses and sites for capitalist profit making. House price inflation was one of the most complained about political issues in postwar Japan. To escape high house prices in urban areas, people were forced to either rent private flats in the inner cities or to travel long distances from their suburban area to their workplaces. For the lower income groups, high house prices also forced them into renting poor-quality private apartments in inner cities. In fact by the 1990s the difficulties of private homeownership and the lack of public housing propelled an expensive rental market (table 4.1).

THE ECONOMIC CRISIS OF THE EARLY 1990s AND ITS SOCIAL IMPACT

It should be noted that Japan's current ills must not be confused with the Asian Financial Crisis of the late 90s since it stems fundamentally from a domestic banking problem of much earlier root. The massive bubble was formed in the second half of the 1980s after a chain of events which involved the BoJ's easy money policy, Nakasone's privatization policy to curb the sharp rise of financial deficit,[6] and the deregulation of the banking system[7] that forced banks to practice unregulated lending policies to assets. To halt asset price inflation, the BoJ abruptly terminated the expansionary monetary policy and raised the official discount rate in rapid succession from mid-1989, thus bursting the bubble. As real estate provided the collateral for almost 70 percent of all loans made during the years of the bubble economy (Lee, 1997:59), the asset deflation led to an extraordinary number of non-performing loans on the banks' balance sheets. At first, the MOF adopted a "forbearance policy," allowing banks to hold non-performing loans without special write-offs, in the hope of a quick recovery of the economy and the real estate market (Cargill, Hutchison and Ito, 1997). It is the Asian Financial Crisis, however, which drove home most forcefully the possibility of a major crisis, since on average approximately one-third of all bank loans to Southeast Asia were made out by Japanese banks and the closeness of economic linkages between Japan and Asian countries provided itself the hardest hit (see Lin and Rajan, 1999: table 4). Starting from November 1997, a series of bankruptcies of large financial institutions occurred, including those of the Hokkaido Takushoku Bank, the largest bank in Hokkaido, and Yamaichi Securities, one of the "big four" security companies in Japan. Since then, one rescue package after another was devised by the Japanese government trying to revitalize the economy. Concurrently, the BoJ adopted the now infamous zero interest rate policy from February 1999 to ease the money supply. It seems, however, that their effects have failed to raise the growth potential of the economy. By now, the economic crisis is more than ten years old and is aptly dubbed "the world's slowest crisis" (Mattione, 2000). In fact, fears about the future of Japan's economy and weakness in asset values have brought an increase in the savings rate in Japan that has lengthened the duration of the crisis (Nakagawa, 1999). Throughout the crisis, the land and housing prices have been continuously falling. Figure 4.2 shows that the fall is especially large in the six major cities, including Nagoya, Osaka, and Tokyo. Between 1991 and 1993, for example, the national residential land value recorded an average drop of 7.3 percent, but land prices in six major cities fell by 33.3 percent. Currently, average prices in residential areas match levels registered in 1986 (*The Japan Times*, September 22, 2004). Residential land around railway stations in Tokyo is down four-fifths from its 1990 peak (Tokyo Statistical Association, 2004, table 167). In terms of housing prices, it witnessed even steeper reductions in the latter half of the 1990s. With 1994 as the base year, nominal residential real estate prices fell in Japan from 97 in 1995 to 91 in 1998. In real terms, they fell from 97 in 1995 to 89 in 1998 (Forrest, Izuhara, and Kennett, 2000b, p.14). By January 2004, the average price of flats in new condominiums in the Tokyo Metropolitan Area was around 40 million yen, compared with an exorbitant 75 million yen in 1991 (JREI, 2004).

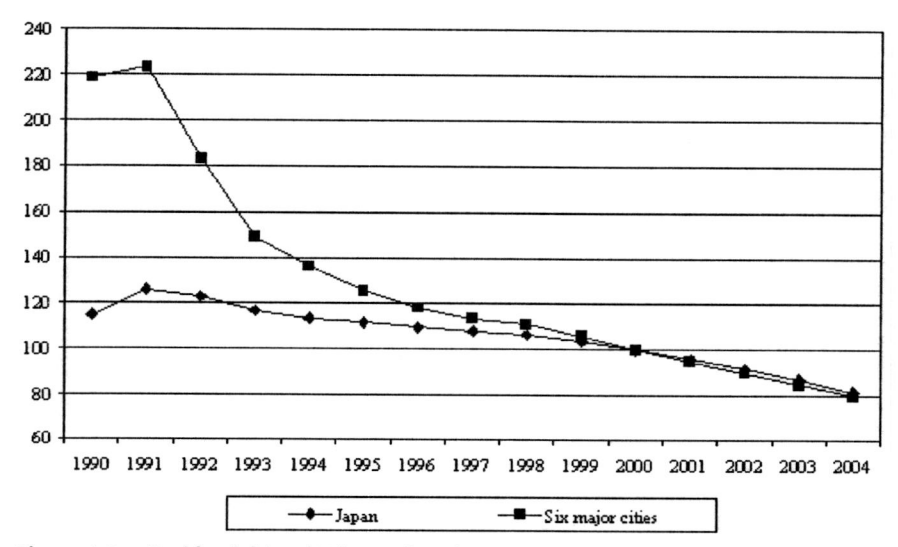

Figure 4.2. Residential Land Price Indices in Japan, 1990–2004

The continuous downward trend of housing prices, for the first time, has led to the formation of negative equities in post-war Tokyo. Using simulation models, the Nippon Credit Bank Research Institute in 1999 estimated that 280,000 households who had purchased a condominium in the Tokyo area between 1988 and 1994 had negative equity (cited in Forrest, et al., 2000: 52). Among them, those purchased in 1990 and 1991 had the highest levels of negative equity and were most severely affected. On average, the negative equity was as much as 12 million yen (Hirayama, 2001: 94). The total amount of negative equity for all metropolitan areas was estimated to be around 1.4 trillion yen, and the capital loss was 6.6 trillion yen. With the recession lingering, more and more households were unable to repay their housing loans. The total amount of outstanding loans swelled from 48,229 billion yen in 1980–1981 to 191,203 billion yen in 2000–2001, which was equivalent to 37.3 percent of the Gross Domestic Product (GDP; Hirayama, 2003). Over half of them (53.8 percent) were outstanding mortgage loans of private financial institutions, and another 40 percent were GHLC loans. Compared with the British experience,[8] the negative equity problem in Japan is surprisingly mild. This may be attributed to a greater contribution from buyers' own savings and family financial assistance in Japanese society. In Japan, the basic route to homeownership is to first purchase a condominium, then followed by a later move to a suburban family home. After that, "trading-up" is achieved by rebuilding on the same site rather than moving to another house.

Indeed, the secondary housing market is small in Japan.[9] The number of used houses that were purchased in 1992 was 137,000 in Japan, and the corresponding number was 3,520,000 in the United States (Kanemeto, 1997, p.634). Thus, the negative equity problem has reduced mobility from the condominium to single-family home in Tokyo. In 1990, 59 percent of second-hand condominiums traded were less than ten years old. By 1998, this figure had dropped to 28.5 percent (Forrest, et al., 2000a: 53). Lower income households occupying low value condominiums on the periphery of the city, which were built massively during the bubble years when land values were low, suffered the most. Generally, these condominiums are of poorer quality than those located in the city center. Moreover, refurbishment activities have declined, adding to obsolescence and further depressing prices to disproportionately low levels.

While old problems are not yet resolved, new problems surface. The prominent one is the rise of the homeless population. Homeless people have increased steadily in Japan, especially in the second half of the 1990s. They were 16,247 in 1998, 20,451 in 1999, 24,090 in 2001 and about 25,000 in 2003 (Aoki, 2003, p. 361; Schaede, 2004, p. 287). Before 1990, Tokyoites only regarded homeless people as being day laborers who usually stayed in flophouses but occasionally slept rough in the old inner city districts like *Sanya* in the Taitō ward (Ezawa, 2002: 281). Now homeless people are found in both new and old inner cities. They have become increasingly visible inside major urban stations such as Shibuya, Shinjuku, and Takadonobaba, promenades along both sides of the Sumida River, and in public parks and small playgrounds in residential neighborhoods throughout Tokyo. Beyond the typical stranded and aging day laborers, the homeless now include an increasing number of people from other backgrounds. A survey of rough sleepers in March 2000 sponsored by the Tokyo Metropolitan Government (TMG) found that 63.9 percent of the 1,028 homeless persons interviewed once held stable jobs, and 42 percent lived in company houses or workers dormitories before they became homeless (Iwata, 2001, p.47). Clearly, the depression in the 1990s has made many businesses, particularly the small- and medium-sized companies (with 300 or less employees) close down, thus affecting those who lived in the dormitories and company housing. Similar to the "old" homeless, these "new" homeless people are predominately single and middle-aged.[10] As public housing is only available to low-income families with elderly persons, disabled and children of lone mothers, the homeless men without family are largely excluded. Also, because the homeless people have no fixed abodes and are not registered as official residents in Tokyo, they are not eligible for welfare benefits and public housing that is designated for single people. So far, Tokyoites have been hostile and unsympathetic to the homeless, seeing them as a type of social outcast group. They are opposed to the building of shelters for the homeless for fear that this would worsen community life. They even pushed local governments to evict the homeless from public places. Reports of homeless freezing to death during cold winter months did not arouse public sympathy as such incidents are seldom covered in the media. Because of the wounded national pride, Japanese people choose to ignore the homeless problem. Their negative attitudes toward middle-aged males to obtain social benefits without contributing to society dampen the obligation of the central and local governments to provide assistance to homeless people. Accordingly, Japan's homeless have become the most visible "invisible" phenomenon among advanced countries.

HOUSING POLICY CHANGES

Dwindling Public Housing

The Japanese government has been consistently half-hearted in its attempts to deal with the housing problems during the recession years. Indeed, public attention is caught on the bad loan problem in the banking sector.[11] More recently, the economic situation has become politically intolerable, making the government more determined in further reducing its role in the housing system.

As a result of increased public spending on the numerous stimulate packages to revitalize the economy, the combined debts of the central and local governments rose to 703 trillion yen at the end of March 2004, over 150 percent of the GDP (*The Japan Times*, June 26, 2004). In this climate of rising public debts, the government funding to publicly operated housing has been diminishing. Accordingly, the construction of public housing is at a declining trend. Only 40,400 publicly operated housing units per year (2.7 percent of the total; see table 4.2) were planned to supply in the seventh housing construction five-year program covering the period from 1996 through 2000. In Tokyo, the TMG only built around 4,000 units a year (Kikuta, 2000), compared to over 15,000 units a year in the mid-1960s (TMG, 1971, table 13).

Not only is publicly operated housing being pushed outside the mainstream of the Japanese housing system, it has always been residualized by housing policies. First, the Publicly Operated Housing Act was amended in May 1996 to abolish the classification of the public housing. The income criteria for public housing eligibility was lowered. In the 1970s, it covered the lowest 33 percent of households in the country. This percentage, however, was reduced to 25 percent in 1996 (Tiwari and Hasegawa, 2001: 424). Second, the rent for public housing, used to be based on construction cost, is now determined in

Table 4.2. The Sixth and Seventh Five-year Housing Construction Program for Japan, 1991–2000 ('000 units)

	Sixth Five-year Plan 1991–1995			Seventh Five-year Plan 1996–2000		
	Planned	Actual	% Achieved	Planned	Actual	% Achieved
Houses with private funds	3,600	3,516	97.7	3,775	n.a.	—
Publicly-funded houses						
Publicly operated houses[1]	315	333	105.7	202	183	90.8
GHLC houses	2,440	3,139	128.6	2,325	2,722	117.1
UDC houses[2]	140	108	77.1	105	87	83.3
Good quality rental housing for elderly	—	—	—	18	28	156.7
Good quality rental housing leased from private owners	—	—	—	205	142	69.4
Others	605	437	72.2	470	409	87.0
Adjustment	200	—	—	200	—	—
Subtotal	3,700	4,107	108.6	3,525	3,573	101.4
TOTAL	**7,300**	**7,623**	**104.4**	**7,300**	**n.a.**	**—**

Notes:
1. Including renewed housing.
2. Formerly they were HUDC houses, but starting from October 1999, they were renamed as UDC houses.

Source: GHLC (2000) p.41.

accordance with the income of tenants and location of housing. As a result, households with an income of more than a certain amount now pay market rent. However, the income criteria for special public housing could be relaxed up to the lowest 40 percent for aged households at the discretion of local and prefectural governments. The narrowing scope of beneficiaries by applying strict rules to applicants implies that public housing is now solely for the "worthy poor"—the disabled, the elderly, and the very low-income households (Hirayama, 2001, p.90). Third, starting from the early 2000s, housing policy has been notably marginalized from mainstream government social policy. The MOC, which had jurisdiction over housing policy, was merged with the Ministry of Transport to form the MLIT in 2001. The government also decided to terminate the five-year Housing Construction Plan in 2005, meaning that there will be no new public rental housing to be built, although redevelopment of existing stock will continue. This new housing policy signifies the end of Japanese government involvement in direct provision of housing services to the poor.

Homeownership Policy: Stimulating Domestic Consumption and Investment

Even though the economic situation is difficult, the promotion of homeownership is still the core activity of the Japanese housing policy. On the one hand, the expansion of owner-occupied housing can help sustain the construction, housing, and real estate industries. On the other hand, it can stimulate domestic consumption and private investment—a pillar of the LDP's policy to revitalize the economy. To boost house building, the major tool was to increase the availability of low-interest loans provided by the GHLC to individuals and private companies to build owner-occupied housing. First, housing funds from the FILP increased dramatically from 8,366 billion yen in 1990 to 14,193 billion yen in 1995, a jump from 30.2 percent of total FILP to 35.3 percent (Fig. 4.3). To counteract the declining household incomes, the GHLC's loan conditions were further relaxed. The basic interest rate, which was 5.5 percent in September 1990, fell to 2.0 percent in June 2003 (*Jiji Press*

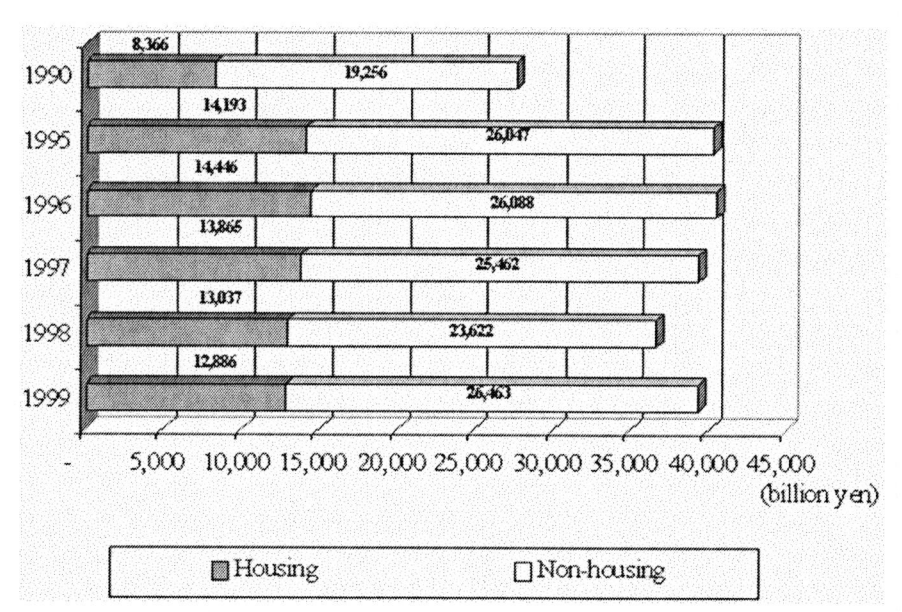

Figure 4.3. Ratio of Housing to Non-Housing Loans from Japanese Government 1990–99

English News, 12 June 2003). In 1993, a new housing loan scheme, *yutori* loans, was introduced to attract more people to take out mortgages from the GHLC. Under this scheme, borrowers took out twenty to thirty-five year mortgages, with very low initial payment for the first five years calculated as if the loan were for fifty years. They then had to pay much higher installments for the rest of the loan's life. The scheme was well received by the public. Nearly a million households took up the offer (*The Economist*, 24 October 1998, p. 131). Over 40 percent of newly built dwellings were financed by GHLC in 1993 and 1994 (see table 4.3 and figure 4.3). The scheme was terminated in 1996 as borrowers began to worry about their ability to pay the more than double repayments starting from the sixth year as the economy was still in recession. Indeed, the number of GHLC loan repayments in arrears rose from 4,820 in 1990, to 15,373 in 1999 and reached 17,958 in 2001 (Tang, 2002, p.475; Hirayama, 2003, p.210).

In Tokyo, backed by the drop in construction expenses and land prices, developers aggressively purchased land in the city center for condominium

Table 4.3. New Dwellings Started by Source of Funds in Japan, 1990–2003

	Private Housing				Public Housing*		
	Privately Funded		Financed by GHLC				
Year	Number	%	Number	%	Number	%	Total
1990	1,219,323	71.4	409,292	24.0	78,494	4.6	1,707,109
1991	925,271	67.6	366,492	26.7	78,363	5.7	1,370,126
1992	847,197	59.7	472,926	33.3	99,629	7.0	1,419,752
1993	799,176	52.9	612,136	40.5	98,475	6.5	1,509,787
1994	787,781	50.5	666,348	42.7	106,491	6.8	1,560,620
1995	857,513	57.8	521,862	35.2	105,277	7.1	1,484,652
1996	922,922	56.6	581,622	35.7	125,834	7.7	1,630,378
1997	839,637	62.6	395,717	29.5	105,993	7.9	1,341,347
1998	716,346	60.7	375,392	31.8	87,798	7.4	1,179,536
1999	687,552	56.1	453,616	37.0	85,039	6.9	1,226,207
2000	762,185	62.8	364,496	30.0	86,476	7.1	1,213,157
2001	828,933	70.7	255,219	21.8	89,018	7.6	1,173,170
2002	885,418	77.3	173,614	15.2	86,521	7.6	1,145,553
2003	924,035	78.7	169,569	14.4	80,045	6.8	1,173,649
Total	12,003,289	62.7	5,818,301	30.4	1,313,453	6.9	19,135,043

*Includes housing units built by UDC, local governments, and local housing supply corporations.

Source: MLIT (2004) *New Dwellings Started*, updated on 12/27/2004 (http://www.mlit.go.jp/toukeijouhou/chojou/ex/juu-e_sy.xls).

building. This boosted the number of condominiums on sale from 44,270 in 1993 to over 80,000 between 1994 and 1996 (*Nikkei Weekly*, 1998). However, after the April 1997 consumption tax increase, strong demand from first-time buyers, who had been encouraged to buy by low prices and interest rates, came to a halt. To restimulate private investment into housing development, the Building Code and the City Planning Law were amended in February 1997 in which special "high rise housing promotion zones" were designated in the center of larger cities to encourage the construction of tower-type buildings for residential use. The legal requirement that each building should enjoy a minimum access to sunlight for three to four hours was no longer applied in the new promotion zones. Homeowners made use of this opportunity to upgrade their dwellings, creating a substantial boom of "indigenous redevelopment" in Tokyo (see Cybriwsky, 1998: 140–141). Then in November 1997, the Japanese government included second dwelling supply promotion measures in its package of economic measures to create new demands for vacation houses in Tokyo and Osaka metropolitan areas (EPA, 1997–1998: p. 26–8). Beyond that, a "housing loan exemption scheme" was established as part of the Fiscal Year 1998 tax system amendments to lift the ceiling and expand the duration of exemption in income tax[12] (MOC, 1998). Furthermore, a new tax incentive was introduced to encourage those who bought a house during the bubble period but have been unable to sell it to purchase another house. To achieve this, the capital loss can be tax-exempted in the repurchase of designated owner-occupied property. On the other hand, there are new housing demands from a special group of single women who are looking for condominiums in large cities. Subsequently, real estate companies in Tokyo have started to construct and sell condominiums exclusively to single women (Hirayama, 2001, p. 95). All these "created" and "natural" additional housing demands generated another condominium boom after 1994. Condominium sales rocketed to 182,000 units in 2000, the highest point after the collapse of bubble economy. In central Tokyo, the number of newly developed condominium towers reached 3,944 in 2000—a rise of 150 percent from 1999 (Fuyuno, 2001).

Meanwhile, the boom of large-scale construction of high-rise apartment blocks of over 20 stories in the city center of Tokyo has been accelerating the deflation of "suburban bubble condominiums," which were developed in the 1990s but still with a lot of unsold houses remaining. The housing market has begun to split urban space into "hot places" and "cold places" (Hirayama, 2003, p. 215). This post-bubble spatial fragmentation has been amplified after the relaxation in building and urban planning rules first in 2000 and later in 2002 which gave private sector an eminent position in urban redevelopment.

Large-scale private urban renewal projects are mushrooming in various parts of central Tokyo, including the Marunouchi district in front of Tokyo Station as well as Roppongi, Shinagawa, and Shiodome. The new redevelopment boom has exacerbated the house price gap between urban and suburban areas. In Tokyo, for example, the condominiums in the central areas (the Chiyoda, Minato, and Chuo wards) cost over 100 million yen per unit, while those located between 20 kilometers and 50 kilometers from the city center are only several million yen. Overall, the expansion of government housing loans and the encouragement of private urban redevelopment have sustained the high level of housing construction. Over the last fourteen years from 1990 to 2003, Japan's housing starts averaged 1.37 million (see table 4.3), equivalent to those of most advanced countries (e.g., 1.37 million in the United States; Corporate Information, 2000) in their property boom years.

The sales of high-rise condominiums, which enjoyed wide popularity until recently, are now losing steam. The housing market is facing oversupply of condominiums that were built in the past few years. Albeit the heavy fall of housing prices has improved affordability significantly and the government's various attractive policy measures have enhanced the accessibility to homeownership, the expansion of owner-occupied housing has been stretched to its limit. The homeownership rate remains around 60 percent (table 4.1). In Tokyo, it is below 42 percent (see table 4.4). When people anticipate that the long-term security of income is increasingly rare in all sectors of the labor market, the preference for homeownership is thus adversely affected (Doling and Ford, 1996: 170). In the long run, the demand for homeownership may decrease when private renting becomes more and more popular.

Table 4.4. Housing Tenure in Tokyo, 1988–1998

	1988 ('000)	%	1993 ('000)	%	1998 ('000)	%
Owned houses	1,782.5	41.4	1,845	39.6	2,051	41.5
Rented houses						
Private rental	1,723.4	40.0	1,825	39.2	2,054	41.6
Public rental	227.2	5.3	241	5.2	253	5.1
HUDC houses	183.0	4.3	182	3.9	195	3.9
Company houses	197.5	4.6	300	6.4	241	4.9
Subtotal	2,331.1	54.2	2,547	54.7	2,743	55.5
Others*	191.3	4.4	268	5.8	147	3.0
TOTAL	4,304.9	100.0	4,660	100.0	4,942	100.0

*Included tenure not reported.

Sources: Tokyo Statistical Association (1999) Table 77; Kikuta (2000) Table 1.

Private Renting: Promoting Private Initiatives to Upgrade Housing Conditions

In adhering to its role in housing provision, the Japanese government plays an indirect role in upgrading the quality of the housing stock. In each housing construction five-year plan, the government decides the specific goals for housing conditions in each type of dwelling to be built by both the private and public sectors. Housing built with GHLC loans have to conform to the Building Standards Law as well as to meet the targeted housing standards established by the MLIT. However, in order not to deter private housing construction, the government's requirements and standards are so lax that few take them seriously. After the Great Hanshin Earthquake in 1995,[13] it became apparent that areas with a dense concentration of deteriorating housing are vulnerable to disaster since most of them were built before the Building Standards Law was amended in the 1980s, which required that all buildings must withstand earthquake destruction, and though they did not meet the standard they were allowed to remain. Because of the reluctance of the government officials to impose strict regulations on the housing construction industry, even after decades of government efforts, there are abundant poor quality rental units persistently remaining. According to the 1998 Housing Survey of Japan, the number of substandard rental houses in Tokyo was about 501,000, roughly 10 percent of the total (table 4.5).[14] They were mainly wooden tenement houses, which were constructed prior to World War II and concentrated in areas that escaped war damage. They were dominated by the lower-income groups, but since the 1980s, newcomers such as migrants from China often lived together in one-room wooden rental apartments.

In view of the seriousness of the problem, the Japanese government amended the Land and House Lease Laws to encourage the supply of good-quality private rental housing. Traditionally, Japanese tenancy laws had been highly protective of tenants. There was no generally accepted principle that tenants must vacate when the term of a lease ends. Instead, a lease was considered to be renewable indefinitely, and tenants could not be easily evicted. Japan has not had a strict rent-control law; rent increases were typically small.[15] What is more, the owner could not evict a tenant who refused a rent increase. All rent disputes must be resolved by the court on a case-by-case basis. Because rent increases were difficult to enforce, the supply of rental housing was limited to very small units of inferior quality, which barely met the minimum housing standards, in order to discourage tenants from long occupancy. To remove the obstacle in the provision of high-quality rental properties, fixed term tenancy provisions were enacted in the 1999 amendment of the Land and House Lease Laws. Under the new law that became effective on March 1, 2000, there is no restriction on the duration of the tenancy and no legal right

Table 4.5. Households Living below the Minimum Housing Standards in Tokyo in Comparison with Japan, 1998

	Tokyo			Japan		
	Below Minimum Housing Standard		Total No. of Households	Below Minimum Housing Standard		Total No. of Households
	('000)	%	('000)	('000)	%	('000)
Owned houses	64.4	3.1	2,051.3	351.6	1.3	26,467.8
Public rented houses (owned by local governments)	40.7	16.1	252.8	283.7	13.6	2,086.7
Public rented houses (owned by public corporations)	37.3	19.1	195.3	132.9	15.4	864.3
Private rental wooden houses (facilities used exclusively)	184.8	23.0	802.1	676.3	12.9	5,248.9
Private rental wooden houses (facilities used jointly)	32.0	63.0	50.8	91.3	51.5	177.3
Private rental non-wooden houses	179.4	14.9	1,201.3	583.2	8.8	6,623.6
Company houses	26.8	11.1	241.0	124.4	7.2	1,729.2
TOTAL	**565.4**	**11.8**	**4,794.6**	**2,243.4**	**5.1**	**43,922.1**

Sources: Statistics Bureau (2000a) Table 72; (2000b) Table 46.

for tenants to renew the tenancy automatically. Also, there is no obligation that landlords and tenants can change the rent after the tenancy expires, but landlords can include the condition of automatic rent increase in the fixed-term tenancy agreement. Recent data showed that landlords of detached houses and bigger condominium units preferred the new tenancy arrangements.[16] For example, in June and July 2000, only 2,300, or 3 percent of 75,000 private rental transactions, were under this new tenancy agreement. Of the 2,300 private rental transactions, 60 percent adopted a fixed term tenancy of more than three years (Tang, 2002: p. 484) as landlords could choose the good tenants and have an option to repossess the units after the expiration of lease.

HOUSING SYSTEM AND ITS INERTIA FOR CHANGE

The bursting of the asset bubble in the early 1990s brought about phenomenal changes in the political environment of Japan. Then the Asian Financial Crisis deepened the economic crisis and brought about the changing perceptions about economic growth, income stability, and job security. These changes have led to the modification of some of the Japanese housing program and schemes. However, its housing policy tenets remain unchanged. Despite the appointment of an unconventional prime minister, Junichiro Koizumi, the change to the housing sector remains limited although the relationship between the financial sector and the property sector remains close. The Japanese government sticks to the homeownership policy as a strategy to counteract the adverse effect of the economic crisis. The provision of housing loans continues to be the major policy tool to spark homeownership. Indeed, the strong tie between the finance market and the property market has forced the Japanese government to invent necessary measures to increase the demand for homeownership as a means to stabilize the banking sector. The pro-ownership policy has remained a major part of the economic policy.

On the production side, both bureaucrats and the LDP politicians had to retract the public housing program under political pressure. The HUDC was reorganized into the UDC in October 1999 as part of the administrative reform because private developers and the housing industry strongly criticized the housing supply of HUDC (Hirayama, 2001: p. 94). The UDC now stops selling houses, reduces the supply of rental housing, and promotes only basic urban redevelopment. It also increases rents, which were already over 120,000 yen for 60 square meters of floor area, and increases the sale prices of its many unsold units to a level higher than those of private condominiums (Hayakawa, 2002: 33). The Japanese government intends to reduce the UDC's housing production and expects that in five to ten years' time, the development of housing commodities will be taken over by the private sector (Tanaka, 1999). It is clear that the Koizumi administration has followed the footstep of Nakasone and further intensified the privatization policy to stimulate economic recovery. While the privatization policy of the Nakasone administration aimed at dealing with the urban fiscal crisis and accidentally triggered the bubble economy, Koizumi's policy aims to use it as a means of economic stimulation and to dispose of bad performing loans (Hirayama, 2003: 217). This heavy reliance on private initiatives allies with Japan's pro-producer policies which have emphasized increasingly on private productivity to assure sustained economic growth on the one hand, and the LDP's aims to guarantee the unflagging political support from the big contractors as well as small- to medium-sized firms in the construction industry on the other (Woodall, 1996).

Finally, at the beginning of the 2000s, the Japanese government has intensified the use of the private sector and further lessened its role in the housing system. First, it cuts the link between the FILP and the GHLC.[17] Under the newly reformed FILP, funds from the pension system and postal savings are not deposited automatically to the FILP (see figure 4.1). The MOF needs to raise funds from the market for the FILP. In other words, public institutions that received FILP funds have to find new sources of capital. Thus, starting from 2000, there has been a gradual reduction of FILP funding to the GHLC and UDC. For example, FILP funds allocated to the GHLC were slashed first to 145.6 billion yen in 2003, then to 75 billion yen in 2004 (*The Japan Times*, December 21, 2003, and December 21, 2004; see figure 4.3 for comparison). To compensate for the diminishing public financing, the GHLC issued 600 million yen of government bonds with a view to raise 50 billion yen through the securitization of housing loans (JICA, 2000: 10–11). Also, in order to scale down the government involvement in home mortgage business, the Koizumi administration plans to replace the GHLC by a new independent administrative corporation focusing on housing loan securitization in 2006. The scale-back of the GHLC's lending business pushes housing consumers to increase their borrowing from private banks. From 2002 onward, less than 20 percent of newly constructed dwellings were funded by the GHLC (see table 4.3). In this way, the growing private housing loans will become a vital source of income to compensate the loss of loans from enterprises during the recession period and an important means to survive the ailing banking sector.

Although recent policy changes have witnessed the gradual disappearance of two important public agents in the Japanese housing system, the essence of the system is still the same: to channel the massive household savings into the housing market. Instead of being an aggregator of savings and as a distributor of investment funds into housing through the GHLC, the Japanese government will assign a new public agent to pump the postal savings directly into the private market, pushing individuals, private and public developers to find housing finance solely from the banking sector. The housing system will be entirely privately funded and operated under government regulation. Together with the cessation of the public housing program, one could say that the Japanese government's involvement in housing provision will be further shrunk to become a wholly residual housing system. One could also label the Japanese model as wholly liberal as it is the market forces that decide the availability of housing services.

Anticipating a long period of slow economic growth and the issues associated with the increase of the elderly population, the Japanese government has further withdrawn its role and put greater reliance on private arrangements to broaden the financing basis of housing services provision as well as cutting public expenditure on housing. Indeed, the securitization of the GHLC loans is taken as a measure toward market-orientation. Yet, at the same time, the securitization market for housing loans has just opened up with the close of the first residential mortgage backed deal completed in October 2003 (*Asiamoney*, October 2003). What is more, it is expected that GHLC will issue its housing loan backed securities in very large volume. Since most of the large banks in Japan have no additional sources of funding due to bad-loan disposals, the ultimate buyer of the GHLC securities will possibly be the BoJ or the government-backed postal savings system. As a result, the Japanese government is still the major player in its housing system even though its involvement becomes more obscure. In fact, the government push for "more market" replicates the result of every reform measure of the Koizumi administration, which was always accompanied by a counter-reform intended to protect the very target of the initial reform (Schaede, 2004, p. 289). Since the Japanese government is very earnest to keep homeowners from mortgage arrears by relaxing GHLC housing loans conditions continuously, it is not surprising to find that Japan is chasing its own tail, running around in circles.

On the other hand, the termination of the already minimal public housing construction amazingly did not cause any uproar from the public. Currently, Japanese people are obsessed with all the possible harmful effects of the aging population on their lives. Recent surveys consistently reported that social security reforms, particularly those for pension and medical care systems, were the most pressing issue that Koizumi's cabinet needs to address (*The Japan Times*, March 7 and 12, 2005). Housing policy therefore has always been kept at a low position on the social agenda. At the political side, even under the tremendously changing external and internal environments, the core of the Japanese housing system is difficult to change given that it is so pro-production and growth-centered. People gained immense vested interests that have been creating in the system over time; for example, homeowners' interest in mortgage tax benefits, housing producers' interest in housing investment, financial institutions' interest in providing more housing loans, the LDP's interest in gaining more votes, and the bureaucrats' interest in creating more jobs through mass production of housing. These vested interests have become embedded in people's economic lives, and it is politically difficult to take them away, thus they are the most impregnable forces that sustain the inertia of the system. Moreover, the political dimension of the housing system is quite stasis given that the LDP has consistently controlled Japan. The extended slump and recession has witnessed the revival of the emphasis on the moral values of cooperation, diligence, self-reliance, and thrift in facing the economic hardship. Indeed, the persistence of cultural practices in maintaining rather than transforming the prevailing order, and consensus and negotiation rather than direct confrontation, has suppressed the initiation of radical changes. Thus, even though most Tokyoites live in small, cramped houses, they are content to let the situation go on. It will probably take another generation for the Japanese to decide whether they do want their living standard to stagnate.

NOTES

1. The Japanese economy has surged ahead at a frantic pace since late 1986. The so-called Heisei boom—named after the reign of the present emperor, Akihito—is the longest and most powerful expansion in modern Japanese history.

2. The exchange rate in 2003 was US$1 = ¥106.

3. During the era of rapid growth period until the mid-1970s, the Japanese financial system was essentially a bank-based system (see Feldman, 1986). Firstly, the Japanese government blocked the direct flows of funds from households to firms by setting low interest rates on bonds, relatively to personal savings accounts, and by strictly regulating bond issues. Secondly, classes of banks were segmented by function and size of customer. Deposit-taking institutions included city banks, long-term credit banks and trust banks, which together comprised the main banks, lending mainly to large corporations; and co-operatives, credits associations, mutual savings banks, and local or regional banks, lending mainly to individuals, and medium and small businesses. The smaller banks however could not compete with the postal system because they were not allowed to offer tax concessions and higher interest rates to individuals in making deposits.

4. Before 1972, FILP was under the complete control of the MOF. Since then, a FILP plan is submitted to the Diet for discussion and approval annually. Because it is created at the same time as the main budget and because the amount of the Fiscal Investment and Loan Fund is about two-thirds of that of the main budget, it is known as "the second budget."

5. During the second half of the 1960s and the 1970s, the national pension was also the major source of the FILP. The state pension schemes built up huge financial surpluses largely because they were at an "immature" stage where contributions paid rose steeply above current payments. As Japan's population is aging, the role of national pension in the FILP is diminishing.

6. To eliminate national deficit financing, Yasuhiro Nakasone, prime minister from November 1982 to November 1987, pursued a series of neoliberal reforms. This included privatization, welfare reforms, and reform of the diverse public corporations. Nakasone's privatization policy, the deregulation of land use and urban planning, the disposal of public land and the increase of public works projects, were aimed at stimulating economic development of the private sector in areas which the public sector has traditionally played a key role. This contributed to the reduction of budget deficits

that had been accumulating during the 1970s after the oil crises. However, it caused further chaos in the land and housing markets (see Hayakawa and Hirayama, 1991) and evoked the spectacular asset inflation caused by speculation in land and securities.

7. The deregulation process, started in the late 1970s, has been steady but gradual, and still continues today. The aims of the deregulation were: the creation of new financial instruments, the development of a vigorous, competitive bond market, the breaking down of market segregation, and in general the promotion of competition among all financial institutions. For more details about Japanese financial deregulation carried out in the 1980s, see Osugi (1990); Takeda and Turner (1992).

8. Between 1988 and 1991, around 11 percent, or two million households, held negative equity which involved £2.7 billion. The number of mortgage arrears increased from 10,500 in 1988 to 864,740 at the end of 1991, and the number of repossessions jumped from 15,800 in 1989 to 75,540 in 1991 (Hamnett, 1994, p.290; see also Dorling, 1994; and Gentle, Dorling and Cornford, 1994).

9. The major contributing factor for the inactivity of the secondary housing market is: neither the GHLC nor banks in the private sector are willing to provide loans for the purchase of older houses.

10. There is a relative absence of women and families among the homeless because the Japanese government provides allowances and other support to lone mothers (but not fathers) and their children under the maternal and child welfare law. Women's shelters, homes for mothers and children, and subsidized public housing units provide a greater range of options specifically to mothers with financial difficulties, and who lack housing. Women are therefore largely invisible in the homeless population in Japan.

11. Public concerns on the bad loan problem were raised in the autumn of 1995 when all seven *jusen* (housing loans companies set up by the major banks in the 1970s which were specialized to provide small-scale housing loans to individuals) showed signs of bankruptcy. As the parties in power, the LDP and the Social Democratic Party were under strong pressure from the agricultural cooperatives. The governing coalition approved to earmark a grant of 685 billion yen (roughly US$6.85 billion) from the 1996 budget to cover part of the losses. Using the taxpayers' money to compensate for the failure of *jusen* immediately roused public outrage which initially made the LDP leadership extremely cautious and reluctant on spending taxpayers' money to save the banking system. It was only until the autumn of 1997 when the bad-debt mountain grew to crisis proportions (76.7 trillion yen). Since then, the Japanese government introduced succeeding bailout packages to inject public funding into the banking sector. Despite banks' continued efforts to write off non-performing loans, outstanding bad loans are broadly unchanged as new non-performing loans emerge faster than expected. The most recent figure was 22.56 trillion yen at the end of September 2004 (*Japan Today*, 28 December 2004).

12. Under the current scheme, people who buy new houses by the end of 2003 could save up to 500,000 yen a year in income tax payments for ten years. The MLIT intended to extend the scheme to 2004 as a means to promote homeownership as a measure to stimulate the economy (*Jiji Press English News*, 16 July 2003).

13. On January 17, 1995, an earthquake of a magnitude of 7.2 on the Richter scale battered Kobe. Among the 79,283 houses destroyed, over 80 percent were built before 1980 (Noguchi, 2003, pp. 359–360).

14. The 2003 Housing and Land Survey data on Tokyo's housing situations were not available at the time when this chapter was written.

15. The difficulty in carrying out rent increases has created rent differences between new and old tenants. For example, the 1988 Housing Survey of Japan showed that on a nationwide basis, existing tenants who initially leased their residences prior to 1946 paid less than half the amount paid by tenants who leased their homes between 1980 and 1985 (Haley, 1992, p.167).

16. In fact, due to the oversupply of condominiums, Japan's large condominium builders turned their unsold units into rental units and leased to big overseas corporations under the new tenancy arrangement (see JETRO, 1998).

17. Also, as a part of administrative reforms that were carried out on January 6, 2001, the status of the MPT was reduced to the Postal Service Agency within the Ministry of Public Management. The Postal Service Agency was later turned into Japan Post, a public corporation, on April 1, 2003, paving the way to privatize the postal savings system.

REFERENCES

Agus, Mohammed Razali, John Doling, and Dong-Sung Lee. (2002). *Housing Policy Systems in South and East Asia*. Hamsphire: Palgrave Macmillan.

Aoki, Hideo. (2003). "Homelessness in Osaka: Globalization, *Yoseba* and Disemployment." *Urban Studies*, 40(2): pp. 361–78.

Campbell, David W. and Wako Watanabe. (1997). *Housing Saving in Japan*. Discussion Paper Series No. 1997–2008. Tokyo, Japan: Institute for Posts and Telecommunications Policy, the University of Tokyo.

Cargill, Thomas, Michael Hutchison, and Takatoshi Ito. (1997). *Japan's "Big Bang" Financial Deregulation: Implications for Regulatory and Supervisory Policy*. Japan Information Access Project, updated on 20 June www.nmjc.org/NMJC-HTML/jiap/dereg/papers/deregcon/hutchison.html.

Corporate Information. (2000). *Industry Analysis: The Construction Industry in Japan*. Available online at www.corporateinformation.com/jpsector/Construction.html.

Cybriwsky, Roman. (1998). *Tokyo: The Shogun's City at the Twenty-first Century*. Chichester: John Wiley & Sons.

Deyo, Frederic C. (1992). "The Political Economy of Social Policy Formation: East Asia's Newly Industrialized Countries," in Richard P. Appelbaum and Jeffrey Hendersen (eds.) *States and Development in the Asian Pacific Rim*. California: Sage, pp. 289–306.

Doling, John and J. Ford. (1996). "The New Homeownership: The Impact of Labor Market Developments on Attitudes Toward Owning your Own Home." *Environment and Planning A*, 28: pp. 157–72.

Dorling, Daniel. (1994). "The Negative Equity Map of Britain." *Area*, 26(4): pp. 327–42.
Economic Planning Agency (EPA). (1997, 1998). *Economic Survey of Japan (1997–1998)*. Tokyo: EPA.
Ezawa, Aya. (2002). "Japan's 'New Homeless.'" *Journal of Social Distress and the Homeless*, 11(4): pp. 279–91.
Feldman, Robert Alan. (1986). *Japanese Finance Markets: Deficits, Dilemmas, and Deregulation*. Cambridge: MIT Press.
Forrest, Ray, Misa Izuhara, and Patricia Kennett. (2000a). "Home-ownership in Japan's Troubled Economy." *Housing Finance*, 46: pp. 50–5.
———. (2000b). *Home Ownership, Economic Change, and the Japanese 'Social Contract'*. Paper presented at the Hong Kong Research Network Conference on Housing Policy and Practice in the Asia Pacific, Convergence and Divergence, July, 13–15 in Hong Kong.
Fuyuno, Ichiko. (2001). "Tokyo's Condominium Revolution." *Far Eastern Economic Review*, May 31, p. 55.
Garon, Sheldon. (1997). *Moulding Japanese Minds: The State in Everyday Life*. Princeton, NJ: Princeton University Press.
Gentle, Christopher, Daniel Dorling, and James Cornford. (1994). "Negative Equity and British Housing in the 1990s: Cause and Effect." *Urban Studies*, 31(2): pp. 181–99.
Goodman, Roger. (1998). "The 'Japanese-style Welfare State' and the Delivery of Personal Social Services." In Roger Goodman, Gordon White, and Huck-ju Kwon (eds.) *The East Asian Welfare Model: Welfare Orientalism and the State*. London & New York: Routledge, pp. 137–58.
Government Housing Loan Corporation (GHLC). (2000). *Statistics on Residential Market 2000*. Tokyo: GHLC (in Japanese).
Haley, John O. (1992). "Japan's New Land and House Lease Law." In John O. Haley and Kozo Yamamura (eds.) *Land Issues in Japan: A Policy Failure?* Seattle, WA: Society of Japanese Studies, University of Washington.
Hamnett, Chris. (1994). "Restructuring Housing Finance and the Housing Market." In Stuart Cambridge, Ron Martin, and Nigel Thrift (eds.) *Money, Power and Space*. Oxford, England and Cambridge, MA: Blackwell, pp. 281–308.
Hayakawa, Kazuo. (1990). "Japan." In Willem van Vliet (ed.) *International Handbook of Housing Policies and Practices*. Westport, CT: Greenwood Press, pp. 671–94.
———. (2002). "Japan." In Mohammed Razali Agus, John Doling, and Dong-Sung Lee (eds.) *Housing Policy Systems in South and East Asia*. Hamshpire: Palgrave Macmillan, pp. 20–37.
Hayakawa, Kazuo and Yosuke Hirayama. (1991). "The Impact of the *Minkatsu* Policy on Japanese Housing and Land Use." *Environment and Planning D: Society and Space*, 9: pp. 151–64.
Hirayama, Yosuke. (2000). "Collapse and Reconstruction: Housing Recovery Policy in Kobe after the Hanshin Great Earthquake." *Housing Studies*, 15(1): pp. 111–28.

———. (2001). "Housing Policy and Social Inequality in Japan." Paper presented in the Anglo-Japanese Workshops: Social Policy in the Twenty-first Century, School of Social Policy, The University of Bristol, March 15–16.

———. (2003). "Housing and Socioeconomic Change in Japan." Paper presented in the First APHR Conference on Housing and Sustainable Urban Development, University of Malaya, Kuala Lumpur, July 1–4.

Holliday, Ian. (2000). "Productivist Welfare Capitalism: Social Policy in East Asia." *Political Studies*, 48: pp. 706–23.

Horioka, Charles Yuji. (1993). "Consuming and Saving." In Andrew Gordan (ed.) *Postwar Japan as History*. Berkeley and Los Angeles: University of California Press, pp. 259–92.

Ito, Takatoshi. (1994). "Public Policy and Housing in Japan." In Yukio Noguchi and James M. Poterba (eds.) *Housing Markets in the United States and Japan*. Chicago & London: The University of Chicago Press, pp. 215–37.

Iwata, Masami. (2001). "Homelessness in Contemporary Japan." Paper presented in the Anglo-Japanese Workshop: Social Policy in the Twenty-first Century, March 15–16, School for Public Studies, University of Bristol.

Jain, Purnendra. (1989). *Local Politics and Policymaking in Japan*. New Delhi, India: Commonwealth Publishers.

Japan External Trade Organization (JETRO). (1998). "Overseas Companies Bullish on Japanese Real Estate." *Japan Focus*, May. Available online at www.jetro.go.jp/it/e/pub/focus/98_05_5.html.

Japan International Cooperation Agency (JICA). (2000). "Housing Loan." Paper presented on seminar of Housing Policy II, 10 November.

Japan Real Estate Institute (JREI). (2004). *Monthly JREI Report*, November.; Available online at www.reinet.or.jp/e/mjr/index.html.

Kanemeto, Yoshitsugu. (1997). "The Housing Question in Japan." *Regional Science and Urban Economics*, 27: pp. 613–41.

Kikuta, Toshihara. (2000). *Housing Situation and Policy in Tokyo Metropolitan Government: Focused on Publicly-Operated Housing*. Unpublished document.

Kirwan, Richard M. (1987). "Fiscal Policy and the Price of Land and Housing in Japan." *Urban Studies*, 24: pp. 345–60.

Lee, Jongsoo. (1997). "The 'Crisis' of Non-performing Loans: A Crisis for the Japanese Financial System?" *The Pacific Review*, 10(1): pp. 57–83.

Lin, Chang Li and Ramkishen S. Rajan. (1999). "Regional Responses to the Southeast Asian Financial Crisis: A Case of Self-help or No Help?" *Australian Journal of International Affairs*, 53(3): pp. 261–81.

Mattione, Richard P. (2000). "Japan: The World's Slowest Crisis." In Wong Thye Woo, Jeffrey D. Sachs, and Klaus Schwab (eds.) *The Asian Financial Crisis: Lessons for A Resilient Asia*. Cambridge, Massachusetts: MIT Press, pp. 185–201.

McGuire, Chester C. (1981). *International Housing Policies: A Comparative Analysis*. Lexington: Lexington Books.

Ministry of Construction (MOC). (1998). *Housing Policy in Japan*. Unpublished document. Japan: MOC.

Ministry of Finance (MOF). (1999). *FILP Report 1999*. Tokyo: MOF. Available online at www.mof.go.jp/zaito/zaito99e.html.

Ministry of Land, Infrastructure, and Transport (MLIT). (2004). *New Dwellings Started*. Updated on December 27. Available online at www.mlit.go.jp/toukeijou hou/chojou.

Nakagawa, Shinobu. (1999). "Why Has Japan's Household Savings Rate Remained High Even During the 1990s?" Research papers, Research and Statistics Department, Bank of Japan, July. Available online at www.boj.or.jp/en/ronbun/ron9907.htm.

Noguchi, Masa. (2003). "The Effect of the Quality-oriented Production Approach on the Delivery of Prefabricated Homes in Japan." *Journal of Housing and the Built Environment*, 18(4): pp. 353–64.

Osugi, K. (1990). *Japan's Experience of Financial Deregulation since 1984 in an International Perspective*. BIS Economic Papers No. 26, Basle: Bank of International Settlements.

Pempel, T. J. (1998). *Regime Shift: Comparative Dynamics of the Japanese Political Economy*. Ithaca, NY: Cornell University Press.

Schaede, Ulrike. (2004). "What Happened to the Japanese Model?" *Review of International Economics*, 12(2): pp. 277–94.

Statistics Bureau, Management and Coordination Agency. (2000a). *1998 Housing and Land Survey of Japan, Volume 1: Results for Japan*. Tokyo: Japan Statistical Association.

———. (2000b). *1998 Housing and Land Survey of Japan, Volume 5: Results for Prefectures, Part 13, Tokyo-to*. Tokyo: Japan Statistical Association.

———. (2005a). *2003 Housing and Land Survey of Japan, Volume 1: Results for Japan*. Tokyo: Japan Statistical Association.

———. (2005b). *Japan Statistical Yearbook 2004*. Tokyo: Japan Statistical Association.

Takahashi, Mutsuko. (1997). *The Emergence of Welfare Society in Japan*. Aldershot: Avebury.

Takeda, Masahiko and Philip Turner. (1992). *The Liberalisation of Japan's Financial Markets: Some Major Themes*. BIS Economic Papers No. 34, Basle: Bank of International Settlements.

Tanaka, Hiromichi. (1999). "Reorganization of Housing & Urban Development Corporation and Some Innovative Approaches Adopted by Japan." Paper presented in the Hong Kong Housing Conference 1999, November 24–25, Hong Kong.

Tang, Connie P. Y. (2002). *A Comparative Analysis of Housing Systems in Tokyo and Hong Kong*. Unpublished Ph.D. dissertation, Centre for Urban and Regional Studies, University of Birmingham.

Tiwari, Piyush and Hiroshi Hasegawa. (2001). "Welfare Effects of Public Housing in Tokyo." *Journal of Policy Modeling*, 23: 421–31.

Tokyo Metropolitan Government (TMG). (1971). *Tokyo's Housing Problem*. Translated by Tokutaro Nakagawa, edited by Martin C. Davidson. Tokyo: TMG.

Tokyo Statistical Association. (1999). *Tokyo Statistical Yearbook 1997*. Tokyo: Tokyo Statistical Association.

———. (2004) *Tokyo Statistical Yearbook 2002*. Tokyo: Tokyo Statistical Association.

Urban Development Corporation (UDC). (2000). *UDC 2000*. Tokyo: UDC.

Woodall, Brian. (1996). *Japan Under Construction: Corruption, Politics, and Public Works*. Berkeley and Los Angeles: University of California Press.

5

Globalization, Regime Transformation, and Social Policy Development in Taiwan

Wan I. Lin and Wen-Chi Grace Chou

Since the 1960s Taiwan has experienced rapid economic growth. This growth has been paralleled by a favorable pattern of income equality, low unemployment rates, and the near elimination of poverty. The national developmental policy of "growth with stability" has been emphasizing economic imperatives since the 1970s (Li, 1988; Gold, 1986). Most remarkable of all, this "economic miracle" also occurred in other newly industrialized countries of East Asia, such as South Korea, Singapore, and Hong Kong in the 1980s (Deyo, 1987). Moreover, with the successful political democratization since the end of the 1980s, Taiwan has presented itself as a unique case of regime transformation in the Third World (Ku, 2002).

The 2000 election in Taiwan that swept President Chen Shiu-bian into office had succeeded in realignment of its underlying political power structure that had been weakening for the past 50 years, since Chiang Kai-shek's Chinese Nationalist Party (KMT) withdrew to Taiwan in 1949. Taiwan's economy is at one of its best periods since the failing of the world technology sector and the terrorist attack on the U.S. in September 11, 2001. In tandem with economic development, Taiwan's social welfare sector has also been gaining grounds. Social welfare spending in Taiwan (including social welfare, community/environmental protection, and pension and survivors' benefits) as a percentage of total government expenditure has increased from 4.7 percent in 1966 to 12.0 percent in 1981, largely owing to the fact that pension expenditures and survivors' benefits for government employees and military servicemen accounted for half of all social welfare expenditures. Social welfare advocacy groups and scholars in Taiwan have argued that social welfare spending should be distributed more equitably among all sectors. Consequently, social welfare expenditures have been recast in a narrower definition. According to the new definition, Taiwan's social welfare spending as a percentage of general government net expenditure has increased almost three-fold, from 5.5 percent in 1982 to 16.9 percent in 2000.

Studying the relation between the social welfare and economic growth from the 1960s to the 1980s, some scholars have argued that Taiwanese social welfare development was an inevitable and beneficial consequence of industrialization, a conclusion similar to that found in Wilensky and Lebeaux's (1965) analysis of the U.S. experience. For instance, Chan's (1979) comparative study of social welfare in Hong Kong, Singapore, and Taiwan suggests that the development of social security in these countries was a result of economic growth. Further, Peng (1983) points out that industrialization and the development of social welfare during the period of 1963 to 1982 were inseparable. However, studies of the achievements of the four little tigers found that social welfare development over the same period had generally been lagging behind economic and industrial development (Midgley, 1984). Lin's (1991) empirical study found that though industrialization-related variables were strongly associated with the welfare effort, in estimating the historic determinants of Taiwan's welfare development, the growth of the nonagricultural population had greater explanatory power than indicators such as GNP, proportion of aged population, or urbanization. From a political economy perspective, Tsai and Chang (1985) argue that the enactment of three major pieces of social welfare legislation in 1980 was in part a response to the Kaohsiung political riot in 1979. But in order to answer the question why Taiwan's social welfare developed sluggishly during even a boom period, Lin (1991) suggests that one reason might be the lack of collective working-class mobilization to some extent minimized the pressure on the state for social protection development.

Nonetheless, the 1990s saw growth in social spending and passing of a number of important social legislations. Ku (1997) points out that in order to gain voters' support in a democracy, the KMT spearheaded in the direction of increasing state welfare. However, capitalist development also made the KMT wary of the economic burden of radical increases in state welfare, and hence the party always hopes that the private sector will progressively share the welfare burden. Accordingly, Holliday (2000) identifies Taiwan as one of the East Asia's "Productivist Welfare Capitalism" state, that is, a growth-oriented state with the subordination of all aspects of state policy, including social policy, to economic/industrial objectives.

Arguing from a political perspective, Aspalter (2002) argues that Taiwan's recent efforts in the field of social policy could be interpreted as the direct outcome of the democratization process. Judging from political mobilization, the rightists' inhibition of welfare efforts and the leftists' boosts to the welfare are both acknowledged, but the difficulty remains as to judging the relative impact of various parties (Hicks, Misra and Tang, 1995; Hicks and Misra, 1993; Papadakis and Bean, 1993; Hicks and Swank, 1992; Korpi, 1989; Esping-Andersen, 1985; Hicks and Swank, 1984). Chen Shui-bian of Taiwan's DPP defeated Lien Chan of the ruling KMT and James Soong, an expelled KMT member running as an independent candidate, to win the presidency of Taiwan in March 2000. Chen's victory was significant in that political power at the national level had been transferred peacefully from one party to another for the first time on the island and indeed in any territory where ethnic Chinese rule. Although the DPP was not identified by itself or the public as a leftist party, President Chen fashionably adopted the slogan of the "Third Way" from the English sociologist Anthony Giddens (1998, 2000, 2001) as his political manifesto. As Scanlon (2001) criticizes, the Third Way is not simply the pursuit of social democratic objectives by the other means, but a recapitulation of social democracy to the requirements of global capital that, in terms of the parameters of existing political debate, represents more of a jump to the Center-Right rather than a step to the Left. Many cognoscenti have also questioned whether Taiwan's social policy in the name of "New Middle Way" could have developed toward the Center-Left since 2000.

In this chapter, we will first analyze the political economy of Taiwan's transformation, followed by an examination of the characteristics of recent regime transformation in Taiwan. Then we will investigate the development of social policy in Taiwan after the transfer of political power, particularly during the period of the economic crisis. Finally, we will make a preliminary assessment of Taiwan's social policy development and try to glimpse what will follow on from this.

TAIWAN'S ECONOMIC DEVELOPMENT IN THE GLOBAL ECONOMY

The data on Taiwan's economic development up to the end of the 1990s shows not only GDP growth rates but also structural change and deepening of industrialization. The GDP growth rate was 8.9 percent in 1966, 12.9 percent in 1971, and 13.9 percent in 1976. In the last two decades, the GDP growth rate dipped slightly to 8.2 percent on average in the 1980s and 6.3 percent in the 1990s.The per capita GNP in US dollars was $237 in 1966, $443 in 1971, $2,669 in 1981, $8982 in 1991, and $13,235 in 1999. The 1999 value of per capita of GNP was 56 times that of 1966. During this period, the economy underwent a noticeable structural change as the contribution of industry outstripped agriculture in the early 1960s and the leading sectors of industry changed as well, from processed food and textiles to electronics, machinery, and petrochemical intermediates. Since 1986 the structure of domestic production has changed again from industrial to service-oriented. Taiwan has a record of equitable income distribution, with Gini coefficients decreasing from 0.323 in 1966 to 0.28 in 1976, and then increased to 0.343 in 2003. In terms of the times of disposable income quintile was 5.25 in 1966, 4.18 in 1976, 4.60 in 1986, 4.97, 5.38 in 1996, and 6.07 in 2003. The unemployment rate has been kept low, averaging 2.1 percent over the last two decades.

Following its past steps, Taiwan's economy has continued to concentrate on heavy chemical and technology-intensive industries since 1996, while the service sectors and information industries are also growing. Yet, with expanding economic liberalization and globalization, Taiwan's economy has been closely related to other economies in the region. This being the case, any single economic incident could trigger a chain reaction. For example, Taiwan's economy was affected by the financial crisis of 1997, although the harm was insignificant compared with that sustained by other Asian countries such as South Korea, Malaysia, Thailand, and Indonesia (Lee, 1998; Chou, 1999).

Fortunately, the economic turmoil sweeping East Asia in 1997 did not significantly impact Taiwan's economy. On the contrary, it served to propel Taiwan's inherent economic and political resilience. Taiwan came through the financial windstorm in 1997 relatively unscathed, and the November 1997 election for magistrates and mayors speedily gained the normalcy of a mature democracy. Taiwan's diplomatic efforts have demonstrated pragmatic flexibility in building upon her already substantial trade and investment relations to raise her international profile.

Even though Taiwan's economic growth in 1997 was slightly affected by the financial crisis of Asia, the domestic economy still grew 6.68 percent, slightly higher than growth rates for 1995 and 1996. This is primarily because Taiwan's economic fundamentals were in good order, enjoying a current-account surplus, a negligible foreign debt of $100 million, and possessing more than $82 billion in foreign-exchange reserves. The domestic economy grew only 4.33 percent in 1998, slightly faster than in 1982, the year of the second oil crisis. The economic growth rates in 1999 and 2000 were 5.32 percent and 5.78 percent respectively, picking up as the world economy eased into the new millennium. For Taiwan, the September 11 attacks were yet another challenge. Indeed, before the incident, the global technology recession had hammered hard the island, whose economy relies heavily on sales of PCs, semiconductors, and other information-technology products to the United States. Over 40 percent of Taiwan's exports are electronics-related. Such technology emphasis helped protect the island during the regional slumps in 1997, but this is no longer the case. Sadly, in 2001, the second year of Chen's presidency, the economic growth rate was minus 2.18 percent, something that had not occurred since Taiwan became one of the newly industrializing countries. The economy mildly recovered in 2002 with a GDP of 3.94 percent, a rate higher than that of Japan (–0.3%), Hong Kong (1.9%), Singapore (2.2%) and the United States (1.9%), but lower than that of Malaysia (4.1%), Thailand (5.3%), South Korea (7.0%), and China (8.0%). The unemployment rate has climbed from 2.72 percent in 1997 to 5.17 percent in 2002 and down to 4.44 percent in 2004. The per capita GNP dropped from US$14,114 in 2000 to US$12,798 in 2002 and US$14,032 in 2004. Obviously, Taiwanese had to be accustomed to living in a smaller way.

In addition, income distribution was worse, with Gini coefficients increasing from 0.325 in 1999 to 0.35 in 2001, the worst record since the 1960s. A greater number of unemployed people and the new poor were in great need of assistance than those in the 1990s, and this posed a great challenge to Chen's administration.

CHARACTERISTICS OF REGIME TRANSFORMATION

Before the great shift in political power, under the rule of martial law from 1947 to 1987, Taiwanese political participation had not expanded to the national level until December 1969, when eleven members of the Legislative Yuan and fifteen delegates to the National Assembly were directly elected by the people of Taiwan. During the first twenty years or so of ROC government on Taiwan, the island was strictly under the control of an authoritarian regime, empowered by the practice of martial law. Not only were political parties forbidden, except the ruling KMT and its two allied parties (Chinese Youth Party and Chinese Democratic Socialist Party) but also a number of political freedoms, such as free speech, publication, and assembly, were strictly restricted.

Taiwan's politics turned to a new page when Chiang Ching-kuo, son of Chiang Kai-shek, became premier of the ROC in 1972; he was key in implementing the first stage of political reform in Taiwan. Chiang Ching-kuo gradually relaxed controls on civil rights and political freedoms in spite of the practice of martial law. He gradually loosened controls over politics because of the economic development in the 1960s. Benefiting from greater affluence and universal education, Taiwanese increasingly expected to have more political participation. In November 1977, two years after the death of Chiang Kai-shek, the Chungli Incident occurred in response to suspicions of election fraud. It was the first time that civilians used violence against the authoritarian KMT government. This incident in Chungli can be seen as a landmark of growing political opposition in Taiwan. Afterwards, in June 1979, the United Office of Popularly Elected Tang wai (non-KMT) Officials, a political party-like organization, was born. Two months later, in August 1979, the *Journal of Formosa* was published for the first time.

On December 10, 1979, on the Human Rights Day, a public speech by the opposition movement in Kaohsiung was turned into street riots that left dozens of policemen injured. This event became widely known as the Kaohsiung Incident. The Kaohsiung Incident constituted a major setback for the opposition movement, as almost the entire elite of the *Journal of Formosa*, including Huang Hsin-chieh, Shi Ming-teh, Lin Yi-hsiung, Yao Chia-wen, Lu Hsiu-lien, Chen Chu, and Lin Hung-hsuan, were in a military tribunal and received long-term jail sentences.

The crucial moment for Taiwan's political liberalization and democratization was the lifting of martial law in July 1987 shortly before the death of President Chiang Ching-kuo. Thereafter, the right to form political parties was guaranteed. Indeed, on September 1986, the first real opposition party, the Democratic Progressive Party (DPP), was formed by the pre-party people at the risk of their political careers. On January 1988, Taiwan experienced another successful political transition when vice president Lee Teng-hui, a native Taiwanese, succeeded Chiang Ching-kuo as the president of the Republic of China. With the formation of political parties and the practice of more political liberalization, the KMT government, under President Lee's leadership, continued to implement political reform. Afterward, the speed of Taiwan's political democratization shifted into high gear. All members of the National Assembly and the Legislative Yuan have been democratically elected since 1991 and 1992 respectively. Moreover, based on the revised constitution of 1996, Lee Teng-hui was elected as the first directly elected president of the ROC in mid-March 1996. This was another significant political change in Taiwan.

Along with national elections, social welfare issues were raised, such as the issue of social rights in the elections for the National Assembly of 1991 and the national old-age pension scheme in the election for the Legislative Yuan held in 1992. Even in the election for city mayors and county magistrates in 1993, which was only a regional election, a demand for a national old-age pension scheme was strongly presented by the DPP candidates. Thus, social welfare became a hot issue together with cross-strait relations in various elections in the 1990s. The so-called "welfare check" (a form of regular welfare screening procedure to determine status) was vindicated by the DPP and social welfare movement organizations, such as the League of the Disabled and the League of the Older People in Taiwan.

Since 1996, Taiwan's political democracy has been further consolidated (Ku, 2002). The votes for non-KMT candidates were growing, a trend especially evident in the 1997 general elections for city mayors and county magistrates. The DPP grabbed 43 percent of the votes by taking twelve cities and counties, whereas the KMT's share of the votes dropped to 42 percent over only eight cities and counties. In the 1998 mayor election, the DPP lost the mayorship of Taipei to Ma Ying-jiou, the popular KMT candidate. After his defeat in the mayoral race, Chen was nominated as the DPP candidate in the 2000 presidential election. In the March 2000 presidential campaign, Chen marginally won the race (see table 5.1).

On May 2000, President Lee peacefully handed his presidency over to Chen Shui-bian. Although the DPP won the presidential election, the KMT was still the majority party in the Legislative Yuan. This situation meant that President Chen could not implement his policy without opposition. The 2001 Legislative Yuan election was crucial, because it realigned the underlying power structure that has been held firmly by the KMT. Lee Teng-hui, the former president of Taiwan, often-called "the father of democracy," was not running for office, but to form a new party, the Taiwan Solidarity Union (TSU), and to form a coalition with the DPP. This coalition allowed Chen a stronger position in the Legislative Yuan. The divided government in the first year was thus terminated. The Taiwan people are prepared to give Chen a chance to prove his leadership.

The very different political style of the KMT and the TSU hold a key to the changing political landscape of Taiwan. TSU is popular among the people who live in southwest, an area that is heavily ethnic Taiwanese. The supporters of KMT live in the industrial north. The most important difference is that the TSU inspires its followers with slogans like "Taiwan ruled by Taiwanese." KMT is more favored by Beijing since it advocates eventual unification with China.

Table 5.1. A Brief Description of Recent Elections in Taiwan by Different Parties

Elections	KMT	DPP	James Soong	PFP	NP	TSU	Other
2000 Presidential Election	23.10%	39.30%	36.84%	0.13%	0.63%		
2004 Presidential Election	49.89%	50.11%					
2001 Legislators Election	28.34%	33.87%	18.48%	2.67%	7.81%	8.85%	
2004 Legislators Election	32.71%	36.12%	13.84%	0.13%	7.86%	9.35%	
2001 County Elections	35.06%	45.27%	2.36%	9.95%	7.38%		
2002 Mayoral Election							
Taipei	64.11%	35.89%					
Kaohsiung	47.00%	50.00%					3.00%

Source: Website of Central Election Commission http://210.69.23.140/Excel/candidateDef.asp

After the presidential election of 2000, James Soong formed a new party called the People First Party (PFP). This party recruited many of the elites from the KMT and the New Party (NP), and ranks as the third largest party in the Legislative Yuan. In terms of public policy, especially China policy, the PFP is indistinguishable from the KMT. As opposition parties, the KMT and PFP are clearly conspiring for the downfall of the DPP.

SOCIAL POLICY DEVELOPMENT IN TAIWAN AFTER THE REGIME TRANSFORMATION

In May 1997, the big question was whether the election of Tony Blair's New Labor government was leading toward the establishment of a new welfare state after 18 years of conservative leadership (Powell, 1999). This important question came to Taiwan after Chen Shui-bian came to power. To what extent does the policy of Chen's administration differ from the KMT? What are the major changes in social policy? Is globalization undermining the ability of national governments to pursue social policy objectives? (Esping-Andersen, 1996; Mishra, 1998, 1999; Held et al., 1999; Hirst and Thompson, 1999; Beck, 2000; Ó Riani, 2000; Korpi, 2003; Jæger and Kvist, 2003).

These questions are especially intriguing since the DPP used to be regarded as more or less a reformist party (Lu and Lin, 1999) and perhaps can be categorized as a Center party. Unlike the Labor Party of UK, the DPP did not forge a strong alliance with working class people but rather with the disadvantaged groups, including the disabled and elderly. It is now possible for us to see how a Center party fares with the global economy. We will first describe what has been done and in what ways. This is mainly concerned with the extent of Chen's ability to comply with promises made during the presidential campaign. Second, we will point out the other important issues that pose a great challenge to social development in Taiwan, including unemployment insurance, national health insurance, and pensions, which are often regarded as the three pillars of Taiwan social policy.

Social Policy Development Promised by Chen

In 1999, Chen Shu-bian launched his European study tour. During his visit to the UK, he met Anthony Giddens at the London School of Economics. Although Chen's political thinking has been influenced by Giddens' Third Way philosophy, he aspires to merely incorporate the central ideas rather than taking the concept wholesale to Taiwan. Its main distinction in application is that Taiwan is a country that does not possess a history of socialist thinking. Given this background, the New Middle Way places more emphasis on investment in education, vocational training, and life-long learning to meet the challenges from globalization. Moreover, to ease the huge burden of government spending on social welfare, the government should actively cooperate with enterprise to revitalize economy and increase job opportunities. While President Chen proactively pursues a knowledge-based economy or the Green Silicon Island project in the global economy, it should be well understood that such economic projects will worsen social polarization and hence social equality. Therefore, a sound social safety net is an urgent need for Taiwan. However, the current welfare development is not moving toward such direction. For Chen, social welfare and economic development are better off when left mutually exclusive.

Apart from the grand policy guidelines, the presidential election promised the "Triple Three Family Welfare Programs"—which provides free health care for children under three, helps young people to get mortgages at 3 percent interest rate, and provides those age sixty-five or over a monthly allowance of NT$3000 under the National Pension Scheme. He also touted the "Triple Five Women and Children Welfare Programs" which aims to increase the number of babysitters by 50 percent, thus reducing women's caretaker load, and hence the number of victims from domestic violence. On the labor issue, the administration promised to implement a forty-hour workweek in 2002 and to create 100,000 job opportunities and enhance administrative efficiency by morphing the current Employment and Vocational Training Administration into a National Employment Security Administration. But what exactly happened in terms of social development after Chen came to power?

SOCIAL POLICY DEVELOPMENT AFTER THE REGIME TRANSFORMATION

Social Welfare Expenditure

Social welfare spending as a percentage of government expenditure has increased from 16.9 percent in 2000 to 17.5 percent in 2001, but back to 15.1 percent in 2002 (figure 5.1). As can be seen, from 1990 to 2000, government expenditures on social welfare increased continuously and this period was thus labeled as the "Golden Decade" of social welfare development in Taiwan (Investigation Report on Social Welfare Development in Taiwan, 2002).

The honeymoon between President Chen and the labor and welfare advocates did not last long. During a press conference on September 16, 2000, President Chen Shui-bian announced "Economy First, Social Welfare Second," saying that he wanted to postpone social welfare programs and focus

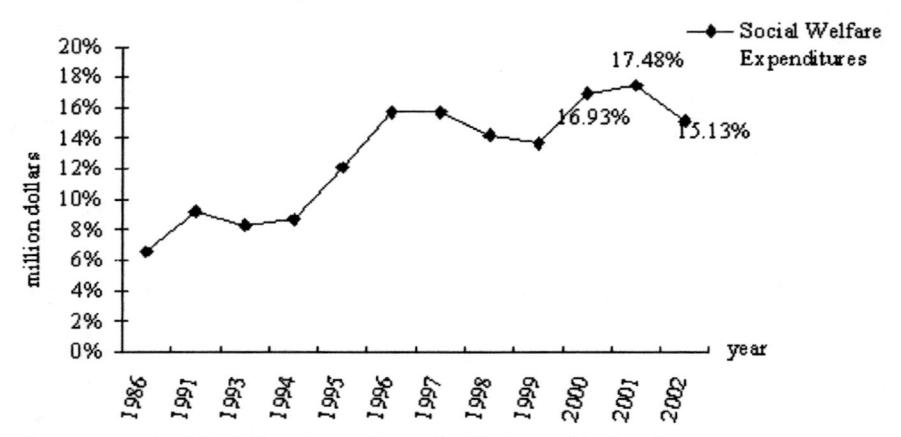

Figure 5.1. Social Welfare Expenditures from 1986–2002 in Taiwan
Source: Ministry of Finance, http://www.mof.gov.tw/default.asp

instead on economic development. This was a sudden shock to the social welfare sector. With a precarious economy and the 921 post-earthquake reconstruction, government debt in 2001 ran as high as NT$2.8 trillion, or 29.4 percent of the GDP (Department of National Treasury, 2002). This situation had a huge impact on later development of social welfare.

Shorter Working Hours and Politics

During the presidential campaign, Chen Shui-bian promised to implement a forty-hour workweek in 2002. On June 16, 2000, the opposition-controlled legislature reversed its previous stance and revised the Labor Standards Law to shorten the maximum working hours to 84 in a two-week period—a more radical shift from the prevailing forty-eight hours per week system. The Council of Labor Affairs had originally reached an agreement with employers and labor groups for a forty-four-hour workweek, rather than the eighty-four hour proposal that was later pushed through by the KMT. In November 2000, the Executive Yuan submitted another bill to the legislature to seek to reverse this decision, arguing that a forty-four-hour workweek was the best option for Taiwan's economy at that time. The legislature voted on December 28, 2000, keeping its June 16 decision to reduce working hours to eighty-four every two weeks, and denying the Executive Yuan its forty-four-hour workweek proposal. The Executive Yuan's amendment was blocked by a vote of 83 to 63, in a joint effort by the KMT, PFP, and New Party. This meant that the eighty-four-hours-every-two-weeks measure would take effect on January 1, 2001. These developments were somewhat ironical. In the past, the KMT had stood against labor issues but now they supported labor but were not really concerned with labor rights. The DPP was seriously criticized by labor groups, accusing them of betrayal. To repair Chen's relationship with labor groups, the presidential office announced a number of pardons, including that of labor rights leader Tseng Mao-hsing. It is clear that this move did nothing in terms of winning support from labor groups.

IMPLEMENTATION OF THE TRIPLE THREE AND TRIPLE FIVE ELECTION PROMISES

Some of the social welfare policies promised by the new government have been realized after a difficult battle, for instance, the "Triple Three Family Welfare Programs" which, among other items, helps young people to get low-interest loans to buy an apartment. Each year, only 10,000 citizens aged twenty to forty from lower-income families who do not own a house are eligible. This measure costs the government one billion dollars each year and will last for seven years. However, critics pointed out that this benefit will be of limited help since the interest rates at private banks have already been lowered, thus rendering the plan unattractive.

The plan also provides for free medical care for children under the age of three. However, when the Executive Yuan sent the budget to the legislature for vetting, the legislature suggested changing the program to include children under the age of 12 from middle- and low-income families. According to official statistics, there are nearly 860,000 children under three years of age nationwide. The government needs to spend NT$1.7 billion to cover the costs of free medical service for children under three. Currently, the National Health Insurance program has already run a monthly deficit of about NT$2 billion (Bureau of National Health Insurance, 2002). This fact led some to question whether the government could afford the new provision, as the new plan took effect since January 2001.

The new government likewise started to allocate a monthly allowance of NT$3000 to the elderly, in order to protect the underprivileged elderly people who are not currently being cared for by anyone. At the moment, Taiwan has 2,026,000 elderly people and if we discount those who already receive public assistance and social insurance benefits, there are approximately 440,000 who could benefit from such a new program, which requires an annual budget of NT$16 billion. The Ministry of the Interior invited relevant government bodies including the Ministry of Finance and city and county governments to discuss the drafting of the Elderly Welfare Allowance Temporary Law in the hope of implementing the subsidies for the elderly program by January, 2002, pending for its abolition with the establishment of the National Pension Scheme. In the end, the measure was finally passed in the Legislative Yuan; however, critics suggested that the Allowance favored retired civil servants and carries inequity problem as most workers under ordinary labor insurance are not eligible for such benefits (*Taipei Times*, June 16, 2002).

Chen also touted the "Triple Five Women and Children Welfare Programs" which aims at increasing the number of babysitters by 50 percent, increasing job opportunities for women and reducing domestic violence. In 2000, Taiwan had a total of 3,751,124 children of whom 1,814,156 were under the age of six. However, only 345,596 children were in public childcare centers and 2,191 in a public nursery school in 2002. Some 72.3 percent of married women need to look after a child under three, according to the 2000 National Survey of Women Employment and Marriage/Childcare. Who provides the childcare and at what price becomes the key issue. Clearly, without appropriate childcare assistance from the state and suitable job opportunities, women cannot be expected to increase their labor force participation. It remains to be seen how the new government can meet their promises coherently.

CONSTRUCTING THE THREE PILLARS OF INSTITUTIONAL WELFARE

In an era of high unemployment, an aging population and deteriorating social inequality: income security, old-age protection, and health insurance have become the three major concerns in welfare development. The following is a brief analysis on the current status of these major welfare programs:

Unemployment, Employment Insurance, and Flexible Labor Market

Unemployment rate in Taiwan has risen from 1.79 percent in 1995 to 5.17 in 2002 and 4.44 in 2004. A total of 454,000 people were unemployed under the ILO definition in 2004. However, if these figures include those who did not actively seek a job, the total unemployment rate increases to 6.54 percent. The number of family members affected exceeded 941,000 in 2004 (Directorate General of Budget Accounting and Statistics, 2005). The unemployment rate among young people between fifteen to twenty-four years old has also increased from 70,000 in 1995 to 120,000 in 2004. The average length of total unemployment has also grown from 17.2 weeks in 1995 to 29.4 weeks (more than six months) in 2004 (Yearbook of Human Resources Statistics, 2005). These figures clearly showed that the unemployment problem must be taken seriously. Not surprisingly, according to recent public polls, the unemployment issue has been rated as a top issue that the government should tackle in the area of social welfare. Taiwan did not start providing unemployment subsidies until January 1999. The long-term unemployment problem was largely neglected under the KMT. However, following a worsening unemployment problem, the KMT government finally implemented unemployment subsidies in 2000. The DPP government further eased restrictions on the subsidies in December 2000. Furthermore, in order to strengthen the link between unemployment insurance payment and vocation training, the Employment Insurance Law took effect in January 2003 to providing six months of unemployment benefits, including subsidies to cover National Health Insurance premium. Currently, the number receiving unemployment benefits decreased to 212,097 and government expenditure down to 3.68 billion, partly due to the success of job creation schemes in recent years (Bureau of Labor Insurance, 2005).

Employment services and occupational training are both weakly organized. The delivery system of employment services is under heavy reconstruction. It remains to be seen whether the government can successfully implement the idea of "Active Labor Market Policies" (ALMP) by providing appropriate employment services and effective vocational training to reduce disincentives to unemployed workers seeking to find a job and help them back to the labor market effectively (Chou, 2005). Another major concern in the unemployment problem is that long-term employment in Taiwan is getting worse. There is a big gap between unemployment insurance benefits and social assistance (Chou, 2005). According to the current Employment Insurance Law, the maximum length an unemployed worker may receive unemployment benefits is up to nine months in two years. This leaves an increasing number of unemployed workers outside the social safety net. The situation is even worse for unemployed workers since the threshold of social assistance (the poverty line) is extremely low. The number of low-income persons entitled to receive public assistance was only 204,216 in 2004, or 0.9 percent of the total population of Taiwan (Department of Social Affairs, 2004).

As far as social policy is concerned, the increase in the unemployment rate and the re-election pressure has propelled the Chen government to seek a special budget of NT$70 billion (about US$2 billion). NT$50 billion was earmarked to expand the public construction program with the hope of boosting the economic growth rate to 3.52 percent, and the other NT$20 billion was aimed at creating 750,000 jobs for people between 35 and 65 years of age through public services, in the hope of cutting the unemployment rate to below 4.5 percent. The latter was conditionally approved by the Legislative Yuan in January 2003 amid hot criticisms including the allegation of blatant "pork-barrel" politics. Between early 2001 and May 2002, the government launched a "Sustainable Employment Project" through job creation by local governments, which created 25,000 jobs. However, the plan was also criticized for lacking sustainability since the jobs were only of 6 to 9 months duration.

While tackling unemployment, the Legislative Yuan continued to deregulate the labor market by passing an amendment to the Labor Standards Law in 2004, extending the period flexi-time workers to fulfill their work quota from two weeks to eight weeks as well as relaxing restrictions on women working at night in the hope of increasing job opportunities for women. Under the new regulations, employers will be able to use flexible working hours in eight-week blocks. The Council of Labor Affairs claims in their White Paper that the government should reconsider its role under the global economy, saying that the government should protect the basic working rights while promoting industrial democracy and the autonomy of union affairs. So, under Chen's administration, the "Gender Equality at Work," "Injured Workers Compensation," and "Protection of Massive Redundancy" laws have all been passed, though the relative success of them were subject to much criticisms.

National Health Insurance and Premium Hikes

The National Health Insurance plan was fully implemented since 1995. Essentially, it is a compulsory social insurance program. The total health expenditure was about NT$504.9 billion, amounting to 5.44 percent of GDP in 1999 and 5.39 percent of GNP in 2002. This figure was higher than those of Turkey and Mexico but lower than South Korea and Japan. Statistics also showed that National Health Insurance was in deficit since 1998 when it was still under the KMT government (Bureau of National Health Insurance, 2002). To remedy the budget, the DPP government therefore wanted to increase the contribution rate from 4.25 percent to 4.55 percent, which represents an average of NT$40 more per person per month, with changes taking effect from September 2002. However, the Legislature voted 118 to 99 in support of a resolution urging the Department of Health to abolish the increase in National Health Insurance contribution and copayment rates. The opposition legislators argued that the government should seek first to crack down on unscrupulous medical service suppliers and mismanagement by the government. The DPP government has been threatened with a vote of no confidence if it doesn't abide by the resolution. Moreover, the opposition parties have threatened to disempower the Department of Health to adjust National Health Insurance contributions if the Department refuses to observe a legislative resolution demanding an end to fee rises. However, legally the Department of Health does not require consent from the Legislature since the insurance premium does not exceed 6 percent of subscribers' monthly incomes. Moreover, the Bureau of National Insurance defended itself on the basis that total administrative expenditures only accounted for 2.06 percent of the medical budget and presented no ground for premium rate increases. The latest development is that the DPP government has proposed allowing people who can't pay their national health insurance premiums to write off outstanding charges and interest accrued on defaulted payments or to halve penalties. If approved by the Legislative Yuan, about 130,000 people would be benefited from the change.

The National Pension Plan and its Related Controversies

The National Pension Plan has been in place for more than ten years. During the presidential election, President Chen promised the implementation of this long-awaited program but was postponed due to the severe 921 earthquake that needed urgent reconstruction expenditure. Since there was a lack of clear policy direction, the Council for Economic Planning and Development (CEPD) has proposed two different plans. One scheme was contributory—the National Savings Insurance. Under this plan, citizens aged between twenty-five and sixty-four would be required to open an individual account and make a monthly deposit of NT$600 in the account. The government will then make up the total with a subsidy of NT$150, or 20 percent of the total. Citizens covered by this plan will then be eligible for a NT$7,500 per month pension upon reaching sixty-five.

Another scheme is a noncontributory basic pension. Under this plan, elderly citizens would receive NT$3,000 every month, with the exception of those who are entitled to other social benefits. These funds would come directly from the administrative budget, lottery revenues, and a planned sales tax to be levied by the Cabinet to fund the expenditures. The latter plan is expected to pose a heavier financial burden on the state since the new government insisted that it would not increase taxes during its term of office. Given the current financial situation, the CEPD prefers the plan using individual saving accounts under the name of "savings insurance." This generated strong criticism from the Federation of Social Welfare Organizations at the National Social Welfare Conference held May 17–18, 2002. Two days later, the Ministry of the Interior modified its stand to favor a social insurance plan based on a flat rate. This scheme will also have more capacity to link with the future revision of current old-age benefits as a lump-sum payment under the Labor Insurance Act. Clearly, the collective voices by social welfare groups did matter to some extent in influencing government's thinking on the National Pension Plan.

Furthermore, the Council of Labor Affairs has also attempted to revise the current retirement payments under the Labor Standards Law and just took effect from July 1, 2005. Under the new Labor Pension Act, employers are required to contribute at least 6 percent to each employee's individual account. Companies with over 200 employees can opt for an *annuity insurance plan*. The old labor retirement payments is a minimum defined benefit-type lump sum when having more than twenty-five years service years or fifteen years if they retire after fifty-five. It has been challenged that this provision is quite illusive in the sense that Taiwan workers seldom fulfill these strict requirements. Several issues have been raised. First, the weakness of this revision lies in its failure to take into account both current old-age pensions and the National Pension Plan. As a result, the reform became too fragmented. Avoiding tax increase has become first priority in planning the National Pension and Retirement schemes. Second, the fact that it is a personal account is bound to worsen the existing social inequality. To make things worse, some employers even cut employees' wages to fulfill the government requirements or reduce the core wages and increase the proportion of bonus in order to reduce their contributions. Third, whether the new pension act would be helpful to middle-wage workers in terms of job seeking is questionable since the age bar is still a serious barrier. Finally, the government has been criticized to use this new reform to avoid state responsibility and shed financial burden, with the aim of pension privatization. These measures have been criticized since they favor enormously the insurance sector.

DILEMMAS AND HARD TIMES FOR THE CHEN GOVERNMENT

Economic, Fiscal, and Tax Issues

Before the new government came to power, the accumulated government debt had reached NT$2,478 billion by the end of 2000. In 2001, the economic growth rate presented a negative growth of −2.18 percent for the first time in years. In 2002, the government social welfare budget decreased to NT$2.50 trillion, down about 10 percent over the previous year. This decline in the social welfare budget has incurred concern from social welfare organizations and scholars. People started to cherish the past "Catching-up Golden Decade" in Taiwan's welfare development where the social welfare expenditure had continued to increase. The total government deficit was NT$398 billion or 4.2 percent of GDP in 2001, and total government debt increased to NT$2,808 billion or 30.3 percent of GDP. Figures for budget deficit are more than 3 percent of GDP and less than 60 percent of GDP for the accumulated national debt under the Maastricht Treaty (Mishra, 1999:40) Table 5.2 provides a brief account of major indicators of economic and social issues between 1999 and 2004.

Table 5.2. Major Economic Indicators and Government Spending

	1999	2000	2001	2002	2003	2004
The World Economic Growth Rate	3.2	4.0	1.4	1.8	2.6	4.1
Economic Growth Rate (%)	5.32	5.78	−2.22	3.94	3.33	5.71
GNP (billion)	9,334	9,752	9,639	9,977	10,173	10,584
GDP (billion)	9,244	9,612	9,447	9,735	9,844	10,205
Per Capita GNP (USD)	13,117	14,114	12,798	12,884	13,139	14,032
Tax Revenues (billion)	1,355	1,930	1,258	1,226	1,253	1,387
Tax Revenues of GNP (%)	14.52	13.20	13.05	12.29	12.32	13.10
Expenditures of GNP (%)	23.75	36.18	25.62	23.34	22.70	21.97
Budget Deficit (billion)	0.29	−356	−375	−318	−336	−300
Accumulated Debt (billion)	−1,218	−2,407	−2,704	−2,934	—	—
Accumulated Debt of GNP (%)	13.05	24.68	28.05	29.41	—	—
Unemployment Rate (%)	2.92	2.99	4.57	5.17	4.99	4.44
Unemployed Persons (thousand)	283	293	450	515	503	454
Ratio of income share of highest 20% to that of lowest 20%	5.5	5.55	6.39	6.16	6.07	—

Source: http://www.dgbas.gov.tw/ct.asp?xItem=9013&CtNode=1348; http://2k3dmz2.moea.gov.tw/gnweb/main.aspx?Page=J http://www.dgbas.gov.tw/ct.asp?xItem=11229&ctNode=1763

If we compare the social welfare expenditure for the same period from 1996 until the present (figure 5.1), it is obvious that social welfare expenditure is not the main reason behind the rise in budget deficits in Taiwan. Another point worth noting is that the average tax revenue as a proportion of GNP has continuously decreased from 14.5 percent in 1999 to 13.1 percent in 2004. The tax burden in Taiwan apparently was relatively lower than in more advanced countries and also lower than Japan and South Korea (National Social Welfare Conference Special Report, 2002). In order to win the election, neoliberal governments tend not to increase taxes during their term of office, and even reduce taxes for some high-income groups. Chen's government did similar moves. The shrinking of the tax base is another pertinent issue. As Mishra (1999:43) suggests, "The ascendancy of neoliberal ideology reinforced by globalization pressures has tended to delegitimize progressive taxation (for fear of capital flight and the increasing unemployment) and changed the ideological climate very much in favor of reducing direct taxation all round."

Besides tax reduction, the introduction of welfare lottery has also been an important source of national income. With the expansion of social welfare, lottery profits will clearly be a big help to the government in its financial difficulties. However, although the implementation of the Public Welfare Lottery seemingly increases public revenue, actual income from this source is not stable, and the lottery worsens the current income gap. To some extent, the lottery can be seen as a kind of "poverty tax."

Politics of Welfare

In spite of the first political regime transformation in Taiwan history, several obstacles still stand in the way of democratization. The performance of social policy development in the Chen era is far from satisfactory. As explained earlier, the DPP is not a leftist party; however it has been called a "reformist party" or "center party." As some critiques suggested, it is perhaps better named as an "opportunist party" in light of its social welfare policy. Clearly, apart from economic and fiscal constraints, the shift of political power, the inner politics of DPP, and the forever inconclusive constitutional debate between president and cabinet, all played a role in its decline.

To take stock, first of all, the minority administration has not really been able to operate smoothly because of continued inter-party political wrangling. Although the DPP won the presidential election, it only controls 71 seats in the 225-seat legislature, whereas the KMT held an absolute majority with 119 seats. In the 2001 Legislative Yuan Election, the DPP increased its hold to 33.4 percent (83) but this was still less than the KMT, 28.6 percent (97) and the newly established People First Party (PFP), 18.6 percent (60). This also leads to a major constitutional problem since the current political system is neither a presidential system nor a parliamentary system. The Chen government suffered tremendously as a result of a series of internal and external conflicts, such as the disputes over the Fourth Nuclear Power Plant, working hours and premium increases for the National Health Insurance, and those battles between the ruling and opposition camps. In fact, many of the policy difficulties over the past six years originated in a Legislative Yuan controlled by the Opposition. Indeed, without the legislature's cooperation, Chen cannot really improve government efficiency. In contrast, during the KMT era, the Legislative Yuan was controlled by KMT legislators and hence a much higher level of legislative efficiency. Moreover, the KMT cannot be totally hands-off of their responsibility for work on important social issues—including unemployment insurance, a sound health insurance plan and the national pension system.

If the DPP government has to learn how to rule a country, the opposition parties have to learn how to be good opposition parties. The KMT is now claiming labor rights. However, the sarcasm lies in the fact that the DPP was also a pro-labor party, but now it has become a target for labor protests. Therefore both parties have demonstrated a degree of inconsistency. The purpose of democracy is to pursue and maximize the people's interests. However, these ideals seem to be compromised by party divisions and incessant political battles. This confusion of partisan roles shows that political values and actions in Taiwan finally boil down to nothing more than strategic considerations.

Second, it takes time and resources to learn politics. KMT was in power for more than 50 years and therefore harbors a large pool of talent through a long process of cultivation. In contrast, the DPP took power only before the development of its own elite group. To gain power in a country is one thing; to rule a country is quite another. DPP's inexperience in handling many politically sensitive issues and in ensuring smooth cooperation between new government and the old bureaucracy is thus central to understanding Taiwan's political dynamics. Moreover, the DPP is rife with factionalism. Only some young party members who have received western education and few senior party leaders who have stepped down (such as Lin Yi-hsiung and Shi Ming-the) are those who wield ideals and long-term vision on social democracy. However, currently President Chen is not a member of this group and therefore has missed this important learning experience. When he launched his own learning trip abroad before the election, he adopted new political fads like the "The Third Way" but unfortunately he did so without a clear understanding, and thus ended up with a bizarre and ineffective implementation. For some critics, President Chen has often been labeled as an "opportunist." His understanding of the meaning and value of social welfare is limited and as such holds reservations in any longer-term institutional change in social policy.

In the 2004 the Legislative election, though the DPP in the end received more votes, it was still difficult to create an alliance to become the majority party in the Legislative Yuan. The deep frustrations of the people and their dissatisfaction have caused serious concerns. Protests from labor groups on pension, objections from social welfare organizations to the National Pension Plan, and peasants against the financial reform toward their local banks show that the DPP is still under a great pressure from civil society.

Political regime transformation is indeed a landmark in Taiwan's history. But it never really ends there. Economic downturns, the decrease of the tax base, increasing government debt and social unrest all pose great challenges to the new government. With an aging population, increasing unemployment, deregulation of the labor market, tax regression, worsening inequality, and increasing poverty, people in Taiwan are expecting better social protection from economic loss and income insecurity in the global economy. However, residual government policies have disappointed both those in corporate circles and the general public. If the Labor Party's embrace of the Third Way was still criticized as a shift to the Center-Right under the pressure of global capitalism, the DPP can hardly escape from this criticism.

In May 2002, the Ministry of the Interior organized the National Social Welfare Conference. At that time, President Chen first changed ideas toward social welfare by proposing "Proactive Social Welfare," meaning that social welfare development should be as important as economic development, and that social justice and economic prosperity should be regarded as two distinct goals pursued at the same time by the government. This significant shift by President Chen arose from the enormous pressure from the grassroots. Clearly, the development of social welfare cannot rely solely on the political manifesto; the collective power represented by disadvantaged and poor groups still plays an important role in pushing politicians to get things right. In the future, it remains to be seen whether the government has the determination to transform these ideals into real practice. Also, "Political Stability, Comprehensive Reform, Economic Revitalization, and Eradication of 'Black Gold' Politics" (i.e., an alliance with capital, gang, and the state) have been frequently claimed as goals by government. We need to further ask what kind of "Welfare Reform" the DPP can provide to the general public. The challenges that beset the DPP are waiting to be handled. Social welfare is not necessarily a kind of consumptive expenditure. The active, positive, and productive sides of welfare functions, such as the accumulation of social capital, enhancement of human capital, and maintenance of social stability, should not be ignored or underestimated. Even amidst the challenges of the global economy, the options for government choices, while constrained, are still open. There is still choice, serious welfare choice to be made! It is therefore high time for the new government to reexamine its welfare policies.

REFERENCES

Aspalter, C. (2002). *Democratization and Welfare State Development in Taiwan.* Ashgate.

Beck, U. (2000). *What is Globalization?* Translated by P. Camiller. London: Polity.

Bureau of Labor Insurance. (2003). *Statistics on Unemployment Benefits.* Available online at 163.29.29.1/cache/content/statistic/.

Bureau of National Health Insurance. (2002). "Why Do We Need to Increase the Premium? Available online at www.nhi.gov.tw/07information/issue/index_prem.htm.

Chan, H. S. (1979). "The Relationship of Social Security System to Economic Development with Special Reference to Hong Kong, Singapore and Taiwan." *National Taiwan University Journal of Sociology*, 13, pp. 139–50.

Chou, W. C. G. (1999). "The Asian Financial Crisis: The Challenge for Social Policy." *Work, Employment, and Society*, 13:3, pp. 759–60.

Chou, W. C. G. (forthcoming). "Trends, Causes, Influences and Policy Response of Unemployment in Taiwan." In Chu Hai-Yuan (ed.) *Social Problems in Taiwan*. Taipei. (in Chinese).

Department of National Treasury. (2002). "Government Debt by Various Years." Available online at 210.69.165.254/business/business209.asp.

Department of Social Affairs. (2003). "Households and Numbers of Low Income People." Available online at www.moi.gov.tw/W3/stat/home.asp.

Deyo, F. C. (1987). *The Political Economy of the New Asian Industrialism*. Ithaca: Cornell University Press.

Directorate General of Budget Accounting and Statistics. (2003). Available online at www.dgbas.gov.tw/census~n/four/n9201.htm.

Esping-Andersen, G. (1985). "Power and Distributional Regimes." *Political & Society*, 14, pp. 223–55.

Esping-Andersen, G. (1996). *Welfare States in Transition: National Adaptations in Global Economies*. London: Sage.

Giddens, A. (1998). *The Third Way: The Renewal of Social Democracy*. London: Polity Press.

———. (2000) *The Third Way and Its Critics*. London: Polity Press.

———. (2001) *The Global Third Way Debate*. Cambridge: Polity Press.

Gold, T. B. (1986). *State and Society in the Taiwan Miracle*. Sharpe.

Held, D., McGrew, A., Goldblatt, D., and Perraton, J. (1999). *Global Transformations: Politics, Economics and Culture*. Cambridge: Polity.

Hicks, A. and Misra J. (1993). "Political Resources and Growth of Welfare in Affluent Capitalist Democracies, 1960–1982." *American Journal of Sociology*, 99:3, pp. 668–710.

Hicks, A., Misra, J., and Tang, N. N. (1995). "The Programmatic Emergence of the Social Security State." *American Sociological Review*, 60, pp. 329–49.

Hicks, A. and Swank D. (1984). "On the Political Economy of Welfare Expansion: A Comparative Analysis of Eighteen Advanced Capitalist Democracies, 1960–1971." *Comparative Political Studies*, 17:1, pp. 81–119.

———. (1992) "Politics, Institutions, and Welfare Spending." *American Political Science Review*, 86, pp. 658–74.

Hirst, P. and Thompson, G. (1999). *Globalization in Question: The International Economy and the Possibilities of Governance,* Second Edition. Cambridge: Polity.

Holliday, I. (2000). "Productivist Welfare Capitalism: Social Policy in East Asia." *Political Studies*, 48, pp. 706–23.

Investigation Report on Social Welfare Development in Taiwan. (2002). "Control Yuan." Control Yuan 2002.

Jæger, M. M. and Kvist, J. (2003). "Pressures on State Welfare in Post-industrial Societies: Is More or Less Better?" *Social Policy & Administration*, 37:6, pp. 555–72.

Korpi, W. (1989). "Power, Politics, and State Autonomy in the Development of Social Citizenship: Social Rights During Sickness in Eighteen OECD Countries Since 1930s." *American Sociological Review*, 54:3, pp. 309–28.

Korpi, W. (2003). "Welfare-State Regress in Western Europe: Politics, Institutions, Globalization, and Europeanization." *Annual Review of Sociology*, 29: pp. 589–609.

Ku, S. (2002). "The Political Economy of Regime Transformation: Taiwan and Southeast Asia." *World Affairs*, 165:2, pp. 59–79.

Ku, Y. W. (1997). *Welfare Capitalism in Taiwan: State, Economy and Social Policy*. London: Macmillan Press.

Lee, E. (1998). *The Asian Financial Crisis: The Challenge for Social Policy*. Geneva: International Labor Office.

Li, K. T. (1988). *The Evolution of Policy Behind Taiwan's Development Success*. New Haven: Yale University Press.

Lin, W. I. (1991). "Labor Movement and Taiwan's Belated Welfare State." *Journal of International and Comparative Social Welfare*, VII: 1&2, pp. 31–44.

———. (1991). "The Structural Determinants of Welfare Efforts in Post-war Taiwan." *International Social Work*, 34:2, pp. 171–90.

Lu, P. C. and Lin W. I. (1999). "Social Welfare Policy in Taiwan: Past, Present and Prospects." In Conference Prague 1999 *Transitional Societies in Comparison: East Central vs. Taiwan*, National Science Council, Taipei, Bonn Office (ed.), pp. 287–308.

Midgley, J. (1984). *Social Security, Inequality, and the Third World*. Chichester: Wiley.

Mishra, R. (1998). "Beyond the Nation State: Social Policy in an Age of Globalization." *Social Policy and Administration*, 32:5, pp. 481–500.

———. (1999). "Social Policy in Retreat Hollowing Out of the Welfare State." *Globalization and the Welfare State*. Cheltenham: Edward Elgar, pp. 36–52.

Monthly Report of Labor Statistics. (2003). "Labor Insurance Benefit by Various Years." Available online at www.cla.gov.tw/acdept/month/tab0610.xls.

Ó Riani, S. (2000). "States and Markets in An Era of Globalization." *Annual Review of Sociology* 16: pp. 187–213.

Papadakis, E. and Bean, C. B. (1993). "Popular Support for the Welfare State: A Comparison Between Institutional Regimes." *Journal of Public Policy*, 13:3, pp. 227–54.

Peng, H. C. (1983). *Industrialization and the Development of Social Welfare in Taiwan, 1963–1982*. Thesis, National Taiwan University (in Chinese).

Powell, M. (1999). *New Labor, New Welfare State? The "Third Way" in British Social Policy*. Bristol: Policy Press.

Scanlon, C. (2001). "A Step to the Left? Or Just a Jump to the Right? Making Sense of the Third Way on Government and Governance." *Australian Journal Political Science*, 36:3, pp. 481–98.

Taipei Times. (2002). "Stipends for Seniors not Really Fair to Everyone." June 16, available online at www.taipeitimes.com/News/editorials/archives/2002/06/16/140600.

Tsai, W. H. and Chang L. Y. (1985). "Politics, Ideology, and Social Welfare Programs: A Critical Evaluation of Social Welfare Legislation in Taiwan." *National Taiwan University Journal of Sociology*, 17, pp. 233–62.

Wilensky, H. and Lebeaux, C. (1965). *Industrial Society and Social Welfare*. NY: The Free Press.

Yearbook of Human Resources Statistics. (2005). *Duration in Average Weeks of Unemployment for Unemployed by Year in Taiwan Area*. Available online at www.dgbas.gov.tw/census~n/four/yrtable21.xls.

Year Book of Labor Statistics. (2002). *Duration in Average Weeks of Unemployment for Unemployed Persons by Year in Taiwan Area*. Available online at www.dgbas.gov.tw/census~n/six/lue5/census-n.htm.

6

The Crisis of Social Security Financing in Hong Kong

Raymond Man Hung Ngan

July 1, 1997, is a major watershed in the history of Hong Kong. Not only did it mark the political reunification of Hong Kong with Mainland China, but very few people would have predicted that "the Pearl of Orient" will soon lose herself to aggravating social problems in the form of rising unemployment, worsening income inequality, rising poverty, and surging welfare expenditures. Regressive social development was evidenced by the study on Social Development Index (SDI-2000) by the Hong Kong Council of Social Service, which suggested: (a) a very substantial social loss recorded on the SDI's Family Solidarity Sub-index (-166); (b) a negative social trend for three population groups: low-income households (-77), youth (-52) and children (-17); and (c) a growing disparitiy in social development characterized by a growing number of low-income households, a sizeable population of troubled youth, and tens of thousands of elderly residents who have not been able to achieve a reasonable degree of security in their old age (Hong Kong Council of Social Service, 2000; Ngan, 2002: 274). The popularity rating of Chief Executive Tung Chee-Hwa had plunged to its all-time low in 2003, climaxed by a mass protest with half a million residents who took to the street to protest against poor governance on July 1, 2003. With the resignation of Mr. Tung on March 10, 2005, "Hong Kong people had watched with a feeling of unease and relief, loss and bewilderment as the last days of Mr. Tung's leadership unfolded after seven years and eight months of weak and chaotic governance," as commented by Chris Yeung, Editor-at-large of the *South China Morning Post* (March 12, 2005).

What had made the Tung Chee-Hwa administration a failed government? For the people from the grassroots, there has been much concern on the government's inability to tackle rising unemployment which climbed to a record level of 7.8 percent in July 2002, with 275,000 people unemployed (*South China Morning Post*, August 20, 2002). The Social Welfare Department recorded 35,639 unemployed people receiving Comprehensive Social Security Assistance (CSSA) in June 2002, compared with 24,114 in June 2001 (*South China Morning Post*, August 20, 2002), an increase of 47 percent in CSSA applications in a year. Instead of launching a massive job-creation program in a declining economy, the government resorted to adopt a policy of welfare cuts. CSSA payment rates were slashed by 11.1 percent in June 2003 and single-parents were forced to seek part-time work before they could receive CSSA benefits. A system of "workfare" is being gradually introduced for able-bodied unemployed CSSA cases and single-parents. But the credibility gap between the ruling government and its poverty-stricken social groups is enlarging. The fiscal environment is less conducive to increased welfare spending through tax change. Noting a record budget deficit of HK$70.8 billion in 2002–2003, the Secretary For Treasury Denise Yue warned that Hong Kong's $369 billion reserves would be used up in 2008–2009 while accumulated government debt will increase to HK$2.66 trillion in 2021–2022 (Hong Kong Government, 2002). It seemed that a crisis in social security financing was imminent. This chapter will examine the possibility of a fiscal crisis in social security financing. It argues that it is not the rise in social security spending that should be blamed. Rather, the problem lies with a unitary financing system which relies solely on taxation and government revenue, without active contributions from workers such as a central provident fund or an old age pension. The chapter identifies a number of structural causes of Hong Kong's welfare crisis that emerge during the Tung Chee-Hwa regime. In conclusion, I argue that neither neoliberalism nor incremental change in the social security system will solve Hong Kong's fundamental social problems. Hong Kong needs a revamp in its social security and long-term care financing. A "multi-pillar" approach is suggested having regard to the successful experiences in Mainland China in its old age pension reform (Ngan & Li, 2000).

INCREASE IN SOCIAL WELFARE AND SOCIAL SECURITY SPENDING

Dr. York Chow, the secretary for health, welfare and food raises a fundamental concern on the doubling of welfare expenditures in the past decade (see figure 6.1):

> Its share in recurrent government expenditure increased from 10 percent to 17 percent . . . Payout in social security is still the single item that enjoys the high-

est growth, at 5 percent, or 114 million (in 2005–2006). We have earmarked HK$24 billion for CSSA in 2005–2006 . . . Faced with an ageing population, we expect that in thirty years, social security payments for the aged will nearly triple, from $11.6 billion to $30 billion. Sustainable development of social services is an issue we simply cannot ignore (*South China Morning Post*, March 24, 2005).

Within a context of prudent public finance in recent years, a large increase in social security expenditure in the last decade apparently became a target of political concern. As remarked also by Mrs. Carrie Yau, the permanent secretary for health, welfare and food:

On welfare spending under Health, Welfare and Food Bureau (which include personal social welfare services and subventions to nonprofit making organizations), there has been a 94 percent increase in recurrent public expenditure between 1996–1997 and 2004–2005. The increase in Comprehensive Social Security Assistance (CSSA) Scheme and Old Age Allowance (OAA) expenditures is also significant during this same period, representing a 104 percent increase. . . . The number of recipients increased by three times from 125,000 to 542,000. Whereas ten years ago, 1 in 50 of the population received CSSA, the ratio now increased to 1 in 12" (Yau, 2005).

It seems that a fiscal crisis on welfare and social security spending is imminent as senior government officials pointed out repeatedly that "the sustainability of our social welfare system is questionable. We cannot afford much longer

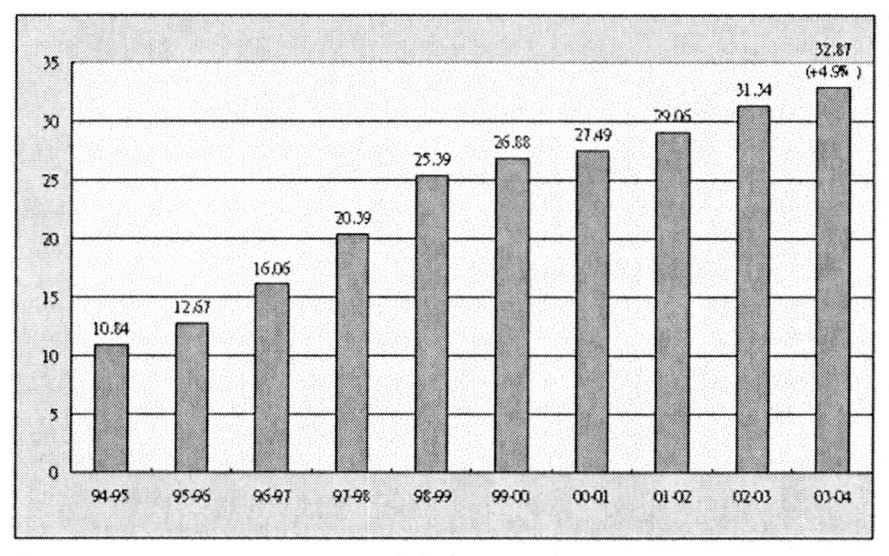

Figure 6.1. Increase in Recurrent Social Welfare Expenditure, 1994–2004 (in HK$ billion)

double-digit growth in welfare spending each year" (Chow, 2005, Lam, 2001; Tsang, 1999; Yau, 2005). This fiscal concern has its pragmatic ground since Hong Kong does not have a wide enough fiscal base to support unlimited increase spending on social welfare. Caught by a low tax regime and a narrow tax base which relies heavily on income and profit tax as well as government revenues to finance welfare spending, Hong Kong does not have a Goods and Services Tax (GST) tax system to widen the sources of government revenue. It has been noted by Carrie Yau (2005) that "in 2003/04, of every $100 we have received from tax revenue, we have spent about $73 on health care, housing, social security and all types of direct social welfare services. This is indeed a very high rate when compared with other OECD economies, which on average spent $57 per $100 tax revenue on these three areas in 1998." It looks as if the woes of the welfare state are already on the policy agenda of senior government officials responsible for welfare. Mrs. Carrie Lam (2001), the former director of social welfare, remarked that "there is a general consensus within the community that we do not wish to see Hong Kong become a welfare state relying on heavy taxes, that there is a limit to how much the government can spend and that the virtues of self-reliance, family cohesion and community support should be preserved." It seems that there is a call to an adherence to the "Confucian welfare state" (Walker and Wong, 2005) or what many have coined the "East Asian welfare model" (Goodman, White, and Kwon, 1998) in which the extended family provides, through cross-generational reciprocity, income support and autonomous care-giving role. The World Bank (1993) claims that East Asian governments had been able to devise social programs minimizing state expenditures while promoting the standard of living for underprivileged social groups.

However, with the onset of the Asian Financial Crisis in July 1997, the mystification of the so-called "productivist East Asian welfare model" (Holiday, 2000) has largely shattered (Li, 2003). Regional financial crisis has brought problems of rising unemployment, increasing income inequality and persistent pockets of poverty (Ngan, 2002). In 1999, the then Financial Secretary Donald Tsang commented, "Hong Kong is facing a major challenge. Many companies have been downsized or closed down. Many people have suffered a pay freeze, a pay cut or even unemployment" (Tsang, 1999). Figure 6.2 shows that the unemployment rate climbed from 2.2 percent in 1997 to 7.4 percent in 2003 (Hong Kong Government Information Services, 2003), and jumped to a record high of 7.8 percent in July 2002, with 275,000 people unemployed (*South China Morning Post*, August 20, 2002). Income inequality is clearly aggravating with more people falling into the poverty trap, an estimated 28 percent of Hong Kong's households (Wong and Lee, 2002). It is found that the poor have only a daily expenditure of HK$35 (US$4.5) for food consumption per head. Be-

The Crisis of Social Security Financing in Hong Kong 129

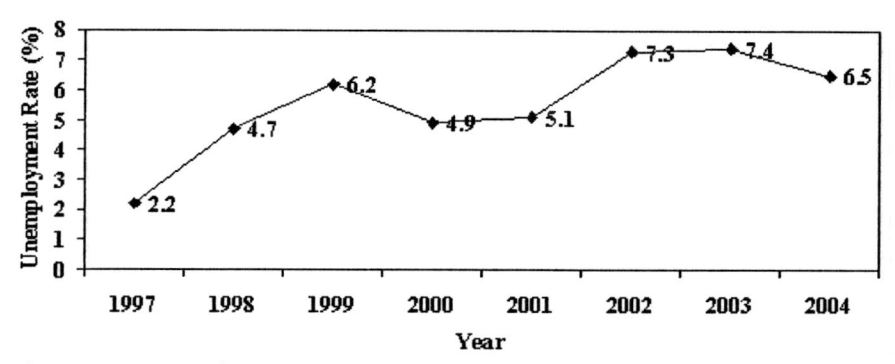

Figure 6.2. Unemployment Rate in Hong Kong, 1997–2004
Source: Hong Kong Census and Statistics Department, 2007

yond that, the Gini coefficient has increased from 0.41 in 1971 to 0.53 in 2001, indicating a widening income gap among the rich and the poor as indicated in figure 6.3 (Census and Statistics Department, 2001).

Nonetheless, faced with economic downturn caused by the Asian Financial Crisis as well as the outbreak of SARS epidemic in 2003 that aggravated the already declining economy, Hong Kong faced a huge budget deficit of HK$78 billion in 2003 (Financial Secretary, 2003). The HKSAR Government's Taskforce Report on Budgetary Problems (Hong Kong Government, 2002) warned that if fiscal policies remain the same and the economy grows at 5 percent a year: (a) the $369 billion fiscal reserves will be used up by 2008–2009; (b) accumulated government debt will increase to $2.66 trillion in 2021–2022; (c) increasing revenue or cutting expenditure by $95 billion a year is needed to achieve a balanced budget in five years; and therefore, (d) the priority should be given to control the growth of public expenditure. Figure 6.4 shows

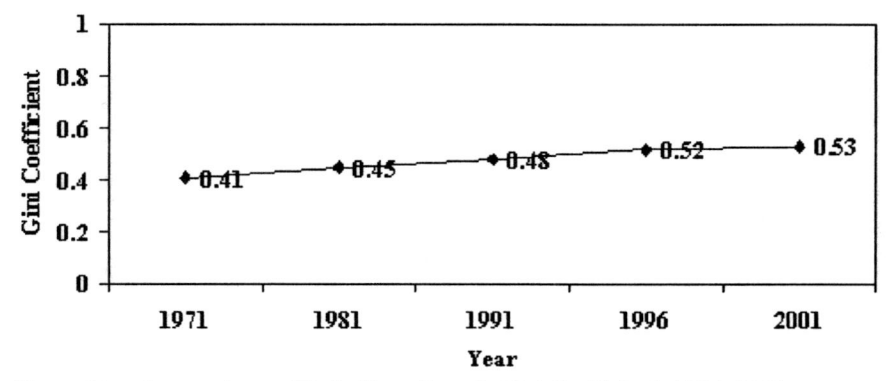

Figure 6.3. Income Inequality in Hong Kong is Gini Coefficient, 1971–2001
Source: Hong Kong Census and Statistics Department, 2007

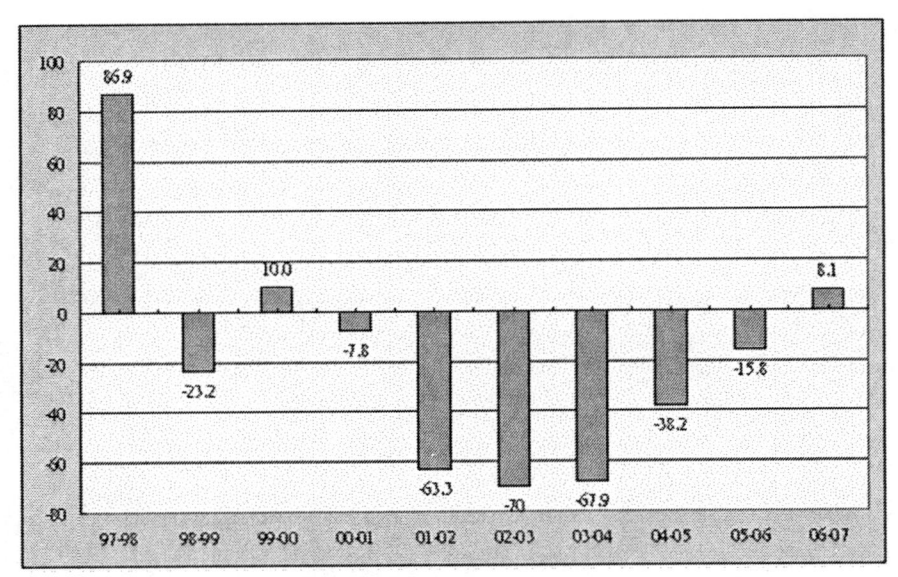

Figure 6.4. Consolidated Deficits of Hong Kong Government, 1997–2007
Source: Hong Kong Government, 2002

the consolidated deficits for the HKSAR government during the years 1997–2007 (Hong Kong Government, 2002). It is thus understandable why the financial secretary announced in the 2004–2005 budget that he would strive to restore fiscal balance in government accounts by 2008–2009, with an expenditure cut of 11 percent (Financial Secretary, 2004).

IS THERE A REAL CRISIS IN SOCIAL SECURITY FINANCING?

If we take the words of senior government officials seriously, it seems that the crisis in social security financing is real, especially when the large budget deficit of $78 billion is taken into consideration. However, the deficit was subsequently found to be a gross overestimate when the financial secretary reported in March 2004, "for 2003–2004, the fiscal deficit will be $49 billion (or 4 percent of GDP), lower than the $78 billion that previously envisaged in October 2003. The economy improved with a 3.3 percent growth in GDP in real terms that is a visible improvement over the 2.3 percent for 2002, and −0.7 in 2001" (Financial Secretary, 2004). In the first quarter of 2005, the GDP increased by 6.0 percent in real terms over a year. It seemed that the economy was on its path to recovery with the budget deficit reduced. The seasonally adjusted unemployment rate declined from 5.9 percent in February–

April 2005 to 5.7 percent in March–May 2005 (Census and Statistics Department, 2005). Nevertheless, it is observed that the total public expenditure for 2004–2005 is 22.5 percent of GDP. This is somewhat higher than the government's target of containing public expenditure at 20 percent of GDP or below (Financial Secretary, 2004: 30), a fiscal requirement stated in the Basic Law of HKSAR which prescribed that the level of public expenditure should not grow at a rate faster than the GDP growth and should not be more than 20 percent of the GDP. Empirical experience shows that this clause is somewhat rigid and restrictive at times of economic adversity with surging unemployment and the outbreak of SARS in early 2003, resulting in more people seeking temporary relief from CSSA. The hardship of socially disadvantaged groups, notably older workers, the disabled, and single-parents, should be dealt with by supportive measures to create suitable employment opportunities, rather than resorting to stern cuts in cost-of-living expenses. Nonetheless, bounded by a declared objective to restore fiscal balance in government accounts by 2008–2009, the financial secretary proposed in March 2004 an 11 percent cut in total government spending by 2008–2009 affecting all government departments. The Hong Kong Council of Social Service finds that this would translate into a cut of more than 30 percent for welfare services since 1997 (*South China Morning Post*, December 15, 2003). The editorial in the *South China Morning Post* commented: "Is it more important to reduce budget deficit or preserve welfare services?"

It seems that the fiscal crisis in welfare spending is caused by both political and economic factors. Politically, the restriction of public expenditure to not more than 20 percent of GDP or increasing at a rate not faster than the growth in GDP is a rigid budgetary constraint set by the Basic Law. This was still evident when, in 1995, a very senior Chinese government official made a metaphorical statement by comparing social security expenditure increases to a high speed car crash (*South China Morning Post*, December 14, 1995). Economically, it is stated in the Basic Law that "social welfare spending has to operate in a low tax environment." (Ngan, 1997). Hong Kong is famous as a "capitalist paradise" with its very low flat rate income and profit tax of 16.5 percent, comparing to over 30 percent for most welfare states in Europe, notably the United Kingdom. In May 2005, two major credit rating agencies—Fitch Ratings and Standard & Poor's—both expressed concern on the volatility of Hong Kong government's revenue base. They cautioned that if the property market or the economy falters, the budget deficit would start to grow again (*South China Morning Post*, June 14, 2005). They recommended that Hong Kong should adopt a Goods and Services Tax (GST) as one of the possible safeguards in steady revenue at times of economic adversity. Yet it seems that Hong Kong government is not keen on the proposal as the financial secretary stated that it was not a good time to introduce GST when the economy had just started to rebound.

There is no question that the crisis in welfare spending is beset by the rapid rise in social security payments over the past ten years as it constituted more than 69.41 percent of the social welfare expenditure in 2003–2004 (Lam, 2001). This is caused by a surge of new applications for CSSA from the unemployed and single-parents, plus mounting expenses spent on payments on the non-means tested universal Old Age Allowance (payable to aged people at seventy and above with five years of residence in Hong Kong). Figure 6.5 shows that there was a marked increase in CSSA cases from 109,461 in 1994–1995 to a peak of 297,145 in 2004–2005, an increase of 2.71 times in eleven years (Social Welfare Department, 2005). How much does this increase in CSSA cases result in government payments? The permanent secretary for health, welfare and food, Mrs. Carrie Yau, notes with concern that "from 1994–1995 to 2004–2005, CSSA expenditure increased by four times, from $3.4 billion to $17.7 billion. The corresponding share in government recurrent expenditure increased from 3 percent to 9 percent. The number of recipients increased by 3 times from 125,000 to 542,000 people" (Yau, 2005). Yet on the demand side for the stepwise increase in people on the dole, it happened at the time when Hong Kong was troubled with economic adversity with rising unemployment resulting from a structural change with more manufacturing industries moving their plants and factories to Mainland China, the downsizing of firms after the Asian

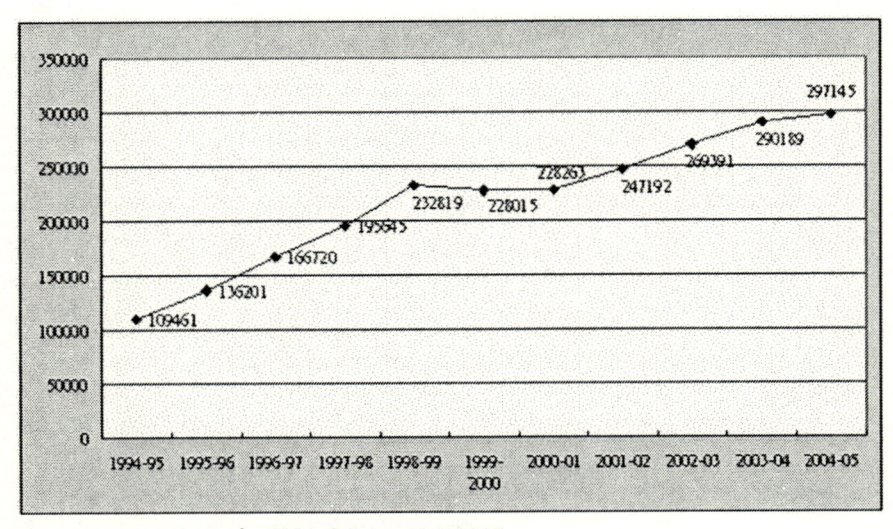

Figure 6.5. Increase in CSSA Cases, 1994–2005
Source: Social Welfare Department Website, www.info.gov.hk/swd/html.org

Financial Crisis in July 1997, and the outbreak of SARS in March to May 2003. This explains why the unemployment rate is on the rise, from 2.2 percent in 1997 to a high 7.8 percent in July 2002, with 275,000 people unemployed (*South China Morning Post*, August 20, 2002). Correspondingly, CSSA cases comprising unemployment, low-income, and single-parent families increased from 11 percent in July 1993 to 32 percent in February 2003 while elderly CSSA cases reduced somewhat from 86 percent of the total CSSA caseload in July 1993 to 66 percent in February 2003. With more people losing jobs, unemployment cases went up to 16 percent of the total CSSA caseload in February 2003, or one CSSA unemployment case per six unemployed workers (*Oriental Daily*, February 26, 2003; Social Welfare Department, 2004). It is evident that the crux of the problem is the lack of jobs in a declining economy rather that the much conflated debate concerning a welfare dependency culture. Unlike Mainland China, Hong Kong does not have unemployment insurance and CSSA is the last resort for relief for those people who lose their jobs.

Apart from the rise in unemployment, low-income and single-parent CSSA cases, the impact of an aging population also plays a crucial role in the impending social policy crisis. Hong Kong suffers from its adherence to a unitary social security system with non-contributory CSSA and non-contributory and non-means tested Old Age Allowance (covering 85 percent of the aged sixty-five and above). Payments are financed by public expenditure relying solely on tax revenue. The total amount of Old Age Allowance increased from $2,141 million in 1992/93 to $3,562 million in 2000–2001, an increase of 66.37 percent (Social Welfare Department, 2001). Although the Mandatory Provident Fund (MPF) scheme was set up since December 2000, it would take a long time to accumulate sufficient contribution from workers for the MPF to become useful as retirement income. Moreover, the MPF does not cover housewives, non-working population or low-pay workers earning less than $5,000 per month, notably disabled and elders on low-paid unskilled jobs (Hong Kong Council of Social Service, 2001). A survey conducted by the Census & Statistics Department (2001) found that 83.3 percent of elderly people aged sixty or above did not have a retirement protection scheme. The Hong Kong Council of Social Service (2003) estimated that the elderly poverty rate (income less than half of median disposal income of the entire population) was on the increase: from 29.5 percent in 1991 to 32.0 percent in 1996 and to 37.9 percent in 2001. It was estimated that with the growth of an aging population, by 2031, about 24.8 percent of elders aged sixty-five and above would possibly be on CSSA, incurring a total expenditure of $30 billion. Can the government afford it in the long run? It is thus understandable why when Dr. York Chow, the secretary for health, welfare and food, alerted the public that "in facing with an ageing population, we expect that in 30 years, social security payments for the aged will nearly triple, from HK$11.6 billion in 2004–2005 to $30 billion in 2035. As public money is funding 90 percent of our public health services (and with frail elders occupying over 52 percent of public hospital beds), we need to study the long-term sustainability of our social welfare development, including health care financing and old-age financial protection" (*South China Morning Post*, March 24, 2005). The impact of an aging population on Hong Kong's non-contributory CSSA payments cannot be underestimated. As commented by Carrie Yau, the permanent secretary for health, welfare and food, "in 2001, 1 in 8 (12 percent or 818,000) of our population is aged sixty-five or above." This ratio is expected to rise to 1 in 4 (about 27 percent) in 2033. This represents a 174 percent increase in the elderly population in Hong Kong in the next three decades. Of the $23.2 billion spent on social security in 2004–2005, about 50 percent (i.e., $11.6 billion) was spent on the elders. Figure 6.6 shows the growth of the aging population from 1981 to 2031 in Hong Kong. The proportion of people aged sixty-five or above increased from 6.6 percent in 1981 to 11.2 percent in 2001, and by 2031, about 24.3 percent of Hong Kong's population will be elderly aged sixty-five and above.

Incidentally, there has been a growing trend in the demand for subsidized long-term care facilities as a result of an aging population, especially the senior aged people seventy-five and above. Thus the discussion on the crisis in social security spending should include the need of financing options for possible long-term care. In 1997, there were a total of 17,000 subsidized residential

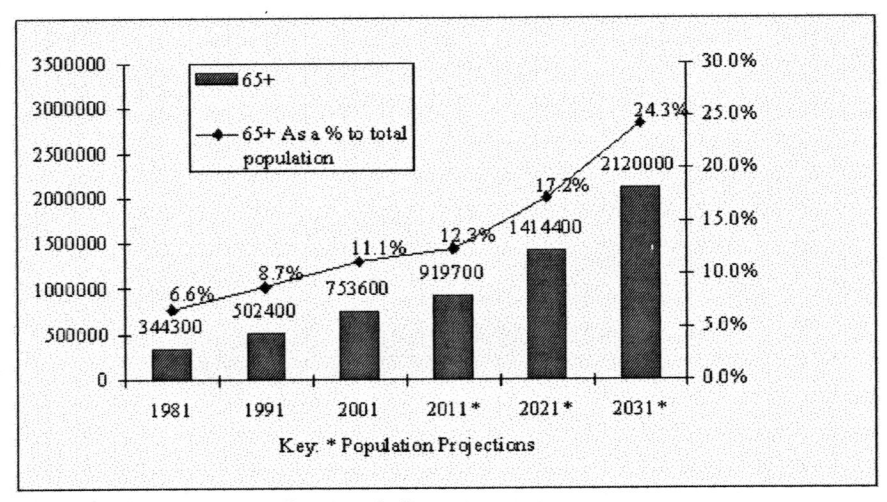

Figure 6.6. Increase in Aging Population, 1981–2031
Source: Hong Kong Census and Statistics Department Website, 2007

care places in Hong Kong, with 19,000 people still on the waiting list (Social Welfare Department, 1997). In December 2002, 52 percent of public hospital-bed occupancy and 39 percent of general outpatient clinic attendance were taken up by elders (sixty and above) (Elderly Commission, 2003). Ho Wing Him, the former deputy secretary for health and welfare said that the Elderly Commission had always been aware of the high cost of long-term care services (2004). Although the annual operating cost of each bed of a care and attention home is more than $100,000, only 20 percent of it is covered by users' fees, with the remaining 80 percent being subsidized in the form of government subvention to the operating welfare agencies. Furthermore, some two-thirds of the residents are CSSA welfare recipients and therefore even the users' fee is paid out from welfare benefits they receive from government. That is, over 90 percent of the cost of the subsidized residential care program comes from public purse. The unit cost for nursing home beds is even higher—at a cost of $150,000 a year—yet with 95 percent of the cost being paid for by public subsidy (Ho, 2004). It should be noted that the total number of subsidized elderly residential places has increased from 17,000 in 1997–1998 to 27,000 on 2004–2005 (Yau, 2005) Plagued by a rapid aging population and the rising cost in subsidized long-term care facilities, the Working Group on Review of the Health Care System (Government Secretariat, 2000, 2005) notes with concern that "the present health care system in Hong Kong is under strain given an ageing population, rising expectations of the community and escalating medical costs. The present level of public services will prove unsustainable in the long run." It calls for the need to adopt three strategic directions for health care reforms: (i) containment of costs and enhancement of productivity; (ii) revamp of public fees structure to better target public subsidies to those in need and (iii) initiating studies to assess the feasibility of establishing a Health Protection Accounts (HPA) scheme in Hong Kong. The concept of HPA has much relevance to the further development of viable options in long-term care financing in the decade to come and will be deliberated in subsequent sections. Basically speaking, HPA is essentially a self-insurance scheme of mandatory savings designed to assist individuals to continue to pay for their health care after retirement (Health Care Financing Study Group, 2004: 4).

THE FISCAL CRISIS

Fundamentally, the funding crisis in welfare is both structural and ideological. The structural defect in Hong Kong's social security system is the lack of a contributory and effective old age pension system that could bring immediate and adequate social protection to old people in need. Another structural

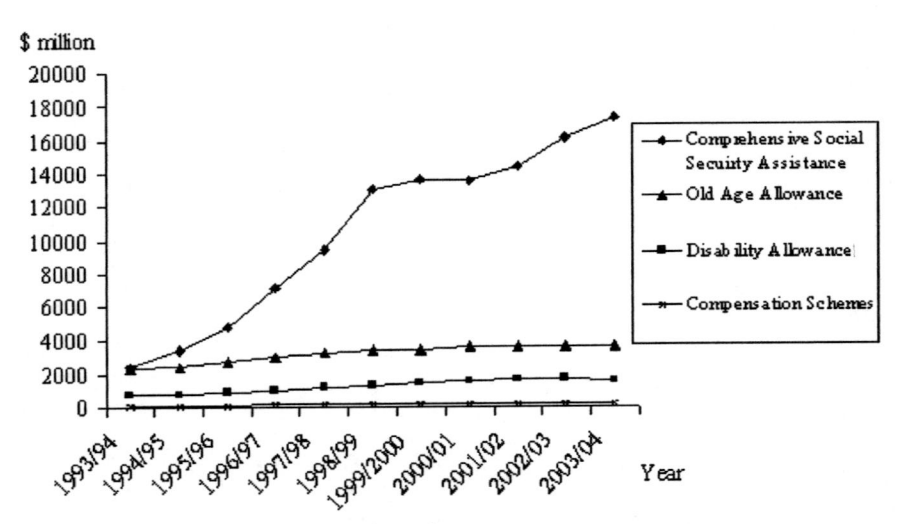

Figure 6.7. Social Security Expenditure in Hong Kong, 1993–2004
Source: Hong Kong Annual Digest of Statistics, 1998–2004

problem is that hitherto the social security system is too rigid and unitary in nature. It relies mainly on a non-contributory social assistance system and its costs entirely borne by the government, including the universal Old Age Allowance (see figure 6.7), resulting in a rapid increase in expenditures for CSSA, as well as total social welfare expenditures (figure 6.8).

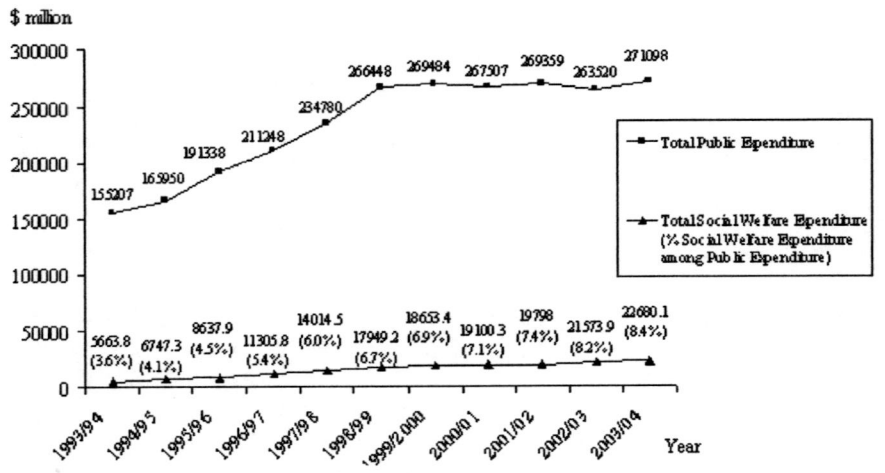

Figure 6.8. Social Welfare Expenditures in Hong Kong, 1993–2004
Source: Hong Kong Annual Digest of Statistics, 1998–2004

The Mandatory Provident Fund introduced in 2000 is not able to bring immediate payments to older workers who do not have a contribution record. Moreover, the amount of contribution, being set at 5 percent of monthly wage contribution from both employees and employers, is in fact quite insufficient as an effective retirement protection for low-pay workers (Ngan and Cheung, 2000). In Hong Kong, social assistance and retirement pension funds work separately from each other. The fact that there is no insurance protection for the unemployed is invariably contributing to widening structural unemployment (Tang, 1997: 72). When more people become unemployed at times of economic adversity, increases in CSSA will become inevitable. Relying solely on taxation and government revenue to finance such payments, policy makers had no alternatives but to introduce cuts and "welfare-to-work" programs. However, the success of such "workfare" schemes for CSSA unemployed persons are negligible due to a fundamental lack of employment opportunities for workers whose skills are made obsolete due to changing market demand for labor (Hong Kong Council of Social Service, 2001). A study by the Hong Kong Oxfam and the Hong Kong Council of Social Service in 2005 found that structural changes in the economy are forcing many women to take up low-paid jobs, especially those who are single parents and whose husbands are unemployed. Besides, the problem of women living in poverty would be exacerbated by the low birthrate and the aging population (Leung, 1999). These women cannot depend on their children when they are old and at the same time they are incapable of saving for their future (*South China Morning Post*, April 7, 2005). There is a pragmatic concern for the government to formulate viable options to revamp Hong Kong's old age financial protection schemes, long-term care financing, and introduce Health Protection Accounts for individual citizens in Hong Kong.

REVAMPING SOCIAL SECURITY SYSTEM AND LONG-TERM CARE FINANCING IN HONG KONG

Before considering suitable proposals for Hong Kong, it is necessary to see how similar Asian countries cope with their rising toll in long-term care expenses and the relationship of pension to long-term care financing. The first country is Japan which set up the Long-Term Care Insurance since April, 2000 (Lai, 2001). It adopts a cost-sharing scheme funded jointly by the people (in the form of premium payments) and the government. Of the 50 percent premium income from the insured population, 17 percent comes from those aged sixty-five and above and 33 percent from those aged forty to sixty-four. The remaining 50 percent is contributed by the central government (25 percent), with prefectural governments and local municipalities each contributing 12.5 percent. The total number of nursing care providers increased by 55 percent when the new Long-Term Care Insurance (LTC) scheme was implemented in April 2000, with most of the increase from private providers (Lai, in press). Yet the new scheme was not without problems: there was an increasing demand for institutional care, while community care was not substantially demanded as expected.

The Republic of Singapore has adopted a lifetime Central Provident Fund (CPF) that allows the transfer of MPF funds to finance long-term care and old age support schemes (Hong, 2001). It uses a "3Ms" approach to finance the health care expenses of senior citizens — 1) Medisave is a compulsory medical savings scheme to pay for hospitalization and outpatient expenses; 2) MediShied is a catastrophic illness insurance scheme, with premiums payable from Medisave and 3) Medifund helps needy Singaporean patients through a medical endowment fund (Ministry of Community Development, 1999). This proves to be a steady and reliable source of funding to finance long-term care. However, the contribution rates for the CPF fluctuates tremendously according to the economy and could be as high as 36 percent of workers' monthly wages, with employees contributing 20 percent and employers 16 percent (Lui, 2001). Such a high contribution rate is unimaginable in Hong Kong as there is a deeply entrenched low tax culture. It is understood that South Korea and Taiwan are in different stages of considering suitable long-term care financing schemes for legislation to be introduced in 2006 (Cheng, 2005). It seems that within the East Asian welfare context it is not conducive to a serious consideration of long term care financing for an aging population. In Hong Kong, there were two contrasting proposals on long-term care financing and reforms in the Old Age Allowance. First is the proposal on Old Age Pension Fund put forth by the Joint Alliance on Universal Protection (2004). It proposes to offer a monthly old age pension of HK$2,300 for senior citizens aged sixty-five and above. The source of financing comes from: 1) government pooling its total expenses on CSSA for old age recipients (those above sixty) and the OAA (aged sixty-five and above); 2) employers surrendering 50 percent of their monthly contribution to workers' MPF accounts and 3) employees saving up to 50 percent of their existing MPF monthly contribution for the future Old Age Pension Fund (Joint Allowance, 2004). While this proposal has the merit of not requiring additional contributions, it might upset the stability of the MPF system.

The second proposal was proposed by a group of academics (Chou, Chow, and Chi, 2004). They recommend that the government issues vouchers to older frail adults for the purchase of long-term care medical services by nongovernmental organizations, or health services provided by the Hospital Authority, with the introduction of services on a self-financing basis, with the government assisting only with capital expenses and part of the initial operating costs. Chou, Chow, and Chi (2004) also suggest combining the CSSA and OAA schemes into one means-tested scheme to provide assistance only to the needy. This selective proposal is substantially different from the one by the Joint Alliance that proposes championed universal provision of long-term elderly care.

There are also other proposals commissioned by the government on medical and long-term care. A major one is the Harvard Report (1999) that proposes a Health Security Plan and Savings Accounts for Long-Term Care, called Medisage. According to the proposal, Hong Kong residents are required to contribute 1 percent of their wages to an individual savings account, which will then be invested and used to purchase individual long-term care insurance policies upon retirement or disability. Similarly, the Health Security Plan is conceived to be a social insurance scheme that requires joint employer/employee contribution of 1.5 to 2 percent of wages. It was intended to cover medical expenses in the event of catastrophic health incidents (Harvard Report, 1999). Yet the proposals met with strong opposition from stakeholders in private medical insurance and were shelved in conjunction with the following comments from the Health Care Financing Study Group in the government: "The radical proposal was not well received by the general public because the scheme involved inter-generation subsidization, and given the ageing population and the declining percentage of young people in Hong Kong, it would put undue funding pressure on future generations" (Health Care Financing Study Group, 2004: 2).

In July 2004, the Health and Welfare Bureau published a report on Health Care Financing for public consultation. It recommends that every working individual from the age of forty to sixty, with a monthly income exceeding $5,000 a month, contributes 2 percent of his salary to a Health Protection Account (HPA) to be drawn upon at the age of sixty-five. The Health Protection Account is to pay for the cost of medical and dental expenses, or alternatively, the savings can be used to purchase medical and dental insurance plans from private insurers (Health and Welfare Bureau, 2004). However, there was concern on the adequacy of the accumulated funds to cover rising costs of long-term care. Besides, in 2004, Hong Kong was still beset with unemployment and a recovering economy in the midst of the fact that workers are already making a 5 percent monthly contribution to the MPF. Thus far there is yet no finalized policy to finance rising demand of long-term care in Hong Kong as the Government still believes that "a medical savings scheme should not be introduced in times when Hong Kong is facing economic difficulties" (Health Care Financing Study Group, 2004: 53).

Plagued by a low-taxation rate and a narrow fiscal base to support a huge rise in social security payments, not only is Hong Kong facing an imminent crisis in social security financing but the financial sustainability of her health care system is also of increasing concern by policy makers. This concern is raised on the ground that in April 2004, the recurrent public health care expenditure for 2004/05 was estimated to be $30.3 billion, constituting approximately 14 percent of the government's total recurrent spending (LegCo Panel on Health Services, 2004). In considering appropriate feasible schemes to overcome these financing problems, a "multi-pillar" system should be explored seriously, following the recommendation by the World Bank (1993).

A "multi-pillar" social security system (World Bank 1993) includes the following three pillars:

1. a universal pension provided by the government;
2. a mandatory, private funded pension scheme; and
3. voluntary personal savings and insurance.

It needs to be pointed out that the CSSA in Hong Kong is not a universal pension provided by the government. It is a public assistance scheme for the most needy and for those who are least able to help themselves. The first pillar could somehow be achieved by combining the CSSA for the aged (sixty-five or above) and the OAA to become an Old Age Pension (OAP) scheme payable to Hong Kong citizens aged sixty-five or above with HK$2,300 as monthly benefits, with a contribution rate initially set at 2 percent each from employers and employees (Education and Manpower Branch, 1994). The OAP should be a better old age protection scheme for the aged if the monthly benefit level of OAP could be set at $2,300, which is above the subsistence level of CSSA and OAA. The level of saved payments in CSSA for the aged and the OAA could then be deposited into the payment accounts of OAP as reserves (Joint Alliance on Universal Protection, 2004). The low contribution rate is to tune in with Hong Kong's hitherto low tax environment. However, it can be increased slightly at a later stage to guarantee balanced payments. Drover (1995) comments, "even with the worst case scenarios, it is difficult to understand why the low level of benefits proposed would have led to significant increases in contributions. Marginal increases, perhaps but with large increases seemed unlikely unless there was a major population relocation." He is suggesting this in the context of commenting on the pension system in Canada where the Old Age Security Pension (OAS) is payable to elders aged sixty-five and above to people who have ten years of residence in Canada, subjected to a surcharge since 1989 so that elders with very high incomes receive only partial payment or no payment (Drover 1995). It seems that Hong Kong's non-means tested OAA (payable to aged seventy and above) should also be combined with the means-tested OAA (payable to aged sixty-five–sixty-nine) to form an *Old Age Pension* (OAP) so that it would become the first pillar of universal public pension system for Hong Kong citizens aged sixty-five or above.

The second pillar would be the retirement pension provided by the Mandatory Provident Fund scheme (MPF). Since its inception in Hong Kong in December 2000, it has already established the rudiment of a mandatory, private funded pension scheme with 5 percent monthly contribution respectively from employees and employers. This will augment the 2 percent basic pension level provided by the OAP in the first pillar.

The third pillar, however, is not about voluntary personal savings and insurance in the general sense. It is proposed that this pillar should contain two schemes: a 2 percent monthly contribution funded scheme for mandatory health insurance and another 1.5 percent for the long-term care insurance. In fact, the mandatory health insurance scheme resembles the 2 percent contribution to a Health Protection Account (HPA) proposed by the government's Health Care Financing Study Group (2004) as described in earlier paragraphs and it differs from the Health Security Plan and Medisage proposal put forth by the Harvard Report (1999) in that it is not a social insurance scheme that requires joint employer/employee contribution. The proposed monthly contribution in this third pillar will be a funded scheme in the individual's own Health Protection Account for his purchase of the needed health care services, either in public or private hospitals but refunded at public sector rates. Such a scheme could be implemented when Hong Kong's economy improves. "Rome was not built in a day." To make the third pillar a feasible and acceptable scheme, it is suggested that the two systems, namely, the mandatory contribution to HPA and the long-term care (LTC) insurance system could be implemented in phases so that workers would not be overloaded with mandatory contributions all at one time. Tax exemption policy should be considered to give people the incentive to make early contributions to prepare for "rainy days."

Summing up, the proposed "multi-pillar" scheme is a "Three-pillar Health Care and Old Age Pension Insurance System" with the following three prominent tiers:

1. a new public universal pension system with the introduction of the Old Age Pension (OAP) payable to Hong Kong citizens aged sixty-five or above;
2. a mandatory, private funded pension scheme formed by the Mandatory Provident Fund (MPF) system and
3. a mandatory health care and long term care insurance system with tax exemption incentives for relevant contributions.

It is also recommended that appropriate actuarial calculations of the long-run financial viability of the proposed "Three-pillar Health Care and Old Age Pension Insurance systems" should be carefully studied by the government.

THE DEMISE OF THE EAST ASIAN WELFARE MODEL

The notion of an East Asian welfare model originated in 1993 with the publication of a World Bank study titled *The East Asian Miracle: Economic Growth and Public Policy*. The ideal model was supposed to achieve a high level of welfare and reduce poverty without involving too much government expenditure. It lauds the spirit of individual and family responsibility as well as the role of the family in providing social insurance and services (World Bank, 1993). However, nowhere is the threat to the East Asian welfare model more evident than the adverse economic performance of the region's economy since the Asian Financial Crisis caused poverty, increasing inequalities and social conflicts emanated by rising unemployment (Ngan, 2002). It seems that the financial crisis has crystallized the difficulties that many families now face in providing long-term care to their frail elderly parents, and income support to their able-body members suffering from prolonged unemployment as a result of the downturn of the economy. To continue ascribing to the universal applicability of the East Asian welfare model would now appear precarious for welfare development in this region. Goodman, White and Kwon (1998) warn that even though East Asian countries and their welfare systems share common features, they are essentially not homogeneous polities, and that it is wrong to oversimplify welfare and social structure here. They point out that East Asian welfare systems have been viable because they have developed within themselves a state-directed growth economy characterized by full employment. They are now under threat because of the onset of rapid societal aging, and are also undermined by recent changes in family structure and economic downturn. If there is an East Asian welfare model, it is largely a model of family care of older people and female caregivers undertaking the bulk of welfare work (Ngan, 2003; Phillips, 1999).

Nowhere is the crisis of welfare and social security spending an urgent concern for policy makers in Hong Kong. The huge budget deficit unfortunately led to welfare cuts which steered welfare development in a highly contentious direction. Structurally, the non-contributory CSSA and OAA programs are aggravating this funding crisis as they rely heavily on government revenues. The welfare crisis will surface in the year 2035 when one in four people in Hong Kong will be aged sixty-five or above. No one can fathom why there has been little development in the Tung Chee-Hwa administrative era on Hong Kong's social security, health care, and long-term care financing, despite the publication of several useful consultancy reports. Perhaps the remarks by the former premier Zhu Rongji are most pertinent: "No decision after consultation and discussion; no action after the decision was made!" (*Apple Daily*, 1999). Plagued by too much worries and concern over a declining economy, the outbreak of SARS epidemic in early 2003, as well as the political controversies over the Public Order Ordinance Amendment Bills, the Tung Chee-Hwa administration has been completely incapacitated to handle such a crisis. How much good faith such a high-powered administrator has on social welfare spending and on integrating economic and social development remains largely unknown (Tang and Midgley, 2002). However, with a neoliberal trend in reign by the government and the capitalists, it is understandable that welfare cuts will continue and workfare is the ultimate goal. In 1996, on forecasting the prospect of a new era of welfare development in Hong Kong, my relevant remarks were: "as long as welfare development still wears the past emperor's clothes and remains remedial, residual, and incremental in outlook and touches little on the structural causes of Hong Kong's ills, it will probably remain an old-fashioned conservative overcoat: welfare development must build on economic growth and neglect the prospect of welfare in stabilizing and promoting the economy" (Ngan, 1997: 429). With the short-term appointment of Donald Tsang as the new chief executive for the HKSAR in July 2005, the prospect of a major change in a remedial welfare policy in the near future is glimpsed.

REFERENCES

Apple Daily, Local News. (1999). "Premier Zhu Talks on Hong Kong's Administrative Indecision." April 13.

Census and Statistics Department. (2001). *Annual Digest of Statistics*. Hong Kong: Government Printer.

——. (2005). *Annual Digest of Statistics*. Hong Kong: Government Printer.

Cheng, M. F. (2005). "The Proposed Direction of Long-Term Care Financing in Taiwan." Paper presented at the Symposium on Long-Term Care Financing, Hong Kong Council of Social Service, June 10, 2005.

Chou, K. L., Chow, N., and Chi, I. (2004). "Preventing Economic Hardship Among Chinese Elderly in Hong Kong." *Journal of Aging and Social Policy*, 16(4): pp. 79–97.

Chow, Y. (2005). Annual Consultation Session with Welfare Sector for Priorities in 2006–2007: Press Release. June 20, 2005. Available at www.hwfb.gov.hk/en/press.

Education and Manpower Branch. (1994). "An Old Age Pension Scheme for Hong Kong: Consultative Paper." Hong Kong: Government Printer.

Elderly Commission. (2003). "Report on Healthy Ageing." Hong Kong: Government Printer.

Financial Secretary. (2003). "The 2003–2004 Budget: Speech by the Financial Secretary." March 2003. Hong Kong: Government Printer.

——. (2004). "The 2004–2005 Budget: Speech by the Financial Secretary." March, 2004. Hong Kong: Government Printer.

Goodman, R., White, G., and Kwon, H. J. (1998). *The East Asian Welfare Model: Welfare Orientalism and the State*. New York: Routledge.

Harvard Report. (1999). "Improving Hong Kong's Health Care System: Why and For Whom?" Consultancy Report by the Harvard University Team. Hong Kong: Hong Kong Special Administrative Region Government.

Health Care Financing Study Group. (2004). "A Study on Health Care Financing and Feasibility of a Medical Savings Scheme in Hong Kong." Health, Welfare and Food Bureau: July 2004.

Ho, W. H. Lawrence. (2004). "Who Pays for Long Term Care in Hong Kong?" Proceedings of the Second World Congress on Long Term Care in Chinese Communities, Taipei, Taiwan, October 28–30, 2004: pp. 29–43.

Holiday, I. (2000). "Productivist Welfare Capitalism: Social Policy in East Asia." *Political Studies*, 38 (4): pp. 706–23.

Hong, P. K. (2001). "The Savings Approach to Financing Long Term Care in Singapore." In Chi, I., Mehta, K. K., and Howe, A. (eds.) *Long Term Care in the Twenty-first Century: Perspectives from Around the Asia-Pacific Rim*. N.Y.: The Haworth Press.

Hong Kong Council of Social Service. (2000). *Results of the Social Development Index 2000*. Hong Kong: Hong Kong Council of Social Service.

———. (2001). "A Research Report on the Implementation of the Support for Self-Reliance Scheme." Hong Kong: Hong Kong Council of Social Service: Research Department (in Chinese).

———. (2003). "Rethinking Income Protection for Elderly People." Paper presented at a Symposium on Retirement Pension in Hong Kong, November 2003.

Hong Kong Government. (2002). "Taskforce Report on Budgetary Problems." Hong Kong: Government Printer.

Hong Kong Government Information Services. (2003). "Press Release: Economic Situation in 2003." Hong Kong Government. Available at www.info.gov.hk.

Joint Alliance on Universal Protection. (2004). "Proposal on Old Age Pension Fund." Hong Kong Council of Social Service.

Lai, O. K. (2001). "Long Term Care Policy Reform in Japan." In Iris Chi, K. K.Mehta, and Anna Howe (eds.) *Long-Term Care in the Twenty-first Century: Perspectives from Around the Asia-Pacific Rim*. N.Y.: The Haworth Press Inc., pp. 5–20.

———. (in press). "Socio-Demographic Changes and Ageing Policy Reform in Japan: Reinventing Long Term Care System in Quasi-Market Domain." In Raymond Ngan and S.Vasoo (eds.) *Social Care Challenges For the Aged in Asia*. Singapore: Marshall Cavendish Academic.

Lam, C. (2001). Director of Social Welfare's Speech at the Tenth Anniversary of the Bachelor of Social Work Program. City University of Hong Kong, June 2, 2001.

Leung, L. C. (1999). *Lone Mothers, Social Security, and the Family in Hong Kong*. UK: Ashgate.

Li, J. (2003). "Housing." In Ian Holiday and Paul Wilding (eds.) *Welfare Capitalism in East Asia: Social Policy in the Tiger Economies*. UK: Hampshire: Palgrave Macmillan, pp. 99–126.

Lui, F. T. (2001). *Retirement Protection: A Plan for Hong Kong.* Hong Kong: City University of Hong Kong Press.

Ministry of Community Development. (1999). "Report of the Inter-Ministerial Committee on Health Care for the Elderly." Ministry of Health: Singapore.

Ngan, R. (1997). "Social Welfare." In Joseph Cheng (ed.) *The Other Hong Kong Report 1997.* Hong Kong: The Chinese University Press, pp. 411–30.

———. (2002). "Economic Crisis and Social Development in Hong Kong Since 1997." *Journal of Comparative Asian Development*, 1 (2): pp. 263–84.

———. (2003). "Long Term Care for Older People and the Social Welfare System in East Asia: Is the East Asian Welfare Model a Myth?" *Social Development Issues*, 25(3): pp. 74–85.

Ngan, R. and Cheung, F. (2000). "The Mandatory Provident Fund Scheme in Hong Kong." Proceedings of the Second Asia Regional Conference on Social Security. January 24–26, 2000. Hong Kong: Hong Kong Council of Social Service, pp. 244–260.

Ngan, R. and Li, B. W. (2000). "Reform in China's Old Age Insurance System: A Lesson to Hong Kong." Proceedings of the Second Asia Regional Conference on Social Security. January 24–26, 2000. Hong Kong: Hong Kong Council of Social Service, pp. 317–26.

Oriental Daily. (2003). Unemployment CSSA Cases on the Rise. February 26.

Phillips, D. R. (1999). "Aging in the Asia-Pacific Region: the Impact of the Ageing and Development Report." *Hong Kong Journal of Gerontology*, 11(2): pp. 22–7.

Social Welfare Department. (2001) (2004) (2005). "Press Release: New Applications in CSSA." Available at www.info.gov./swd.

South China Morning Post. (1995). Local News, December 14.

———. (2002). Pressure Mounts for New Taxes, Feb.22.

———. (2002). Jobless Rate at New High Rate of 7.7 Percent, August 20.

———. (2003). Social Workers Warn of Funding Crisis, December 15.

———. (2004). Shades of 1997 in Optimism about a New Leader, March 12.

———. (2005). Social Welfare Spending: Every Cent Counts. Letters to the Editor by Dr. York Chow, Secretary for Health, Welfare and Food, March 24.

———. (2005). Women Workers Denied in Old Age, April 7.

———. (2005). Local News, June 14.

Tang, K. L. (1997). "Non-contributory Pensions in Hong Kong: An Alternative to Social Security?" In James Midgley and Michael Sheridan (eds.) *Alternatives to Social Security: An International Inquiry.* Westport, CT: Aubum House, pp. 61–74.

Tang, K. L. and Midgley, J. (2002). "Social Policy after the East Asian Financial Crisis: Forging a Normative Basis for Welfare." *Journal of Comparative Asian Development*, 1 (2): pp. 301–18.

Tsang, D. (1999). Speech by the Financial Secretary: Budget 1999–2000. March 1999. Hong Kong: Government Printer.

Tung, C. W. (1997). (2005). The Policy Address by the Chief Executive at the Legislative Council meeting in January 1997 and 2005. Hong Kong: Government Printer.

Walker, A. and Wong, C. K. (2005). *East Asian Welfare Regimes in Transition: From Confucianism to Globalization*. UK: Bristol: The Policy Press.

Wong, H. and Lee, K. M. (2002). A Study of Hong Kong Poverty Line, 1999–2001. Research Report. City University of Hong Kong: Division of Social Studies.

World Bank. (1993). *Averting the Old Age Crisis: Policies to Protect the Old and Promote Growth*. Oxford: Oxford University Press.

Yau, C. (2005). "Is our Social Welfare System Sustainable?" Speech by the Permanent Secretary for Health, Welfare and Food at the Business and Professionals Federation of Hong Kong. March 17, 2005.

7

Age Discrimination in the Labor Market

Barriers to Active Aging in Hong Kong

Raymond Man Hung Ngan, Ping Kong Kam, and Jacky Chau Kiu Cheung

With improvement in medical sciences and the emphasis by policy makers on "Healthy Aging" (Elderly Commission, 2001), it has been found that older people are not just living longer, they are also living healthier and therefore can remain active for many more years in society. As such, there has been a call for the development of a Positive Aging Strategy to improve opportunities for older people to take an active part in the community in the ways they choose (Dalziel, 2001). Hon. Lianne Dalziel, minister for senior citizens, New Zealand, comments that "New Zealanders who are now sixty-five plus are more highly educated and healthier than their predecessors. Their capacity for productive work of all kinds, not necessarily for pay, is a national treasure. Their contribution to New Zealand society is and will continue to be immense. If they are ignored, undervalued, or otherwise excluded from society, New Zealand can hardly be competitive against other countries that have found a way of harnessing this immense resource." (Dalziel, 2001) Similarly, there has been a call for "Productive Aging" in the 1980s in the United States as well as the "Active Aging" movement in Europe in the 1990s (Bass, Caro, and Chen, 1993; Walker, 2005). Apart from the discussions on the increase in elderly productivity, paid or unpaid, there has also been increasing concern among policy makers in finding ways of removing disincentives to labor participation and the lowering of barriers to part-time employment among older workers (European Commission, 1999; Walker, 2000; WHO, 2001). The notion of "Active Aging" goes beyond the conventional emphasis on employment and productivity to include strong emphasis on inclusion and independence, quality of life, and mental and physical well-being amongst older people (Walker, 2005). However, it has been found that age discrimination is still very much a major barrier to active aging (Walker, 2000). In most countries, large numbers of older workers are excluded from the labor market. Older workers tend to occupy low-paid jobs, experience discrimination in regard to job recruitment and training, and are disproportionately represented among the long-term unemployed (Walker, 1997). Research in Europe has shown incidences of discrimination against older workers (Walker, 2001; Walker and Maltby, 1997). There are also cases of such discrimination reported in Hong Kong (Society for Community Organization, 1998). Furthermore, the discrimination may manifest itself in various ways, including early retirement (Ngan, Chiu, and Wong, 1999), which is a form of indirect discrimination and early exit from the labor market (Walker, 2000).

In recent years, the Hong Kong Special Administrative Region (HKSAR) Government has sought to eliminate discrimination in a wide range of social services. However, the Working Group on Age Discrimination in Employment contend that there is little evidence of pure age discrimination by employers due to personal prejudice (Education and Manpower Branch, 1996:4). The Working Group therefore recommends against the introduction of age discrimination in employment legislation on the grounds that it could introduce artificial impediments that would hinder the free play of market forces, imposing rigidities on employers' operations (Education and Manpower Branch, 1996:5). Nonetheless, local studies found that discrimination and stereotyping against older people are still quite common (Chiu and Ngan, 1999; Hong Kong Council of Social Service, 2000; Kam, 2003). Older workers are remarkably less likely to be able to re-enter the labor market (Society for Community Organization, 1998).

Age discrimination in the labor market is often hidden due to employers' screening measures (Walker, 2000), notably the use of job advertisements that implicitly specify an age limit (Walker, 1997). Research has also found the abandonment of full employment policy is likewise accounted for a partial cause of discrimination against older workers (Phillipson, 1998). Another source of discrimination may also be the emphasis on youthfulness as in the energetic competition of Olympic Games by employers (Frerichs and Naegele, 1997). Thus far, there has not been a rigorous updated territory-wide investigation of age discrimination in Hong Kong. Moreover, there is a large research gap concerning the causes and consequences of discrimination against older workers. On the one hand, while social constructionist theory explains age discrimination by way of social construction (Phillipson 1998), few studies present data on the influence of social construction on such discrimination in Hong Kong. On the other hand, while there are data about the harm done by such discrimination on the victim's self-esteem, relationship with friends, and financial conditions (Phillipson, 1998), there is no data concerning impacts of such discrimination on other workers, the organization, society, and legislations. It is within this context this study hopes to contribute. This chapter presents the results of a study conducted in 2002 on the causes and consequences of age discrimination in the labor market at individual, organizational, and societal levels in Hong Kong (Ngan, Kam, and Cheung, 2004). The first part of the chapter briefly introduces the study while the second part presents our major findings.

THE STUDY

Theoretical Significance

As mentioned above, *social constructionist theory* or *political economy theory* regards social construction as a cause of discrimination against older workers (Phillipson, 1998). The theory generally maintains that political and economic institutions create and promulgate ideas to shape common people's beliefs. These ideas and beliefs may not be long-standing or normatively rooted in the culture. They rather serve the interest of the prevailing political and economic institutions. Most people are willing to accept the socially constructed meaning as a way to make sense of reality. The theory rests on the premises that (1) individuals rely on concepts (known as *typification*) to guide their action; (2) these concepts become prevalent in society as a result of *externalization* of these concepts by people, particularly professionals and the government; (3) they are available to individuals through a process of *internalization*; and thus (4) concepts constructed in society can ultimately influence people (Berger and Luckmann, 1966).

In the social construction of old age, the theory suggests that emphasis on modernization, exchange, life course development, privatization, individual responsibility, biomedicalization and the disengagement of older people in society precipitate such discrimination (Walker, 1993, 1996; Phillipson, 1998). These notions either regard older people as incapable and in need of help or emphasize the fact that old people should retire and exit from the labor market. Added to this notion is the Confucius notion of filial piety that emphasizes that aged parents should stop working and be cared for by their children (Ngan, Chiu, and Wong, 1999). The extent to which these concepts consitute age discrimination is a focal concern for the present chapter (Phillipson, 1998).

Practical Significance

Eliminating age discrimination is an important issue for policy making worldwide (Society for Community Organization, 1998; Walker, 2000), because such discrimination is cotradictory to social justice (Frerichs and Naegele, 1997). The issue becomes increasingly relevant because of the increasing capability of working people to extend their work life (Krain, 1996). Lengthening of work life may benefit the organization and society (Koeber and Wright, 2001).

THE RESEARCH

The study is to fill the empirical gap regarding the prevalence of age discrimination in Hong Kong. The specific objectives are to reveal discrimination and stereotyping against workers aged forty-five or above, their causes, impact to workers, organizations and the society, and also impact on related legislations. Apart from unveiling the extent of the problems, our study intends to identify the extent to which social construction is responsible for age discrimination.

METHODOLOGY

This study primarily uses a telephone survey to obtain data from workers. Nine hundred and sixteen working people were interviewed through computer-assisted telephone interviewing (see table 7.1). The sample consisted of 480 persons aged between eighteen and forty-four, 275 between forty-five and fifty-four, and 161 aged fifty-five or above. Workers in the older age group (55 and above) were more likely to be male, born in Hong Kong (34.2%), and married. Older workers take on more temporary jobs (14.8%) and worked in domestic or commercial security services, with part of them in estate housing management (12.4%). They were on average unemployed for a longer time (mean = 2.1 months). The period of data collection was from September to November 2002.

Research Framework

Before the random sampling telephone survey, six focus groups were formed to formulate ideas for the construction of a research framework and also breakdown items for measuring discrimination, stereotyping, and other perceptions. Of the six focus groups, one consisted of seven employers, one composed of eight retrainees who got re-employed after a period of retraining, one of nine retrainees who were taking parts in various job-retraining programs, one composed of twelve elderly job seekers, one composed of thirteen young workers, and the final one consisted of ten union members. Based on the views of the focus groups, the following framework was constructed (see figure 7.1).

Table 7.1. Background Characteristics by Age Range

Category	18–44 (n = 480)	45–54 (n = 275)	55+ (n = 161)	All (N = 916)
Sex				
Male	47.0	46.9	69.6	56.2
Female	43.0	53.1*	30.4	43.8
Age				
18–39	100.0	—	—	52.4
44–54	—	100.0	—	30.0
55+	—	—	100.0	17.6
Birthplace				
Born in Hong Kong	82.9*	55.9	34.2	66.3
Born in Mainland China	15.6	41.9	58.4*	31.0
Marital status				
Married	61.8	92.7*	92.5	76.5
Unmarried	37.2*	5.1	1.3	21.2
Divorced or separated	1.0	1.1	1.9	1.2
Widowed	0.0	0.7	3.1*	0.8
Employment nature				
Permanent job	81.9*	76.7	75.0	79.4
Temporary job	6.4	9.3	14.8*	8.5
Long-term casual job	5.5	8.4	7.8	6.7
Contracted job	6.2	5.3	1.6	5.2
Service work				
Security/housing/facility management	0.2	2.5	12.4*	3.1
Delivery	0.2	0.7	0.0	0.3
Cleaning	1.0	5.5	5.6*	3.2
Domestic helper	0.6	1.1	1.9	1.0
Waiter	1.3	1.5	0.0	1.1
Cashier	0.4	1.1	1.2	0.8

*Significant ($p < .05$) across age groups and highest

In this framework, four factors are presumed likely leading to age discrimination in the labor market. The first factor is the societal factor that addresses the existence of negative stereotypes about older workers. The second and third factors refer to the organizational factor that concerns the goals of the organization: whether the organization is putting emphasis of its goal on profit making rather than social responsibility. The apparent assumption is that organizations normally find aging workers less productive than younger ones. The fourth factor addresses the personal level, which refers to the worker's personal health status. This framework suggests that the consequences of age discrimination are relevant to the individual, organizational, and societal levels. The individual level refers to the harm to older workers

Causal Factors   **Consequences**

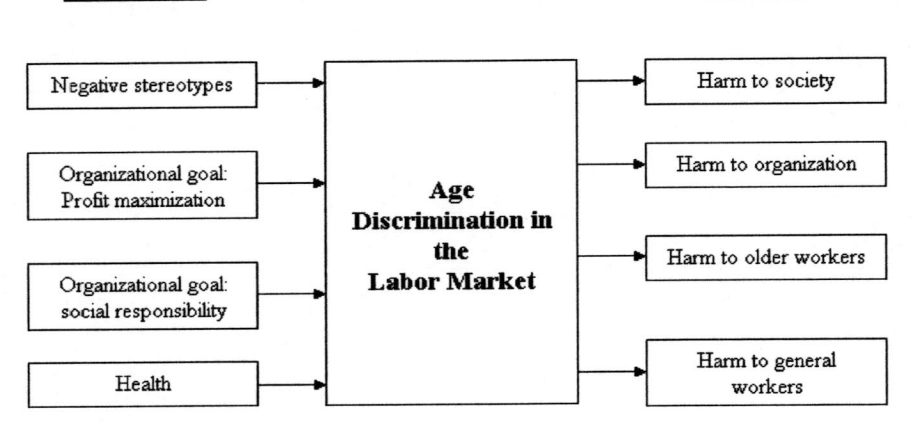

Figure 7.1. Age Discrimination in the Labor Market

and workers in general. The organizational level concerns the harm to the productivity, performance, and image of the organization. The societal level refers to impacts on society as a whole.

Measurement

A structured questionnaire was used in the telephone interview and questions were of a closed-ended nature with predetermined response categories. The questions commonly used five-point scale score measurement. Nine composite scales measured the respondents' perception of age discrimination, the four causal factors, and the four areas of consequences (see table 7.2). Basing

Table 7.2 Internal Consistency (Reliability Alpha)

Composite scale	Number of Items	Alpha
Age discrimination	8	.623
Causal factors		
Negative stereotypes about older workers	11	.722
Organizational goal: profit maximization	2	.803
Organizational goal: social responsibility	5	.630
Health	2	.713
Consequences		
Harm to society by age discrimination	4	.725
Harm to the organization by age discrimination	3	.474
Harm to older workers by age discrimination	4	.741
Harm to general workers by age discrimination	2	.476

on data from the 916 respondents, reliability tests showed that except the Harm to Organization Scale, Harm to Older Workers Scale, and Harm to General Workers Scale, the other six scales attained satisfactory reliability (see table 7.2). The items demonstrated considerable internal consistency in forming composite scores. We will examine each item accordingly.

FINDINGS

Discrimination Against Older Workers in the Labor Market

Table 7.3 shows that from the perception of workers of any age, discrimination against older workers aged forty-five and above was quite prevalent in Hong Kong. With 100 score as the full mark, the four highest discrimination areas included: "older workers are less likely to be hired for a long time;" "older workers are less likely to be rewarded with higher salary;" "older workers have lower chances of promotion;" and "older workers are more likely the first to be laid off."

Table 7.3. Means of Perceived Discrimination Against Older Workers by Age Range

Item	18–44 (n = 480)	45–54 (n = 275)	55+ (n = 161)	All (N = 916)
Older workers are less likely than younger workers to be hired for a longer time	62.4*	57.2	48.9	58.5
Older workers are less likely than younger workers to be rewarded with higher salary	51.3	52.1	57.5	52.6
Lower chances of promotion for older workers	47.0	52.7	63.4	51.6
Older workers are more likely to be laid off first	48.9	48.2	55.7	49.9
Employers refuse to hire older applicants but accept younger applicants	46.2	47.1	55.0	48.0
Employers refuse to hire older job applicants if the age is revealed	44.1	47.1	52.1	46.4
Putting heavier workload on older workers	39.6	46.4	46.0	42.8
Older workers need to take on lower level work but younger workers do not	32.8	35.7	36.9	34.4

*Significant ($p < .05$) across age groups and highest

In addition, the idea that older workers need to adjust to lower level work was subjected to lesser discrimination (mean = 34.4). Except for the questionnaire item on "length of employment" older workers, on average, perceived a higher level of discrimination than younger workers in all other areas. "Lower chances of promotion" was the item showing the highest discrimination against older workers among the eight questionnaire items listed in table 7.3 (mean = 63.4).

Causes of Age Discrimination

Causal Factor I: Negative Stereotyping

Table 7.4 shows that young workers generally exhibited a significantly higher level of negative stereotyping about older workers. That is to say they generally thought that many older workers had negative characteristics in work. Among them, the perception that older workers are "being slow in learning" and "having difficulties taking up new jobs" appeared to be most salient. In contrast, younger workers consider few older workers to be lazy at work. They tend to think that older workers are more reliable and dependable. All the stereotype beliefs of young workers were stronger than older workers' perception. This difference to some extent indicates that the younger workers' attitude toward older workers is negative and stereotypical.

Table 7.4. Means of Negative Stereotypes About Older Workers by Age Range

Item	18–44 (n = 480)	45–54 (n = 275)	55+ (n = 161)	All (N = 916)
Being slow in learning	44.9*	36.1	35.3	40.5
Not enjoying teaching younger workers	40.6*	36.7	34.6	38.3
Having difficulty taking up new jobs	44.5*	33.0	28.6	38.1
Not having good interaction with younger colleagues	40.8	34.1	34.0	37.5
Not cooperating well with younger colleagues	39.5*	28.1	29.3	34.2
Always grumbles about work	40.1*	20.3	20.3	30.5
Being disliked by customers	33.3*	25.8	22.0	29.0
Not feeling responsible for work	32.6*	14.7	10.6	23.1
Not having much work experience	24.2*	18.8	20.2	21.8
Refusing to work overtime	26.9*	14.2	12.9	20.6
Being lazy during work	27.6*	10.4	9.8	19.2

*Significant ($p < .05$) across age groups and highest

Table 7.5. Perceived Organizational Goals by Age Range

Item	18–44 (n = 480)	45–54 (n = 275)	55+ (n = 161)	All (N = 916)
Organizational goal: Profit maximization (average of the following two)	68.4	76.4*	75.1	72.0
Profit making being the most important	71.7	78.7*	78.6	75.1
Emphasize current profit	64.9	73.9*	71.6	68.8
Organizational goal: Social responsibility (average of the following)	46.4	46.2	47.6	46.6
Responsibility to society	52.3	51.9	55.3	52.7
Taking care of workers' needs	47.3	48.8	51.4	48.5
Ensuring that older workers are free from discrimination	46.4	45.5	50.6	46.9
Not reducing investment in labor	44.0	43.2	42.8	43.5
Long-term development of staff	42.0	41.6	38.7	41.3

*Significant ($p < .05$) across age groups and highest

Causal Factor II: Organizational Goals

Older workers tend to think that their organizations emphasized profit maximization (table 7.5). Nevertheless, there was no significant difference in the perception of the social responsibility of their organizations between younger and older workers.

Causal Factor III: Health

The self-assessed health condition of both older and young workers was quite good. Older workers' self-assessed health status was even better than that of younger workers. These data seem to suggest that older people were not in poorer health than were younger ones, and therefore they could perform equally well at work. These results again show that younger working peoples' perception of older workers was excessively negative and stereotypic (see table 7.6).

Table 7.6. Health Situation by Age Range

Item	18–44 (n = 480)	45–54 (n = 275)	55+ (n = 161)	All (N = 916)
Few illness episodes in 2001	71.3	78.6	76.0	74.3
Perceived health status in 2001	71.3	74.8	73.0	72.6

Causal Factors in Regression Analysis

Regression analysis indicates that among all age groups, the organizational goal of social responsibility and negative stereotyping had a significant and stronger effect on age discrimination. Our results show that people working in an organization with greater social responsibility had less discrimination against older workers ($\beta = -.227$), and negative stereotyping led to perception of discrimination against older people ($\beta = .120$). The goal of social responsibility had a stronger effect on perceived discrimination against older workers than did negative stereotyping. Among older workers aged fifty-five and above, the organizational goal of social responsibility was a significant factor (see table 7.7). Among younger workers, those working in an organization holding a stronger goal for profit making perceived more discrimination against older workers ($\beta = .142$). All in all, organizational goals are clearly significant factors affecting perception of discrimination against older workers.

Perceived Causes of Age Discrimination

In the telephone survey, respondents were asked to attribute causes of age discrimination (see table 7.8). Both older and younger workers attributed the major causes of age discrimination to "greater number of job seekers," "increase in the unemployment rate," "poor economic circumstances," and "employers' concern to raise productivity." In contrast, reasons of "older workers' higher salary" and "prevalent reports in society about older people's illness" were placed at a relatively lower level.

Table 7.7. Standardized Effects of Causal Factors on Perceived Discrimination Against Older Workers

Predictor	18–44 (n = 480)	45–54 (n = 275)	55+ (n = 161)	All (N = 916)
Negative stereotyping about older workers	.095*	.193*	.101	.120*
Organizational goal: profit making	.142*	−.044	−.069	.061
Organizational goal: social responsibility	−.268*	−.143*	−.333*	−.227*
Health	−.069*	.010	.064	−.032

Note: The regression analysis also included all significant background characteristics as predictors.
*Significant ($p < .05$) across age groups and highest

Table 7.8. Means of Perceived Causes of Age Discrimination by Age Range

Item	18–44 (n = 480)	45–54 (n = 275)	55+ (n = 161)	All (N = 916)
A great number of job seekers	80.6	79.9	79.5	80.2
Increase in unemployment rate	74.8	77.4	73.2	75.3
Poor economic circumstances	73.5	76.0	75.3	74.6
Employers' concern to raise productivity	66.6	60.6	66.0	64.7
Popular notion emphasizing youthfulness in society	57.8	64.0	67.2*	61.3
Employers' mentality for exploiting workers	60.5	63.2	60.7	61.4
Lack of legislation to protect older worker	55.9	63.3	60.3	58.8
Doubts in older workers' work capability	54.3	55.9	57.2	55.3
Popular notion about the uselessness of older people in society	47.9	52.9	60.5*	51.6
Societal belief about older people's frequent need on medical care	46.7	51.2	60.6*	50.4
Older workers' higher salary	50.8	47.8	53.4	50.4
Prevalent reports in society about older people's illness	42.5	50.8	58.1*	47.7

*Significant ($p < .05$) across age groups and highest

Social Constructionist Attribution of Discrimination Against Older Workers

Among all the perceived causes, four items reflected social constructionist attribution of age discrimination. The four items included: "popular notion emphasizing youthfulness in society," "popular notion about the uselessness of older people in society," "societal belief about older people's frequent need to receive medical care," and "prevalent reports in society about older people's illness" (see table 7.9). Generally, working people's attribution of age discrimination to the emphasis on youth in society (mean = 61.3) was the greatest, and their attribution to reports about older people's illness in society was at the lowest level. Among all these four items, older workers displayed a significantly higher level of social constructionist attribution than younger workers.

Consequences of Age Discrimination

Table 7.10 shows that both younger and older workers perceived a similar and substantial level of harm of age discrimination to society, organizations, older

Table 7.9. Social Constructionist Attribution by Age Range

Item	18–44 (n = 480)	45–54 (n = 275)	55+ (n = 161)	All (N = 916)
Popular notion emphasizing youth in society	57.8	64.0	67.2*	61.3
Popular notion about the uselessness of older people in society	47.9	52.9	60.5*	51.6
Societal belief about older people's need to receive medical care in society	46.7	51.2	60.6*	50.4
Prevalent reports in society about older people's illness	42.5	50.8	58.1*	47.7

*Significant ($p < .05$) across age groups and highest

Table 7.10. Comparison of Perceived Consequences of Age Discrimination by Age Range

Item	18–44 (n = 480)	45–54 (n = 275)	55+ (n = 161)	All (N = 916)
Perceived harm to general workers	69.2	68.4	68.0	68.7
Perceived harm to society	56.2	63.7	62.6	59.5
Perceived harm to older people	58.5	59.6	58.3	58.8
Perceived harm to organizations	55.2	53.4	53.8	54.4

*Significant ($p < .05$) across age groups and highest

workers, and workers in general. In comparison, harm to general workers ranked the first, while harm to society ranked the second, harm to older workers ranked the third, and harm to organizations ranked the fourth.

Reflecting the harm to general workers, the two items of "depriving the sense of belonging in workers" and "reducing stability of staff" showed a rather high level. Their scores were the highest among all other items (see table 7.11).

With regard to the harm done to society, the working people's perceived harm to increasing dissent in society was the greatest (mean = 70.0) among the four aspects of harm to society. On the other hand, their perceived harm

Table 7.11. Perceived Harm of Age Discrimination to General Workers by Age Range

Item	18–44 (n = 480)	45–54 (n = 275)	55+ (n = 161)	All (N = 916)
Depriving the sense of belonging in workers	74.3	74.6	72.1	74.0
Reducing stability of staff	64.1	62.0	63.9	63.4

to causing disturbance in society was the lowest (mean = 42.6), particuarly among the youngest working people (mean = 35.4) (see table 7.12).

Both younger and older workers perceived the harm of age discrimination to older people to be substantial. The harm was particularly greater in terms of impairing older workers' health (mean = 61.0) (see table 7.13).

With regard to the possible harm to organizations, both younger and older workers perceived greater harm in terms of draining away work experience (mean = 61.1) (see table 7.14).

Table 7.12. Perceived Harm of Age Discrimination to Society by Age Range

Item	18–44 (n = 480)	45–54 (n = 275)	55+ (n = 161)	All (N = 916)
Increasing dissent in society	68.8	71.1	71.5*	70.0
Making people lose their confidence in the government	64.3	68.5	65.6	65.8
Disintegrating the society	56.3	64.9*	63.0	60.0
Causing disturbance in society	35.4	50.4	51.2	42.6

*Significant ($p < .05$) across age groups and highest

Table 7.13. Perceived Harm of Age Discrimination to Older People by Age Range

Item	18–44 (n = 480)	45–54 (n = 275)	55+ (n = 161)	All (N = 916)
Impairing older workers' health	60.2	61.6	62.5	61.0
Impairing older workers' job performance	61.3	57.9	57.1	59.6
Engendering the sense of inferiority in older workers	57.4	59.0	57.2	57.8
Worsening the older people's image	55.9	59.7	56.3	57.1

Table 7.14. Means of Perceived Harm of Age Discrimination to the Organization by Age Range

Item	18–44 (n = 480)	45–54 (n = 275)	55+ (n = 161)	All (N = 916)
Draining away work experience	58.5	64.3*	63.5	61.1
Reducing the productivity of the organization	58.5*	51.1	56.0	55.9
Impairing the image of the organization	49.0	44.5	43.0	46.6

*Significant ($p < .05$) across age groups and highest

Table 7.15. Preference for Legislation Against Age Discrimination by Age Range

Item	18–44 (n = 480)	45–54 (n = 275)	55+ (n = 161)	All (N = 916)
Support legislation	71.6	77.1*	75.3	73.9
Legislation being useful	45.3	49.6	51.9*	47.7
Legislation more preferable than education	33.0	39.5*	36.9	35.6
Not difficult to implement the legislation	33.4	39.7*	34.9	35.5
Legislation expected to be implemented within the next two years	30.1	28.8	31.3	29.9

*Significant ($p < .05$) across age groups and highest

Preference for Legislation Against Age Discrimination

All workers expressed strong support for the establishment of legislation to curb discrimination against older workers (mean = 73.9) (see table 7.15). Not surprisingly, older workers were more supportive of legislation than younger ones (mean = 77.1 and 75.3 vs. 71.6). Nevertheless, working people had only a modest belief that the legislation would be useful (mean = 47.7). One can argue that Hong Kong is still in an early stage of social legislation and that the society at large is still ambivalent about its use and effects. Furthermore, they seemed to prefer public education to legislation (mean = 35.6) and predicted great difficulty in successful implementation of the legislation (mean = 64.5). There was also lower expectation that such legislation could be implemented within the next two years (mean = 29.9), confirming a general societal belief that Hong Kong people are highly pragmatic and instrumental in their life outlook.

DISCUSSION

Discrimination against older workers appears to be prevalent in Hong Kong, a common view shared by both younger and older working people. Such discrimination tends to reflect negative stereotyping of older workers, the tendency to weight profit making as the most important aspect of organizational goal, social construction that denigrates older people, and adverse economic conditions. As a result, older workers are likely to become scapegoats in the job seeking process as well as with organizations. In this study, it has been found that age discrimination in the labor market would carry harmful effects onto society, organizations, as well as older and general working people. This is a view shared by younger and older working people at the same time. Although social legislation as a means to curb age discrimination has the support of working people, nonetheless, its effectiveness and ease in implementation is doubted, to the extent that expectation of the effective implementation of the legislation is low. Working people, old and young, generally expressed a preference for education as a more effective means to curb age discrimination.

Statistical analysis of this study indicates that the perception of discrimination against older workers rises with negative stereotyping or negative self-assessment. Hence, working people with negative views of older workers find more discrimination against older workers, which is not surprising. However, this relationship may to some extent reflect the causal effect of negative stereotyping on discrimination when those perceiving more discrimination are also more likely to approve and practice discrimination themselves. Besides, organizations with greater emphasis on profit making rather than social responsibility tend to be more discriminative against older workers than those that treasure social responsibility more. The organizational influences are even greater than that of negative stereotyping since they power to facilitate age discrimination. Henceforth, discrimination could well be seen as an institutional or organizational phenomenon, rooted in collective values or prejudices.

Social constructionist theory provides a possible framework to explain Active Aging and to reduce age discrimination in the workplace. The vision of the Active Aging strategy, as put forth by Alan Walker (1997, 2000, 2005), seeks to encompass the following policy measures: changing the endemic culture of ageism that permeates the labor market; removing age barriers in all walks of life so that people are judged on their competence; developing active age management in employment; aiming at preventing age to become a barrier; keeping older workers in touch with employment; enabling them to maintain their skills so that workability is not reduced; encouraging flexibility in retirement so that the rigid division between employment and retirement disappears; and combating social exclusion especially among older people.

A limitation of the present study is its sole reliance on self-report survey data from working people. Thus, the opinions might be one-sided, lacking corroborating data to support. In the presence of possible bias in personal judgment, self-report data does have its limitation. Apart from the issue of validity, reliability could also be an issue for some measures, particularly those regarding perceived harm to organizations and older and general workers. Besides, the study does not attempt to make a strong claim in terms of generality since the sample is vulnerable to sampling error commonly found in telephone surveys. At best, the sample reflects people accessible by telephone, and at present differences between people accessible and not accessible by telephone remain unknown. It is therefore more appropriate to interpret these findings more to working people accessible by telephone. These findings, nevertheless, are primarily descriptive and they do not involve strong proof of causal relationships concerning age discrimination in the workplace. They at best demonstrate the perceived causes of age discrimination. Empirical analysis of the causes of age discrimination would require testing causal relationships between age discrimination and organizational and managerial characteristics. For instance, it will reveal what type of organization would have greater discrimination against older workers.

CONCLUSION

Compared with other developed countries like the United States, New Zealand, Australia, and Canada, Hong Kong lags behind in the absence of social legislation against age discrimination. The 1996 Education and Manpower Branch Report is quite outdated in concluding that there was no evidence to prove any discrimination in employment against persons of any age group (Education and Manpower Branch, 1996: 2). The present study has found that there is evidence of widespread age discrimination in the labor market as perceived by both older and younger workers (Ngan, Kam, and Cheung, 2004). At the times of economic crises, older workers in Hong Kong are certainly more likely to be unemployed and less likely to be promoted or selected for training than younger workers (Chou and Chow, 2005; Ho et al., 2000). The general view is that these workers are more difficult to train and adapt to a new working environment (Chiu and Ngan, 1999). Hence, these negative stereotypes on the capacities of older people need to be carefully dealt within the boundary of social policy. To eliminate age discrimination, social legislation must be backed up by voluntary initiatives on the employer side; and the identification of best practices in the recruitment, promotion, and training of older workers has to be encouraged (Chou and Chow, 2005; Walker, 1999). All these strategies should be set in the context of promoting "Active Aging" among older workers, changing employers' perceptual bias on older workers' abilities, promoting lifelong education and continuous training by offering incentives to extend working life, and enabling flexible employment and retirement (Walker, 2000, 2005). It is until then could Hong Kong claim to have adopted and developed a Positive Approach to Aging to enhance social welfare.

REFERENCES

Bass, S., Caro, F., and Chen, Y. P. (1993). *Achieving a Productive Aging Society*. Westport, CT: Auburn House.

Berger, P. L. and Luckmann, T. (1966). *The Social Construction of Reality*. London: Penguin.

Chiu, S., and Ngan, R. (1999). "Employment of Chinese Older Workers in Hong Kong: Cultural Myths, Discrimination and Opportunities." *Aging International*, winter, pp. 14–30.

Chou, K. L. and Chow, N. (2005). "To Retire or Not to Retire? Is There an Option for Older Workers in Hong Kong?" *Social Policy and Administration*, 39 (3): pp. 233–46.

Dalziel, L. (2001). *The New Zealand Positive Aging Strategy*. Wellington: Senior Citizens Unit, Ministry of Social Policy.

Education and Manpower Branch, Government Secretariat. (1996). *Equal Opportunities: A Study on Discrimination in Employment on the Ground of Age: A Consultation Paper*. Hong Kong: Government Printer.

Elderly Commission, Hong Kong. (2001). *Report on Healthy Aging Projects*. Hong Kong: Author.

European Commission. (1999). *Towards a Europe of All Ages*. Brussels: European Commision.

Frerichs, F. and Naegele, G. (1997). "Discrimination of Older Workers in Germany: Obstacles and Options for the Integration into Employment." *Journal of Aging and Social Policy,* 9, pp. 89–101.

Ho, L. S., Wei, X. D., and Voon, J. P. (2000). "Are Older Workers Disadvantaged in the Hong Kong Labor Market?" *Asian Economic Journal*, 14, pp. 283–300.

Hong Kong Council of Social Service. (2000). *A Study on the Employment Situation of Middle and Aged Persons in Hong Kong: Research Report*. Hong Kong: Author.

Kam, P. K. (2003). "Powerlessness Among Older People in Hong Kong." *Journal of Aging and Social Policy*, 15(4), pp. 81–112.

Koeber, C. and Wright, D. W. (2001). "Wage Bias in Worker Displacement: How Industrial Structure Shapes the Job Loss and Earnings Decline of Older American Workers." *Journal of Socio-Economics*, 30, pp. 343–52.

Krain, M. A. (1996). "Policy Implications for a Society Aging Well: Employment, Retirement, Education, and Leisure Policies for the Twenty-first Century." *American Behavioral Scientist,* 39, pp. 131–51.

Ngan, R., Chiu, S., and Wong, W. (1999). "Economic Security and Insecurity of Chinese Older People in Hong Kong: A Case of Treble Jeopardy." *Hallym International Journal of Aging* 1(2), pp. 35–45.

Ngan, R., Kam, P. K., and Cheung, C. K. (2004). *Age Discrimination in the Labor Market: Causes and Consequences at Individual, Organizational, and Societal Levels: Research Report*. Hong Kong: Department of Applied Social Studies, City University of Hong Kong.

Palmore, E. B. (1990). *Ageism: Negative and Positive*. New York: Springer.

Phillipson, C. (1998). *Reconstructing Old Age: New Agendas in Social Theory and Practice*. London: Sage.

Society for Community Organization (1998). *Aging with Worth: Research Report on Hong Kong Elderly Working People*. Hong Kong: Author.

Taylor, P. E. and Walker A. (1994) "The Aging Workforce: Employers' Attitudes toward Older People." *Work Employment and Society* 8(4), 569–591.

Walker, A. (1997). *Combating Age Barriers in Employment: European Research Report*. Dublin, Ireland: European Foundation.

———. (1999). "Why the Aging Workforce Demands an Active Response to Public Policy." Keynote lecture for the International Conference on Active Strategies for an Aging Workforce, Turka, August 12–13.

———. (2000). "Towards Active Aging in Europe." *Hallym International Journal of Aging* 2(1), pp. 49–60.

———. (2005). *Active aging: A global strategy for sustainable social protection*. Vincent Woo Distinguished Visiting Scholars Lecture 2005. Hong Kong: Lingnan University.

Walker, A. and Maltby, T. (1997). *Aging Europe*. Buckingham, UK: Open University Press.

World Health Organization (WHO). (2001). *Active Aging: A Policy Framework*. Geneva: World Health Organization.

8

Contradictions of Welfare and the Market

The Case of Hong Kong

Sam Wai-kam Yu

Studies have shown that the relationship between social welfare and capitalism is often marked by contradictions (Ginsburg, 1979; Gough, 1979; Mishra, 1984). On the one hand, social welfare may perform economic and political functions essential to the development of capitalism—for example, securing political legitimacy for capitalist governments, reducing workers' dissatisfaction by improving their quality of life, and promoting capital accumulation. On the other, it may impede the private market functioning. When people are provided with social services that can enable them to maintain a certain standard of living without the need to participate in the labor market, their incentive to work may sway (Esping-Andersen, 1990). Moreover, the government may be required to increase taxes to finance social welfare to an extent that may possibly undermine investors' incentive to invest (Offe, 1984). Hence, in social service provisions, many capitalist governments try to reduce its negative effects on the private market (Walker, 1990; Wilding, 1990). This chapter intends to contribute to this discussion by examining two major social policies adopted by the Hong Kong government to reduce its financial responsibility in social welfare and at the same time seeking to reduce its adverse effects on people's work incentive: 1) the social security reform and 2) health care financing. There are two reasons for this analysis. First, I want to show that the Hong Kong government does not passively face the contradictory relationship between social welfare and capitalism. Instead it has been actively proposing new strategies or modifying existing strategies to reduce the negative effects of social welfare on the market. Second, it is important to note that whatever good intentions by the government to reduce such contradictions, they are doomed to fail. Moreover, the strategies used consequently may not enhance people's incentive to work, or reduce the government's financial responsibilities at all. Furthermore, some social policies carry the functions of promoting capital accumulation and strengthening political legitimacy, and henceforth the government may be unwilling to radically change them.

This chapter is organized into four parts. First I will discuss the features and limitations of the two strategies for reducing the negative effects of social welfare. This is followed by a discussion about the background to the social security and health care finance reforms, including the Hong Kong government's attitude toward social welfare and the economic and social conditions after 1997. The third part is concerned with the substantial contents of the reforms. Finally, I will examine the mixed implications of such reforms on the private market.

THE TWO STRATEGIES

The first strategy used to reduce the negative effects of social welfare on capitalism is to make social welfare a poor substitute for employment. These measures are intended to reconstruct social policies in favor of the residual welfare model, which is based on the assumption that the private market and the family are the natural channels for fulfilling people's needs and that the government should only play a secondary role in providing social services (Titmuss, 1974; Mishra, 1981; Williams, 1989). To keep government's commitment to social welfare contingent, residual social policies are thus characterized by the use of *entry* and *exit devices* to regulate and ration services. An example of an entry device is means-testing. It operates at the pre-consumption stage and its function is to screen out those who can afford to use private services (Yu, 1997a). The exit device operating at the post-consumption stage is responsible for assessing the eligibility of incumbent users and deciding whether to renew or terminate the relationship with them. Its main function is to encourage, by stick or carrot, those who can afford to purchase private services to leave the public sector. The notion of the exit device has been highlighted by Peacock, "The true objective of the welfare state is to teach people how to do without it" (Titmuss, 1974:11). By operating these entry and exit devices, the government seeks to reduce the supposedly adverse effects of statutory social services on the private market, such as reducing people's demand on private services or undermining work incentives.

The second strategy is to link people's entry into the private market with their entry into the statutory social services. This can be achieved by developing *double entry measures*, which refer to arrangements by which the entry devices of statutory social services are linked to people's entry into either the private labor market or the private product market or both (Chau and Yu, 2001). Double entry measures can be categorized into four main types according to different roles played by people in the private market and in the consumption and financing of social services.

The first type of strategies encourages people to consume private services through the provision of government support. An example is the First Time Home Purchase Loan Scheme (Housing Authority 2004), which offers an interest-free loan to people who want to buy a private flat to pay for the down payment. Upon drawing this loan, the service recipients may choose to enter either the public sector or the private market.

The second type of strategy is to encourage people to enter the job market by providing government support, such as providing financial rewards to those who successfully get a job in the private market. As will be discussed in other sections of this chapter, the government, through the Disregarded Earning Scheme (Social Welfare Department, 2006), encourages people on welfare to re-engage in the labor market. If people on welfare choose to take up a job, part of their income will be forfeited in the calculation of the amount of financial assistance given to them.

The third type is to legally oblige workers to contribute a certain proportion of their income to compulsory saving schemes or compulsory insurance schemes to finance social services. An example is the Mandatory Provident Fund, which requires the majority of full-time employees and their employers to contribute to a savings scheme to provide income security for workers after retirement (MPF 2006). Details of this fund will be detailed later.

The fourth type is to legally require people to contribute some money to finance social services when they consume certain kinds of private goods. An example is the Lottery Fund, which is used to finance social services. According to the Gambling Ordinance (Cap. 148) and Betting Duty Ordinance (Cap. 108), a certain proportion of the betting money for horse racing and Mark Six Lottery goes to the Lottery Fund to finance social services. The first two types of double-entry measures can strengthen people's incentive to participate in the private market while the latter two measures may help to reduce the government's financial responsibilities for welfare. However, it is important to note that residualization and double-entry measures may not necessarily be effective in reducing the negative effects of social welfare on the private market. Three points should be noted.

Firstly, in reality it is quite rare, even for right-wing governments, to make all social services purely residual. This is because they may need to provide some social services on a larger scale than that allowed by the residual welfare model in order to promote capital accumulation, seek political legitimac and respond to the petitions from workers and political groups. Facing political reality, they may try alternative but less effective ways of reducing the negative effects of social services on the private market such as: keeping social services as close to the residual welfare model as politically possible by maneuvering the entry or exit device or both. For example, the Hong Kong government has long stressed that public rental housing should be provided for low-income people. Applicants normally need to go through the means-test procedure to determine their eligibility for public housing. However, to enable squatter clearance to be conducted smoothly, it exempts the displaced residents from means-testing when they give up their squatters and move into public rental flats (Yu, 1997b). However, for the purpose of making public rental housing closer to the residual welfare model, public housing tenants are required to go through another means-test to prove that they continue to have the need to live in public rental flats after ten years' residence. Those who fail this means-test are required to pay higher rent or encouraged to move out of their public rental flats.

Second, the effectiveness of the two strategies is affected by the conditions in the private market, which may not be within the government's control. For example, the deterioration of job market or a sharp rise in the price of market goods may change social services from an inferior to an attractive substitute to market goods and/or employment in the job market. In order to reduce the attractiveness of social services, the government may need to further residualize social services.

Third, residualization measures and double entry measures may not be able to reduce the costs of social welfare and its negative effects on people's incentive to participate in the private market at the same time. It is not unusual to see that these measures meet one goal at the expense of the other. For example, the government may need to spend a lot of money on strengthening the entry and exit devices in order to make social welfare an inferior substitute to employment. Another example is that the government can secure a stable source of revenue by requiring workers to make contributions to the Mandatory Provident Fund. However, this attempt may discourage workers from entering the labor market because part of their disposable income is taken away by the government.

THE HONG KONG GOVERNMENT'S ATTITUDE TOWARD SOCIAL WELFARE

The Hong Kong government has long been establishing a pro-capitalist investment environment and tries to achieve this by identifying itself as a defender of free capitalism and its minimum role in terms of intervention in the economy (Yu, 1996). When Hong Kong was a British colony before July 1997, government officials always openly championed that the private market is the best mechanism for allocating resources. John Copperwaithe, the former financial secretary, highlighted:

> It is still the better course to rely on the nineteenth century's hidden hand than to thrust clumsy bureaucratic fingers into its sensitive mechanism (*Hong Kong Hansard*, 1962, p. 133).

Such view was shared by Chris Patten (1995, p. 13), the last governor of Hong Kong:

> government controls and arbitrary interference with the price mechanism would only depress confidence, deter investment and damage the efficiency of our free market economy.

Under the banner of "One Country Two Systems," the postcolonial Hong Kong government is as enthusiastic in associating its rule with the identity of "defender of capitalism" as before. Its status as a capitalist economy is stipulated in the Basic Law:

> The socialist system and policies shall not be practiced in the Hong Kong Special Administrative Region, and the previous capitalist system and the way of life shall remain unchanged for fifty years (Basic Law Drafting Committee 2006).

In his 2001 budget speech, the financial secretary cited the principle *one country two systems* as the simple and low tax regime with both efficient and effective market-regulatory system as the competitive edge of the Hong Kong economy (Hong Kong SAR Government, 2002a). Concomitant with this the Hong Kong government emphasizes low intervention in the economy which is characterized by the absence of a central bank, extremely low public debt, free movement of capital, and low tariffs (Castells, 1992; Owen, 1971; Lau, 1982). The government's unwillingness to intervene extensively in the economy is also reflected in its financial policy. Direct taxation is low—the standard rates of income tax and profit tax were respectively 15 percent and 16.5 percent in 2002. Moreover, it favors a budget surplus policy to a budget deficit policy where there were only six financial years with some form of budget—1949 to 1997. Furthermore, the Basic Law stipulates that

> The Hong Kong Special Administrative Region shall follow the principle of keeping expenditure within the limits of revenues in drawing up its budget, and strive to achieve a fiscal balance, avoid deficits and keep the budget commensurate with the growth rate of its gross domestic product (Article 107).

SOCIOECONOMIC CONDITIONS AFTER 1997

In the light of its ruling identity and economic policy, it is reasonable to assume that the Hong Kong government is wary of the negative effects of social welfare on the private market. In fact, some senior government officials argue that the welfare state is unsuitable for Hong Kong because the "welfare disease" may spread and undermine the incentive to work (Chiu and Wong, 1998). In the White Paper on *Social Welfare into the 1990s and Beyond* the government stresses that social services should be improved without "creating the sort of dependency culture that has emerged in some developed industrialized societies" (Hong Kong Government, 1991:14). Notwithstanding such views, the government has created one comprehensive welfare system in East Asia. For example, over half of the total population is either living in public rental flats or enjoying publicly assisted home ownership. More than 90 percent of the hospital services provide the local population with subsidized medical care (Hong Kong SAR Government, 2000b). In addition, the government provides basic education for all young people aged 16 or below by establishing a nine-year universal, free, and compulsory education system, including six years of primary education and three years of junior secondary education (Education and Manpower Bureau, 1981).

The government's commitment to the social welfare system has attracted the attention of a number of social analysts. Apart from tracing the causes of such development to the pressures exerted by pressure groups and political parties, their studies emphasize the contributions of social welfare to capitalism—these include reducing people's dissatisfaction with the government, ensuring a steady supply of healthy and productive labor and making available opportunities for capitalists to earn money through the provision of a relatively comprehensive welfare system (for example, building public housing for the government) (Castells, Goh and Kwok, 1990; Scott, 1989; Chau and Yu, 2003). However, these analysts also suggest that social welfare is a mixed blessing to the government since it produces negative effects on the private market and to some extent explains why there is always a gap between what the government professes and what it practices when coming to actual social welfare provision (Chau and Yu, 2005). It is interesting to note that this gap did not arouse serious discontent among capitalists in the past or cause serious financial problems since not only capitalists benefited from the provision of social welfare but also the government was able to draw on abundant revenue supply during boom periods (Chau and Yu, 1999). However, welfare expansion was nonetheless paralleled by a rise in income disparity—Gini-coefficient increased from 0.43 in 1971 to 0.525 in 2001 (Census and Statistic Department, 2001). Why could the government keep taxation low and still secure a surplus budget for a long period of time? When recounting his experience of governing Hong Kong, Chris Patten (1998, p. 46–47), the last governor, highlighted the colony's unique public finance situation.

> one had to make few difficult decisions about resources; spending on one priority programme did not require cuts in the money spent elsewhere. Since the economy had grown without check for three and a half decades, there was usually enough money for the things we wished to do.

However, drastic changes in economic and social conditions in recent years have enabled the government to be more aware of its commitment to social welfare. Since 1997 Hong Kong has experienced severe economic depression. In the years between 1998 and 2004, Hong Kong experienced deflation and negative economic growth. Since November 1998, the consumer prices suffered a sixty-eight-month prolonged fall. Between the fourth quarter of 1997 and the first quarter of 2004, the median household income fell by 23 percent. At the lowest point, residential property had lost nearly 70 percent of their value (Tang, 2000; Yu, 2006). Moreover, the unemployment rate increased from 2.2 percent in 1997 to 5.7 percent in 2005. In 2003, the unemployment rate was as high as 8.5 percent. These economic problems not only made it difficult for the government to raise sufficient revenue from the economy but also created an increasing demand for social services (Tang, 2000). The total number of Comprehensive Social Security Assistance (CSSA) cases increased from 289,694 in November 2003 to 295,703 in September 2004. The increase in cases came not only from those old aged applicants (from 146,770 to 149,217) but also from those suffering from low earnings (from 13,259 to 15,688) (Social Welfare Department, 2004).

Besides the economic problems, the government also faces the challenges of an aging population. The proportion of people aged sixty-five or above steadily rose from 7 percent to 12 percent in the period of 1985 to 2001. It is estimated that it will further increase to 13 percent by 2016 and 20 percent by 2036. The ageing population is expected to create a huge demand on social and medical services, as backed up by the following statistics: in 2004 over 50 percent of CSSA recipients were older people and the overall inpatient utilization rate for the group aged seventy-five and above was 80 percent higher than the group aged fifteen to twenty-four (Social Welfare Department, 2006).

Coupled with the aging population is the decline in the caring capacity of the family. The average household size continued to decrease, from 4.2 persons in 1976 to 3.7 persons in 1986 (Phillips, 1992). At the same time the extended family has also been gradually replaced by the nuclear family system.

In 1986 over 70 percent of families were nuclear families, while less than 15 percent were extended families. Such change reduces the pool of potential caregivers in the family (Chau and Yu, 1997). Hence, it is not surprising to see that an increasing number of older people lack sufficient care and support from their families. The Association for the Rights of the Elderly (2002) estimates that over one-tenth of people aged over sixty live alone. The decline in the family's caring capacity implies that more and more older people need caring support from the government. Facing a growing demand for social services, the government reluctantly carried out deficit financing from 1998 to 2004. Worse still, the government estimated that if the deficit budget continued, Hong Kong's $369 billion fiscal reserves would be wiped out by 2008–2009 (*South China Morning Post*, 2002).

MEASURES TO REDUCE THE NEGATIVE EFFECTS OF SOCIAL WELFARE ON THE PRIVATE MARKET

In response to the changes in economic and social conditions, the government has taken an active role in restructuring social welfare. While it stresses the importance of securing social stability and giving the public an image of social protection, it does not want to see a souring welfare budget, as this may eventually lead to tax increase. Moreover, it emphasizes an individual approach in dealing with the unemployment problem. Instead of making structural improvements in the labor market, it focuses on encouraging people to adjust to the conditions of the labor market through various training programs. Various retraining opportunities are provided for the unemployed to learn new skills in the job market. The government's eagerness to reduce pressure on its financial commitment and promote people's incentive to participate in the labor market is reflected in the reforms of the Comprehensive Social Security Assistance scheme (CSSA), the introduction of the Mandatory Provident Fund, and the reforms of medical finance.

Social Security

Long before Hong Kong's economic and social problems surfaced, the government has been wary of the negative effects of CSSA on the labor market and much effort has been spent to ensure that it is an inferior alternative to employment. First, applicants aged sixteen to fifty-nine are required to register for job placements at the Labor Department unless they can demonstrate that they are unable to work. The amount of financial assistance offered by the CSSA is kept below a level at which recipients can enjoy a decent standard of living (Chiu, 1997; Chan, 1999). MacPherson (1993) has noted that households on the CSSA spend more than 70 percent of the benefits on food and therefore lack sufficient money to meet other essential needs. Chiu (1997) estimates that the real value of the benefits offered by the CSSA was reduced by 10 percent while average wage doubled during 1981 to 1991. Furthermore, CSSA recipients are accorded low social status. A significant proportion of respondents in a study complained about the negative attitudes of staff of the Social Welfare Department towards them and attributed this to their difficulties in receiving the help that they need (Chan, 1998).

Certainly, the means-testing mechanism, the requirement of registering with the Labor Department, the low level of welfare benefits, and the stigma attached to welfare recipients, all serve to discourage people from leaving the labor market to live on welfare. Users should be under pressure to stop using services if they have the opportunity to get a job in the labor market, however inadequate or inappropriate the job may be. However, the poor performance of the economy has no doubt increased the attractiveness of the CSSA to its potential recipients. Since it is increasingly difficult to get a job in the private market, unemployed people have no alternatives but to apply temporary relief from the CSSA. As a result, the number of unemployment CSSA cases increased from 3,500 in September 1993 to 37,038 in July 2002. The government was concerned that the increase in CSSA benefits had outpaced the general growth in wages (Hong Kong SAR Government, 1998). In order to reduce the reliance of the unemployed on CSSA, the government considered it necessary to reduce its attractiveness as an alternative to employment. In the review of the CSSA in 1998, it suggested:

> Obviously, we should avoid the possible emergence of a dependency culture in which there is a tendency for some employable adults to consider reliance on welfare assistance a preferred option even when there is employment available. International experience tells us that long-term dependency is likely to develop when the benefit level has become equal or close to what can be earned in a job. (Hong Kong SAR Government, 1998, p.6).

Three exit devices hitherto introduced were: the Active Employment Assistance program, the Community Work program and Disregarded Earnings Program (Social Welfare Department, 2002b: 25). Both the Active Employment Assistance Program and Community Work Program are aimed at encouraging able-bodied unemployed CSSA applicants (including those earning less than $1,610 or working less than 120 hours per month) to develop a work habit and re-enter the job market. Under the Active Employment Assistance Program, CSSA applicants are required to apply for at least two jobs per fortnight, attend fortnightly workplan progress interviews, and update their individual plans. Moreover, they are required to sign a Job Seeker's Undertaking. Under the Community Work Program, CSSA applicants are required to take part in community work for up to one full day or two half-days per week while they are looking for a job. The community work includes jobs such as simple library/clerical work, general counter duties, laundry work, cleaning country parks, gardening and collecting recycled paper. These two schemes by nature are exit devices of the residual welfare model. They not only serve to encourage CSSA recipients to re-enter the private market but also convey the message that the CSSA will only provide temporary assistance. In the long run, CSSA recipients are expected to strengthen their employability and get a job in the labor market. In order to further strengthen the effectiveness of these devices, Lam Cheng Yuet-Ngor, the then Director of the social welfare, warned that the government might stop CSSA payments to those who are not enthusiastic in job seeking or carrying out community work (*South China Morning Post*, 2002).

The aim of the Disregarded Earning Scheme is to give financial rewards to those CSSA recipients who are willing to participate in the labor market although such earnings are small. The maximum amount of earnings to be disregarded is $1,805 per month. The formula is shown in table 8.1.

In the short run, this scheme can be seen as a double-entry measure since participants can receive government support and wages from the private market at the same time. However, in the long run the government expects participants to stop relying on the CSSA and fully meet their financial needs in the job market. In this sense the government sees this scheme more as an exit device of the residual welfare model than a double-entry measure. As shown in table 8.2, older people are the main group of CSSA recipients. To lessen its financial responsibilities for providing social welfare, the government has attempted to reduce the reliance of older people on the CSSA through the introduction of the Mandatory Provident Fund in 2000.

Whether and how Hong Kong should establish a pension scheme for all older people has been discussed and debated for decades. In the early 1990s, only a few years before the return of Hong Kong to China, the government

Table 8.1.   Disregarded Earning Scheme under CSSA

Earnings	Level of Earning to be Disregarded	Maximum Amount to be Disregarded
First $451	totally disregarded	$ 451
Next $2,708	disregarded by half	$1,354
$3,159 or above	the first $451 and half of next $2,708	$1,805

Source: Social Welfare Department (2002b), *A Guide to Comprehensive Social Security Assistance,* Hong Kong SAR Government: Government Printer.

Table 8.2. Composition of CSSA Recipients in 2001–2002

Type of Recipients	No. of Recipients	Percentage
Old age	139,288	56.35
Unemployment	31,602	12.78
Single Parent	29,534	11.95
Ill-health	20,082	8.12
Mentally Ill	9,208	3.73
Low Earnings	9,140	3.7
Physically Disabled, Blind and Deaf	4,520	1.83
Others	3,818	1.54
Total	**247,192**	**100**

Source: Social Welfare Department (2000a), *Annual Report 2001*, Hong Kong SAR Government: Government Printer

surprisingly took an active role in establishing an old age pension scheme (OPS) based on the pay-as-you-go principle (Education and Manpower Branch, 1995). The proposed scheme was designed to give HK $2,300 to all eligible senior citizens (aged sixty-five plus). The level of benefits received by eligible users would be indexed to the official Composite Consumer Price Index. It was proposed that the source of money would come from the compulsory contributions from employers and employees (Tan, 1998). However, the government dropped this proposal in 1994 in response to strong criticisms from business groups and the Beijing government. In the following year, the government made preparation for the setting up of the Mandatory Provident Fund by way of setting up the Mandatory Provident Fund Authority and the Fund was formally established in December 2000. It is a compulsory retirement saving scheme which requires almost all full-time employees aged between eighteen and sixty-five, and their employers to contribute respectively five percent of the employees' earnings, to a recognized private provident fund each month. Employees earning less than $5,000 a month do not need to contribute but their employers have to contribute 5 percent of the employees' income. For employees earning more than $20,000 a month, mandatory contributions are capped at $1,000. Workers are not allowed to receive the money until they reach the age of sixty-five. By promoting redistribution of individual resources over time, the government wants to see more people rely on their savings instead of relying on the CSSA to maintain their livelihood after retirement.

The Mandatory Provident Fund is an example of a double entry measure because entry into this compulsory saving scheme is associated with entry into the labor market. Whether this scheme undermines or enhances the importance of the private market in the allocation of resources is subject to debate. However, it is quite clear that the extent to which workers participate in the labor market is closely related to the amount of protection they can receive from the Mandatory Provident Fund—how much participants can save through this scheme depends on how long they have been a member of the scheme and how much they have earned in the labor market.

Reforms of Health Finance

A number of studies have predicted that public health expenditure will increase faster than general public expenditure because of advances in medical technology and increasing specializations in medicine (Hong Kong Government, 1993; Harvard Team, 1999). It is estimated that the total health expenditure will increase from 4.6 percent of GDP in 1996 to 6.4 percent of GDP in 2016, and public health expenditure will increase from 2.1 percent of GDP to 4 percent of GDP (Fan, 1999). As mentioned above, the government is the largest provider of medical and health services. And these public medical and health services are financed almost entirely through taxation. In order to tackle these financial challenges, the government commissioned a research team from Harvard University (the Harvard Team) to explore the possibility of introducing health insurance and health saving schemes. The Harvard Team published its report in 1999. The government later published its own report to comment on the Harvard Team's proposals and made counter-proposals. Both the Harvard Team and the government's proposals on the financial reforms are highlighted as follows.

The Harvard Team's Proposals

The Harvard Team proposed to set up the Health Security Plan and MEDISAGE. The Health Security Plan is a compulsory insurance plan intended to cover major unexpected medical costs and to pool risk within the population through a pay-as-you-go mechanism. It provides a benefit package for inpatient hospital services and outpatient services for specific illnesses, such as cancer and stroke. Employers and employees share the cost of this benefit package, which equates to 1.5 percent to 2 percent of an employee's wages. Under this plan, patients are allowed to choose from either public or private medical service providers.

MEDISAGE is an individualized accumulative fund. Employers and employees are both required to contribute an amount equivalent to 1 percent of the employee's wages to the Fund. The money is then used to purchase an individual long-term care insurance policy for retirement or disability, including a combination of nursing home, visiting nurse services, and also home-aid visits. The purchase of this long-term care insurance is mandatory at the age of sixty-five. The Harvard Team also suggested that the government should fully subsidize the Health Security Plan premium and MEDISAGE for the poor and unemployed, and provide partial subsidy for the Health Security Plan premium for the elderly and those on a low income.

The Government's Suggestions

In a policy document published in 2000, the government supported the principles of MEDISAGE and promised to form a research team to study the technical details of its implementation (Hong Kong SAR Government, 2000b). However, the government also proposed to replace the Health Security Plan with the Health Protection Account. This requires every individual between the age of forty and sixty-four to put approximately 1 to 2 percent of their earnings into a personal account to cover the cost of future medical needs. Such savings cannot be withdrawn until the person reaches the age of sixty-five (earlier if they suffer a disability). The savings can be used either to pay for medical and dental expenses at public sector rates, or to purchase medical and dental insurance plans from private insurers. If the person chooses services in the private sector, he/she will still be reimbursed only at public sector rates from the accumulated savings.

Similar to the Mandatory Provident Fund, the MEDISAGE and Health Protection Account are examples of a double entry measure. Evidence shows that the government is keen to introduce the Health Protection Account, first by setting up a working group to study its political and financial feasibility, and then to raise people's awareness of the importance of setting up a mandatory saving scheme by raising the medical fees and charges steadily. At the end of 2002, the charges for inpatient and outpatient services were increased respectively by 47 percent and 22 percent respectively (*Hong Kong Daily News*, 1 December 2002). On the same day, it also introduced new charges such as fees for using accident and emergency services and admission fees in hospitals.

THE MIXED IMPLICATIONS OF THE REFORM MEASURES ON THE PRIVATE MARKET

The above measures in social security and health care reforms are intended to reduce the government's financial responsibility and promote incentive to participate in the private market. They carry mixed implications on the private market. On the one hand, the government is keen to retain the private market as an important mechanism for allocating resources. These measures to a certain extent promote the importance of market values and secure a favorable environment for the private market to function in the allocation of resources. On the other hand, they fail to erase all the negative effects of social welfare on the private market. As mentioned above, the Hong Kong economy has been seriously hampered by the Asian Financial Crisis, and as a result the government finds it increasingly difficult to gain sufficient revenue to cover its expenditure. Instead of exploring the possibility of fundamentally reforming the market economy (for example turning it into a socialist economy), the government assumes a purely neoliberal perspective in that the private market will be considered the most efficient and effective mechanism for creating and distributing wealth in Hong Kong. This is evidenced by maintaining its ruling legitimacy as a defender of the free market by maintaining a low taxation policy and a free port. Hence, it is not surprising that the government continues to encourage CSSA recipients to re-enter the labor market through the introduction of new social security measures and is asking people to share more financial responsibility for health and medical services through the proposed reforms to health finance.

Some reform measures indeed serve to strengthen market values such as individualism and inequality. For example, the Mandatory Provident Fund associates people's personal contribution to the quality and quantity of services they receive—the more people earn in the labor market, the more they can save for their retirement. As a result, the social inequality created in the labor market is reinforced. The Active Employment Assistance Program and Community Program convey a message that unemployment is an individual problem rather than a social problem. In order to solve it, the unemployed should make personal changes such as developing a work habit and spending more time job seeking.

However, the reform measures are not able to reduce all the negative effects of social welfare on the private market. The Active Employment Assistance Program, Community Work, and Disregarded Earnings Scheme show that the private market alone cannot effectively allocate jobs or resources. That is why the government needs to play an active part in helping CSSA applicants to re-enter the job market. Moreover, the government's attempts to encourage CSSA recipients to re-enter the private market through the Disregarded Earnings measure challenges the fair competition principle supported by advocates of the free market. Furthermore, the administration costs on these schemes should not be overlooked, though the government may think that it is more cost-effective to spend money on these schemes than providing direct welfare payments to CSSA recipients in the long term.

There has been great concern that the Mandatory Provident Fund, MEDIS-AGE, and Health Protection Plan may undermine people's incentive to work or to invest. Since many workers are required to make contributions to these saving schemes, they will have less disposable income and henceforth may be discouraged to take an active part in the labor market. Moreover, employers are also required to make contributions for their employees in some of these schemes and therefore may have to bear a higher cost of production. Their incentive to invest in Hong Kong may thus be reduced too.

Kwun (1998) points out that most small companies did not have any form of employee benefit arrangements such as group life insurance or medical insurance before the introduction of the Mandatory Provident Fund. Statistics have shown that only 15 percent of small companies had a group medical insurance program set up for their employees in 1998 and it is thus not surprising to see that many of them are strongly opposed to the establishment of this Fund (Chapel, 2001). When the Hong Kong economy was seriously affected by the outbreak of the Severe Acute Respiratory Syndrome (SARS) in 2002, some industries, such as tourism and hospitality, even attempted to pressurize the Hong Kong government to suspend this Fund for one year. (Mackay, 2003). Moreover, studies also showed that employees are not willing to put too much money into the compulsory saving schemes including the Mandatory Provident Fund and medical saving schemes especially during economic recession (Ngan and Cheung, 2000; Health, Welfare and Food Bureau, 2004).

It is important to note that the public have already been discontented with a lot of government policies such as the handling of the bird flu crisis in late 1997, the new Hong Kong International Airport fiasco in mid-1998, and the outbreak of the SARS epidemic in 2002 (Chau and Wong, 2002; Chow and Fan, 1999). The discontent was so severe that it led to two mass demonstrations on July 1, 2003 and 2004 (Chau and Wong, 2002; Chow and Fan, 1999). This is why despite a number of studies showing that the contribution rate of the Mandatory Provident Fund is too low to ensure participants' a decent retirement, the government is still unwilling to raise the contribution rates (Chau and Yu, 2001; Ngan and Cheung, 2000).

There is no doubt that the Hong Kong government is aware of the contradiction between social welfare and capitalism. This awareness is evidenced by its eagerness to reduce the negative effects of medical services and the CSSA on the private market through residualization measures and double entry measures. However, these measures are far from effective in reducing all these effects. The ineffectiveness of these measures indicates the ideological, political, and financial difficulties faced by the government when dealing with the contradictory relationship between social welfare and the private market. In addition, Hong Kong, as well as other East Asian countries, have benefited tremendously from a long growth period with high income, to the effect that the welfare system has been mystified as being uniquely resilient to the ups and downs of a globalized economy. My example of the those entry and exit measures in social security and health care policies have failed to provide evidence to suggest that Hong Kong's social policy is less vulnerable to those stresses and strains that are commonly experienced by all Western economies. Nonetheless, what is deeply troubling is the strong domination by neoliberal values, firmly upheld both by the government and the capitalists in any social policy discussions. The accumulated effects of this could pave the way for an impending crisis in welfare, one characterized by the unpreparedness of the welfare system as well as government's failure to capture the importance and symbiotic nature of the society's relationship between welfare and the economy.

REFERENCES

Association for the Rights of the Elderly. (2002). *The Second World Assembly on Ageing: The Other Hong Kong Report*. Hong Kong: The Association for the Rights of the Elderly.

Basic Law Drafting Committee. (2006). *Basic Law of Hong Kong Special Administrative Region of the People's Republic of China, 1996*. Hong Kong: Joint Publishing (H. K.) Company, Ltd.

Castells, M. (1992). "Four Asian Tigers with a Dragon Head." In R. P. Applebaum and J. Henderson (eds.) *States and Development in the Asian Pacific Rim*. Newbury Park, CA: Sage.

Castells, M., Goh, L. and Kwok, R. (1990). *The Shek Kip Mei Syndrome: Economic Development and Public Housing in Hong Kong and Singapore*. London: Pion.

Census and Statistics Department. (2001). *Hong Kong 2001 Population Census Main Report*. Hong Kong SAR Government: Government Printer.

Chan, C. K. (1998). "Welfare Policies and the Construction of Welfare Relations in a Residual Welfare State: The Case of Hong Kong." *Social Policy and Administration*, 32(3), p. 278–91.

Chan, K. W. (1999). "Conclusion: Social Policy and Social Inequality." In K. C. Li, W. S. Chiu, L. C. Leung, and K. W. Chan (eds.) *New Social Policy*. Hong Kong: The Chinese University of Hong Kong (in Chinese).

Chapel, C. (2001). "Too Little, Too Late." *Asian Business*, 37(1), p. 53.

Chau, C. M. and Yu, W. K. (1997). "The Sexual Division of Care in Mainland China and Hong Kong." *International Journal of Urban and Regional Research*, 21(4), p. 607–19.

———. (1999). "Social Welfare and Economic Development in China and Hong Kong." *Critical Social Policy*, 19(1), p. 87–107.

———. (2001). "Making Welfare Subordinate to Market Activities: Reconstructing Social Security in Hong Kong and Mainland China." *European Journal of Social Work*, 4(3), p. 291–301.

———. (2003). "Marketization and Residualization: Recent Reforms in the Medical Financing System in Hong Kong." *Social Policy and Society*, 2(3), p. 199–207.

———. (2005). "Is Welfare UnAsian: The Case Study of Hong Kong and Mainland China." In A. Walker, and C. K. Wong (eds.) *Eastern Welfare States in Transition*. Bristol: The Policy Press.

Chau, L. and Wong, C. K. (2002). "The Social Welfare Reform: A Way to Reduce Public Burden." In S. K. Lau (ed.) *The First Tung Chee-hwa Administration*. Hong Kong: The Chinese University Press.

Chiu, W. S. (1997). "Poor and Rich." In W. K. Yu, W. Shui, and D. Lai (eds.) *Social Policy in Hong Kong in the 1990s: An Alternative Analysis*. Hong Kong: Hong Kong Policy Viewers (in Chinese).

Chiu, W. S. and Wong, V. (1998). "Social Policy in Hong Kong: From British Colony to Special Administrative Region of China." *European Journal of Social Work*, 1(2), p. 231–42.

Chow, L. and Fan, Y. K. (1999). "Introduction." In L. Chow and Y. K. Fan (eds.) *The Other Hong Kong Report, 1998*. Hong Kong: The Chinese University Press.

Education and Manpower Branch. (1995). *Assessment of Public Opinion on the Consultation Paper: An Old Age Pension Scheme for Hong Kong*. Hong Kong: Government Printer.

Education and Manpower Bureau. (1981). *Overall Review of the Hong Kong Education System*. Hong Kong: Government Printer.

Esping-Andersen, G. (1990). *The Three Worlds of Welfare Capitalism*. Cambridge: Polity Press.

Fan, R. P. (1999). "Freedom, Responsibility, and Care: Hong Kong's Health Care Reform." *Journal of Medicine and Philosophy*, 24(6), p. 555–70.

Ginsburg, N. (1979). *Class, Capital, and Social Policy*. London: Macmillan.

Gough, I. (1979). *The Political Economy of the Welfare State*. London: Macmillan.

Hang Seng Bank. (2004). "Returning Balance to the Residential Market." *Hang Seng Economic Monthly*, June 2004.

Harvard Team. (1999). *Improving Hong Kong's Health Care System: Why and For Whom?* Available online at www.hwfb.gov.hk/hw/text/english/consult/hcs/hcs.htm.

Home Affairs Bureau. (2001). *Consultation Paper on Gambling Review, (June 2001)*. Hong Kong: Government Printer.

Hong Kong Government. (1991). *Social Welfare into the 1990s and Beyond*. Hong Kong: Government Printer.

———. (1993). *Towards Better Health: A Consultation Document*. Hong Kong: Government Printer.

Hong Kong Hansard. 1962. Report of the Meetings of the Legislative Council of Hong Kong, p. 133.

Hong Kong SAR Government. (1998). *Report on Review of the Comprehensive Social Security Assistance Scheme (December 1998)*. Hong Kong: Government Printer.

———. (2000a). *Lifelong Investment in Health, A Consultation Document on Health Care Reform*. Hong Kong SAR Government: Government Printer.

———. (2000b). *The 2002–2003 Budget*. Available online at www.budget.gov.hk/2002/eindex.htm.

Housing Authority. *Annual Report 2004–2005*. Hong Kong: Corporate and Community Relations Sub-Division.

Kwun, C. (1998). "The Mandatory Provident Fund and Small Companies." In B. Rogers (ed.) *Funding The Future*. Hong Kong: Euromoney Publications.

Lau, S. K. (1982). *Society and Politics in Hong Kong*. Hong Kong: The Chinese University Press.

Mackay, A. (2003). "HK Upholds Pensions Plan in Spite of SARS Pressure." *Financial Times*. London, UK: April 24, 2003, p. 21.

MacPherson, S. (1993). "Social Security in Hong Kong." *Social Policy and Administration*, 27(1), p. 50–7.

Mishra, R. (1981). *Society and Social Policy: Theories and Practice of Welfare*. London: Macmillan.

———. (1984). *The Welfare State in Crisis: Social Thought and Social Change*. Brighton: Harvester Whearsheaf.

MPF. (2006). www.mpfahk.org/eindex.asp.

Ngan, R. and Cheung, F. (2000). "The Mandatory Provident Fund Scheme in Hong Kong." Paper Presented at the Second Asia Regional Conference on Social Security organized by the Hong Kong Council of Social Service and the Social Welfare Department of the Hong Kong SAR Government.

Offe, C. (1984). *Contradiction of the Welfare State*. Cambridge, MA: MIT Press.

Owen, C. N. (1971). "Economic Policy." In K. Hopkins (ed.) *Hong Kong: The Industrial Colony: A Political, Social, and Economic Survey*. Hong Kong: Oxford University Press.

Patten, C. (1995). Speech at the Spring Reception of the Hong Kong Council of Social Services on Tuesday, February 14, 1995.

———. (1998). *East and West*. London: Macmillan.

Phillips, D. (1992). "Hong Kong: Demographic and Epidemiological Change and Social Care for Elderly People." In Phillips, D. (ed.) *Ageing in East and South-east Asia*. London: Edward Arnold.

Scott, I. (1989). *Political Change and the Crisis of Legitimacy in Hong Kong*. Hong Kong: Oxford University Press.

Social Welfare Department. (2002a). *Annual Report 2001*. Hong Kong: SAR Government Printer.

———. (2002b). *A Guide to Comprehensive Social Security Assistance*. Hong Kong: SAR Government Printer.

Social Welfare Department. (2004). "Statistics and Figures on Social Security." Available online at www.swd.gov.hk/en/index/site_pubsvc/page_socsecu/sub_stat/.

———. (2006). *Departmental Website*. Available online at www.swd.gov.hk/en/index/site_pubsvc/page_socsecu/sub_supportfor/index.html.

South China Morning Post. (2002a). "Tsang Makes Case for Tax Increases." 2/23/2002, p. 1.

——. (2002b). "Welfare Chief Warns of Drastic Cuts." 12/11/200, p. 2.

Tan, P. (1998). "An Overview of the Mandatory Provident Fund." In B. Rogers (ed.) *Funding The Future*. Hong Kong: Euromoney Publications.

Tang, K. L. (2000). "Asian Crisis, Social Welfare, and Policy Responses: Hong Kong and Korea Compared." *The International Journal of Sociology and Social Policy*, 20(5/6), p. 49–71.

Titmuss, R. M. (1974). *Social Policy: An Introduction*. London: Allen & Unwin.

Walker, A. (1990). "The Strategy of Inequality: Poverty and Income Distribution in Britain 1979–1989." In I. Taylor (ed.) *The Social Effects of Free Market Policies: An International Text*. New York: Harvester Wheatsheaf.

Wilding, P. (1990). "Privatization: An Introduction and a Critique." In R. Parry (ed.) *Privatisation?* London: J. Kingsley.

Williams, F. (1989). *Social Policy: A Critical Introduction: Issues of Race, Gender, and Class*. Oxford: Basil Blackwell.

Yu, W. K. (1996). "The Nature of Social Services in Hong Kong." *International Social Work*, 39(4), p. 411–30.

——. (1997a). "The Sale of Public Rental Housing: The Britain and Hong Kong Experience." *International Social Work*, 40, p. 209–23.

——. (1997b). "The Hong Kong Government's Strategy for Promoting Home Ownership: An Approach to the Reducing of the Decommodifying Effects of Public Housing Services." *International Journal of Urban and Regional Research*, 21(4), p. 537 and 553.

——. (2006). "The Reforms of Health Care Finance in Hong Kong and Urban China—A Mixed Attitude to Social Welfare." *Critical Social Policy* 26(4), p. 843–64.

9

Managing the SARS Crisis in Hong Kong

Reviving the Economy or Reconstructing a Healthy Society

Kam-wah Chan and Lai Ching Leung

Severe Acute Respiratory Syndrome (SARS) is believed to have started in southern China at the end of 2002. It then spread to Hong Kong in February 2003, before moving on to neighboring Asian countries, and subsequently to North America and Europe, although on a lesser scale. This deadly disease created social panic in many countries, and was seen as a serious global threat to people's lives and well-beings. By the end of June 2003, the total number of infected cases had reached 8,458, with a death toll of 807 worldwide (WHO, 2003a). The major strategy of the Hong Kong Special Administrative Region Government (HKSAR Government) to tackle the crisis was built on a scientific and economic rationality paradigm—a typical approach to policy making in many global cities around the world. HKSAR Government depended greatly on advance medical technology and managerial control to manage the disease, while at the same time trying to revive the badly hit economy. The aim of this chapter is to critically review the effectiveness of this managerial-economics led strategy in dealing with the SARS crisis in particular, and more broadly, to ascertain how such strategy affects social policy making.

Among various theoretical approaches to the study of risk and social crises, Ulrich Beck's conception of risk society (Beck, 1992, 1999; Beck et al., 1994) has particular relevance and has significant implications on policy strategy in tackling social risks in a global city like Hong Kong (Adam et al., 2000; Elliott, 2002; Turner, 2001). This chapter starts with a brief sketch of the development of the SARS crisis in Hong Kong and how the HKSAR Government reacted to the problem. The economic rationality paradigm underpinning the HKSAR Government's strategies will then be scrutinized. Using Ulrich Beck's concept of risk society, the study will focus on such relevant issues as the unequal distribution of risks and "individualization" of social inequalities, in order to demonstrate that the HKSAR Government's policy is ineffective in dealing with these problems. The next section, based on the notion of "reflexivity," will reflect on alternative strategies to develop a healthier society, with emphasis in two arenas: health and work. Finally, this chapter concludes by calling attention to a fundamental review of managerial-economic led policy making in global cities, which places greater concern on economic growth, rather than healthy living.

NEW CHALLENGE, OLD RESPONSE

The response of the HKSAR Government was passive and bureaucratic, especially at the beginning of the crisis. When SARS broke out in southern China at the end of 2002 (at that time identified as "atypical pneumonia"), the HKSAR Government was overconfident that modern medical technology was fully capable of dealing with the disease. Even when SARS was confirmed as having spread to Hong Kong in February 2003, the HKSAR Government still tried to tune down public concern by insisting that everything was under control. With the outbreak at the Prince of Wales Hospital on March 11, 2003, the government claimed that this could be easily contained within the hospital. On March 17, however, despite repeated warnings from medical professionals at the Prince of Wales Hospital that the disease had already spread to the community, the Secretary for Health, Welfare, and Food, Dr. Yeoh Eng-kiong, publicly denied that there was an outbreak of SARS in the city, and refused to step up preventive measures against the disease. On March 26, a massive outbreak in Amoy Gardens, an old private housing estate, which eventually infected more than 300 residents within a few days, shocked Hong Kong and confounded the experts. It was not until in late March, with hundreds of people infected and the number of deaths increasing (see figure 9.1), that the government began to step up measures to fight against SARS. Publicity program were launched to educate the public. For the first time, people were advised to wear facemasks, to wash their hands frequently, to clean their homes with diluted bleach water, and to practice good hygiene. Schools were suspended starting from March 27 and those who had had close contact with SARS patients were required to be quarantined. Body temperature checks were conducted at airports and on other border crossings, all in an attempt to prevent the import and export of SARS.

In view of the sudden outbreak, on April 2, the World Health Organization (WHO) issued a travel advisory against Hong Kong. This had a tremendous impact on tourism and related businesses, which led to the most serious eco-

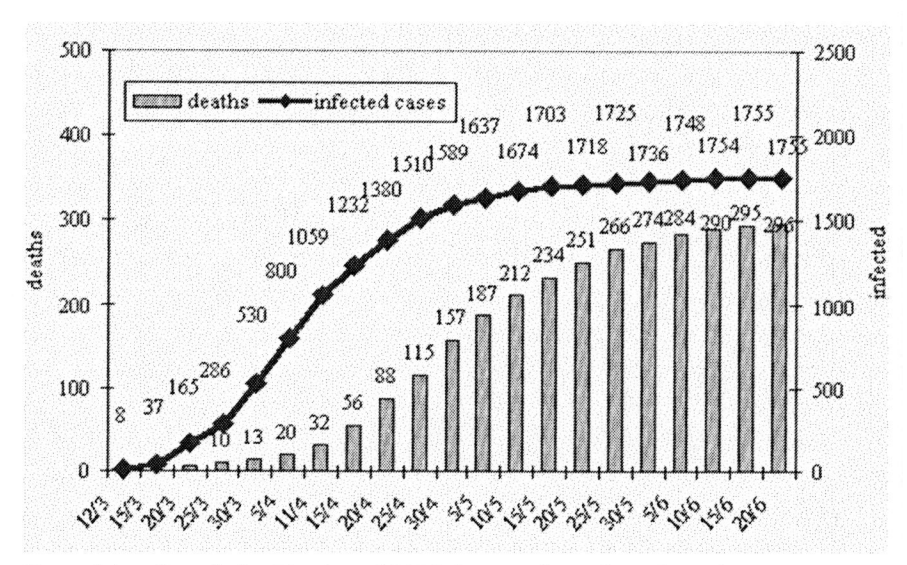

Figure 9.1. Cumulative Number of SARS Cases and Number of Deaths

nomic downturn in Hong Kong since the 1997 Asian Financial Crisis. A study by Oxford Economic Forecasting estimated that Hong Kong would lose close to HK$28 billion (£1=HK$12, approximately) in tourism and related businesses as a result of the crisis (Oxford Economic Forcasting, 2003).

By mid-May, it seemed that the situation was under control and by the end of June, the spread of SARS had come to a halt. Up to June 20, the cumulative number of SARS cases were 1,755 and 296 lost their lives (see figure 9.1). The World Health Organization lifted the travel advisory on May 23 (WHO, 2003b), and a month later, Hong Kong was removed from the list of SARS infected areas (WHO, 2003c).

Eventually, it seemed that Hong Kong had gotten over the crisis. The major focus of concern was then shifted from fighting against SARS to rebuilding the economy. At the end of April, the government announced a HK$11.8 billion package to revive the economy and to provide for hardship relief. Campaigns like "We Love Hong Kong" were launched to promote business, attract tourists and encourage local people to spend. In early May, the chief executive of the HKSAR Government appointed two working groups, one for reviving the economy and the other for promoting a "Clean Hong Kong Campaign." This was augment by another special committee to evaluate the government's strategy in tackling the SARS crisis. Ironically, this committee was headed by the Secretary of Health, Welfare, and Food, Dr. E. K. Yeoh,—the person who had initially denied that SARS was a public threat and could be contained within hospitals. Dr. Yeoh had also been the recipient of numerous complaints from the public on the handling of the outbreak. Although eventually he was removed from the Chair under public pressure, public confidence in the outcome of this committee was much hampered.

THE LIMIT OF ECONOMIC RATIONALITY IN A RISK SOCIETY

The response of the Hong Kong government was largely characterized by a managerial-economic led strategy, which has been the dominant ideological framework in social policy making in many global cities over the last decade. With rapid advancement of globalization and international competition, the state is perceived as incapable of providing comprehensive welfare even if it so desires (Taylor-Gooby, 1997). The free market is taken to be the most efficient form of production and distribution of social resources while the state is seen as the dominant force in promoting "workfare" to enhance individual employability or competitiveness. Social welfare has now come to be replaced by "workfare" as citizen's rights are replaced by individual obligations and social equality. Interestingly, this realignment of the individual's role in modern governance is ironically dubbed as "social inclusion" (Lund, 2002; Levitas, 1998). To solve the problems created by the "marketization" of social services, or to speed up marketization, managerial control is thus relentlessly pursued. It is believed that through scientific management and quality control, substantial savings on social services expenditure could be made without affecting the quality of services provided.

However, in the last decade there have been powerful analyses about the negative impact of "managerialism" (Clarke et al., 2000), 'marketization' (Mooney, 2001; Drakeford, 2000), as well as the impact of globalization, (Dominelli and Hoogvelt, 1996; Taylor-Gooby, 1997) on social services and social policy. Similarly, there have also been numerous critiques of the "modernism" paradigm and the principle of scientific and economic rationality (Beck, 1992; Hewitt, 1994; Penna and O'Brien, 1996; Carter, 1998). Studies on risk society in recent years (Beck, 1992, 1999; Beck et al., 1994; Adam, 2000; Elliott, 2002), especially those relating to social policy, (Kemshall, 2002; Edwards and Glover, 2001; Culpitt, 1999; Manning and Shaw, 2000; Ring, 2003), could somehow provide help in terms of demystifying this deeply entrenched policy orientation.

Ulrich Beck's notion of risk society (Beck, 1992, 1999) suggests that the world has entered a stage of second modernity, which is characterized by such risks as nuclear hazards, environment pollution, health crises and unemployment. Beck argues that policy making has become over-concerned with the efficiency of production of wealth, which inevitably also produces risks without being aware of it. New ways of food production, genetic technology, high density living in cosmopolitan societies, over-working, over reliance on technology and managerial control, have all contributed to producing or exacerbating risks. In other words, risk is produced in social policy and social practice with its dependence on economic rationalism, technocratic development and managerial logic. The Bovine Spongiform Encephalopathy (BSE) crisis in the UK in 1996 and the SARS crisis in Asia 2003 provide a good fit for analysis.

In Hong Kong, the managerial and economic led strategy has proved to be ineffective in dealing with the SARS crisis. Instead it may even have exacerbated the problem. One of the underlying reasons for the government's reluctance to step up measures to fight against SARS during its early stages concerned the adverse effect this would have on the economy, especially tourism and foreign investment. The government did not implement a quarantine policy or suspend schools until the end of March, when the outbreak was already out of control. This was in direct contrast to other countries, such as Singapore, Vietnam, Australia, and Canada, which implemented quarantine policies long before Hong Kong did, even though their problems were far less serious. No wonder then, that the Dean of the Faculty of Medicine of the Chinese University of Hong Kong, Professor Sydney Chung Sheung Chee, accused the government of being more concerned about the economy, than with human life (*Ming Pao*, May 5, 2003) when quarantine measures were not enforced against infected hospitals in mid-March.

The low-key approach in handling the SARS crisis did not help to pacify the public. On the contrary, the lack of information led to social panic. A rumor, spread through the internet on April 1, which claimed that Hong Kong would be declared an "infected port," sparked off panic buying in supermarkets and somehow the stock market to fall. (*South China Morning Post*, April 2, 2003). At the same time, the lack of risk consciousness and health knowledge to deal with infectious diseases, especially during the early stage of the crisis, helped the SARS to spread.

Over reliance on managerial control in hospitals with SARS patients is another issue we will attempt to analyze. In March and April 2003, many doctors, nurses, and other medical workers complained about the lack of protective gears for themselves. It was discovered later that in fact there was no shortage of protective gears, but that some mid-level managers had limited the supply of equipment in order to maintain a "reasonable" stock, as stipulated by management guidelines. Similarly, many medical workers complained about insufficient manpower, unreasonable workload, long working hours, confusing or impracticable guidelines, and the lack of proper equipment and facilities. This constitutes one of the major reasons why medical workers kept on getting infected even well into mid-June 2003, when the government had already claimed that SARS was under control (*South China Morning Post*, June 8, 2003). Such problem might be rooted in the managerial culture developed under hospital administrative reforms in Hong Kong since the mid-1980s, which resulted in cutbacks of frontline medical professionals and workers. In this top down management system, senior managers in hospitals were insensitive to the problems and grievances of frontline medical workers. The "reforms" reduced the hospitals' ability in dealing with crises and actually endangered the safety of, not only medical professionals and health workers, but also the public as patients.

This economic-led orientation becomes even more apparent when the government launched a HK$11.8 billion package to revive the economy and provide hardship relief in late April. Most of the measures provided in the package were geared toward helping the business sector with such incentives as tax rebates, rate concessions, waiver of water charges, sewage charges, and business registration fees, providing loans for businesses facing hardship, and generally making available a generous budget for promoting businesses locally and internationally. This stood in stark contrast to the HK$1.5 billion that was allocated to develop mechanismd to control future SARS outbreaks. This is contrasted with the meager HK$432 million set aside for employee retraining and the creation of jobs, which represent a mere 16 percent of the revival package of resources set aside to the control of SARS.

Dominated by economic rationalism, this managerial-economic led strategy reflects a high degree of insensitivity toward "unequal distribution of risk," thus resulting in relief and remedial actions failing to target those hardest hit. Even more detrimental, some measures tend to "individualize" social inequalities, putting the blame on the disadvantaged.

Unequal Distribution of Risk

One of the more important implications of Beck's study on risk society is the unequal distribution of risk. Beck argues that risk cuts across class and that "risk[s] display a social *boomerang effect* in their diffusion: even the rich and powerful are not safe from them" (Beck 1992: 37). However, this does not imply that risk undermines class society.

> like wealth, risks adhere to the class pattern, only inversely: wealth accumulates at the top, risks at the bottom. To that extent, risks seem to *strengthen*, not to abolish, the class society. Poverty attracts an unfortunate abundance of risks. By contrast, the wealthy (in income, power and education) can *purchase* safety and freedom from risk (Beck 1992: 35).

Everybody is susceptible to risk, irrespective of his class position. However, those at a disadvantageous position with respect to class, gender, race, ethnicity, and age are more likely to bear the burden. Although most Hong Kong people were affected by the SARS crisis irrespective of class position, some groups were at higher risk than others, for example medical workers. Until the end of June 2003, 386 doctors, nurses, and health workers had contracted the disease (Hong Kong SAR Government, 2003a). This amounted to 22 percent of the total number of infected cases, which was the highest number occupational group infected. It should also be noted that most of these health workers were frontline medical workers, with the exception of a few senior doctors infected during the early stage.

Different age groups also faced different levels of risk. Statistics on June 4, 2003, (see table 9.1) showed that amongst the 283 fatal cases, 63 percent (178 cases) were older people aged sixty-five or above. Up to June 17, there were 1,755 infected cases, of which 18 percent were aged sixty-five or above (see table 9.1). Although there were no further updated statistics on age distribution of fatal cases, what became apparent was that the death rate for older people was extremely high as compared to the overall death rate of 22 percent in Hong Kong, or 9.5 percent worldwide (WHO, 2003a). Although a higher death rate for older people was generally expected, an exceptionally high death rate as such begs questions. No wonder there was rumor that lesser medical care and attention had been given to those infected older people.

Gender is another social dimension worth further investigation within the SARS context. Statistics showed that 56% of those infected were female (Hong Kong SAR Government 2003a). Although more detailed statistics are required to better understand the situation, it should be noted that

Table 9.1. Age Distribution of Infected and Fatal Cases

Age Group	Infected Cases (as at June 17, 2003)	Fatal Cases (as at June 5, 2003)
0–14	4%	0%
15–24	10%	0%
25–34	24%	3%
35–44	21%	12%
45–54	15%	12%
55–64	8%	10%
65–74	8%	24%
75–84	10%	26%
85 or above		13%
Total	N=1,755 100%	N=283 100%

Source: Hong Kong SAR Government (2003a, 2003b)

women were at higher risk due to the fact that greater burden of hygiene and health care services are mostly undertaken by women both in the public and private spheres. Frontline workers such as nurses, health care workers, cleaners, and home-helpers are mostly women. More unfortunately, many of these lower rank employees were not provided with adequate protective gears. Similarly, homemakers were required to pay extra effort to clean their homes without state support. This extra risk and burden on women is not reflected in official statistics.

Beck-Gernshim (2000: 129) has pointed out that health responsibilities could lead to oppression, as people are often compelled to take up a heavier burden "voluntarily." One example of this is from the Women's Commission of Hong Kong, which appealed to women to pay extra effort in cleaning their homes. A lengthy list of "useful tips for women as carers for the family" was also issued, to teach women how to take care of their families.

> The Commission believes that women who are the carer[s] of the family should . . . take the opportunity to lead their family members to establish a healthy lifestyle, strengthen ties with their children and enhance family cohesion . . . At the neighbourhood and community level, women can assume the role of health ambassadors. The Commission appeals to all women in Hong Kong to step up efforts in keeping their home and public environment clean to prevent the spread of atypical pneumonia (Women's Commission 2003).

The caring role of women was emphasized repeatedly, while men and other family members were not encouraged to become involved, nor was the government urged to provide extra support and resources for home carers. This reflected the fact that most members of the Women's Commission were appointed by a very conservative government, generally lacking gender consciousness. An unintended consequence of the SARS outbreak, therefore, was reinforcing gender division with women as the primary carers.

Another point that draws our attention is the different impact the SARS outbreak had on employees at different ranks. Although nearly all walks of life suffered from the economic downturn linked to the SARS crisis, lower rank staff suffered most. Many employees had their salaries slashed, were forced to take no pay leave, or were even dismissed. According to a survey by the Census and Statistics Department in the week ending June 21, 2003, on average, 89 percent of employees in Hotels, 66.7 percent in airline companies, 50 percent in travel agencies, and 24 percent in restaurants had to take no pay leave (Census and Statistics Department, 2003a). The unemployment rate rose to 8.3 percent in the March–May quarter of 2003 (Census and Statistics Department, 2003b), which was considered a record high for Hong Kong. Our suggestion is that this had not been fully reflected as an impact of the SARS crisis.

Ethnic and racial inequalities were another interesting dimension at SARS. In Western societies, the SARS crisis exacerbated discrimination against Asian ethnic minorities, whereas in Hong Kong new immigrants from the Mainland China and ethnic minorities from countries such as Pakistan, India, and the Philippines were placed in a disadvantaged position. For example, new immigrants from the Mainland were blamed for spreading the disease, while ethnic minorities from other Asian countries had less access to information or resources regarding the prevention of SARS. To date, studies and discussions in these areas are extremely thin, and these problems remain largely invisible.

Individualization

Why and how was this unequal distribution of risk perpetuated? Beck (1992) argues that there is an increasing trend of individualization of social inequalities in late modernity. Unlike risk in traditional societies that is perceived as natural and mostly unavoidable, risk in late modernity is regarded as manageable or insurable. Consequently, individuals who failed to avoid risk are blamed, and the "problem[s] of the system are lessened politically and transformed into personal failure" (Beck, 1992: 89). This individualization process could be structured in social policies and social practices, as Beck points out, in the context of state welfare:

> individualization is a structural concept, related to the welfare state; it means "*institutionalized* individualism." Most of the rights and entitlements of the welfare state, for example, are designed for individuals rather than for families . . . . By all these requirements people are invited to constitute themselves as individuals: to plan, understand, design themselves as individuals and, should they fail, to blame themselves (Beck, 1999: 9).

This individualization process was clearly reflected in the management of the SARS crisis. Although state intervention was inevitable to fight this epidemic, the emphasis was on individual, rather than on social or public responsibility. Victims of SARS and their families were not entitled to any publicly funded social assistance, unless they were qualified for Comprehensive Social Security Assistance that was already designated for the most vulnerable. As an alternative, four senior female government officials launched a fund raising campaign to help the children of those who died of SARS. This appears to be paradoxical. On the one hand, individual and voluntary efforts to help the SARS victims should be encouraged; yet on the other hand, this became an excuse for the government to renege on its responsibilities. Contracting SARS became an "individual misfortune" rather than a social responsibility that should have been taken care of by public revenue. Furthermore, there was the added negative implication that this type of charity work was women's business.

Another typical example of "individualization" is the Clean Hong Kong Campaign, which was launched in mid-May 2003. Of course, it is important to improve environmental hygiene to prevent another outbreak of SARS. However, instead of promoting health education and improving urban services, the government took on a high profile role through the penalization of those who littered and spat in public. Penalties were raised from HK$600 to HK$1,500. Repeat offenders living in public housing are liable to eviction. Studies on risk society have pointed out that risk could lead to social panic, which could end up in scapegoating the disadvantaged (Hier, 2003). Emphasis on health responsibility in a risk society could lead to the blaming of individuals who failed to live up to emphasized "standards" (Beck-Gernsheim, 2000), and could also result in greater surveillance and regulation of individual lifestyles (Kemshall, 2002: 42–64). More importantly, individualization diverts attention away from social and structural problems, such as the lack of health education, low quality of urban service and poor working conditions of cleaning workers. The outbreak of SARS was largely the result of structural and social problems, rather than individual failure.

Increasing exploitation of manual workers is one reason for the deterioration of environmental hygiene. As reports from the World Health Organization and the HKSAR Government have pointed out, poor environmental hygiene, faulty sewage systems, as well as the low quality of cleaning and maintenance services were the most important factors leading to the massive outbreak of SARS in Amoy Gardens (WHO, 2003d; Hong Kong SAR Government, 2003c), which infected more than 300 residents within a few days. This deterioration of hygiene is partly related to the casualization of work in cleaning and maintenance services. It is unrealistic to expect high quality services for low-paid and unstable jobs. Under the "individualization" discourse, issues relating to low pay, poor working conditions, and lack of employment security for cleaners and maintenance workers have been sidelined.

REFLEXIVITY: KNOWLEDGE OR UNAWARENESS

This individualization of social inequalities will not help to solve the problems of modern society. Conversely, the lack of reflection and the unintended consequences created could further exacerbate the risk in the modernization process. It is in this sense that 'reflexivity' becomes a key to future social development. Beck, Giddens, and Lash (Beck et al., 1994) points out that the world is developing from the first modernization, or the industrial model of development, to a second modernization, that they have labelled "reflexive modernization." However, the meaning of "reflexivity" is ambiguous, even among these authors. Roughly there are two positions, of which Giddens and Lash belong to the first and Beck to the second.

> In the first view . . . . "reflexive" modernization is bound in essence (in keeping with the literal meaning of the words) to knowledge (reflection) on foundations, consequences and problems of modernization process, while in the second one, . . . it is essentially tied to unintended consequence of modernization (Beck, 1999: 109).

The first position emphasizes "reflection," which is concerned with knowledge, information, calculating, and insurance against risk in late modernity. The second position emphasizes the unintended consequence, uncontrollable outcome, and unpredictable risk in this second modernization. Of course, these two aspects are not mutually exclusive, but rather two sides of the same coin.

An important implication for policy analysis is critically rethinking the development of a "knowledge-based society" to reveal the unintended consequence of policy making. To develop an effective strategy of the present epidemic disease and to rebuild a healthy society, the HKSAR Government should reflect on policy making at least in two arenas: health and work.

Rethinking Health: Medical Model vs. Community Health

In recent decades, health services in Hong Kong have very much relied on technological and professional knowledge (Wong, 1999; Gauld and Gould, 2002) which assumed that with advances in technology, coupled with quality management, we could solve most pressing health problems. Medical models and the domination of professionals in health services have long been criticized in western literature (Doyal, 1979; Illich, 1976; Navarro, 1986; Purdy, 1999; Turner, 1995). A community approach to health has always been part of an important debate in Western societies (Davies, 1999; Wilkinson, 1996). However, this is severely underdeveloped in Hong Kong. Public health education is lacking and people are not encouraged to develop a healthy life pattern. As a consequence, people tend to rely heavily on the professionals to cure when sick, hence perpetuating social risk.

A review of the hospital services in 1985 (Hong Kong Government, 1985) was a watershed in Hong Kong, which further shifted the health care system toward hospital services. Although a Report on Primary Health Care was published in 1990 (Hong Kong Government, 1990) and several paragraphs on primary health care and preventive care were included in the consultative document on Health Care Reform published in 2000 (Hong Kong SAR Government, 2000), the recommendations were never systematically implemented. As Gauld and Gould (2002: 20–22) pointed out, of the HK$30.8 billion in recurrent public expenditure spent on health in 2000–2001, only 11 percent was allocated to the Health Department, while the rest went to hospital services. As a result of the limited budget of the Health Department, only about one-third is spent on disease prevention and health promotion. Health Care Reform in Hong Kong is still largely focused on introducing managerial quality control, shifting toward a "mixed economy" to deal with rising costs, and hence much victimized by the domination of professionalism and scientific-economic rationality.

This "hegemony" of scientific knowledge has also contributed to the marginalization of herbal medicine in Hong Kong, which has thousands of years of practical experiences in Chinese society. It is ironic to see that traditional Chinese medicine, which focuses on strengthening the immune system, prevention of illness, and maintaining a balance between the nature and the human body, was largely neglected in fighting SARS. However, it is interesting to note that various prescriptions for Chinese herbal tea, soups, and medicines to prevent SARS did become popular among the public, as people somehow lost faith in 'scientific knowledge."

Research and development in Chinese medicine was not encouraged until fairly recently, when the government wanted to develop a "world class" Chinese Medicine Research Center. However, the qualification of traditional Chinese medical doctors was not fully recognized until 2002, when a registration system was set up. Ironically, changes in recent years simply seem an extension of scientific rationality logic that aims at developing a professional and technocratic form of Chinese medicine as health care, rather than a shift toward community-based health services, as well as generalizing health knowledge among the public.

In the post-SARS era, instead of promoting a healthy lifestyle, the HKSAR Government has launched several economic revival campaigns to encourage spending and consumption, such as, eating out in restaurants, shopping, watching movies, and traveling. To a certain extent, the present health crisis was an unintended consequence of an overconsumption and overproduction society. It is easy to see that mass consumption activities are promoted as a solution to this crisis, further reflecting the fact that the HKSAR Government has learned very little from the SARS crisis, and lacks the consciousness of promoting a healthy lifestyle. In connection with the promotion of health consciousness, we need to pay attention to a number of unintended consequences. First, the emphasis on health risk could lead to a form of "voluntary compulsion" (Beck-Gernsheim, 2000: 129), surveillance and a regulation of lifestyle (Kemshall, 2002: 42–64). Second, the rising concern of health does not necessarily challenge dominant scientific rationality. On the contrary, this could lead to further dependence on scientific knowledge, such as the development of genetic engineering in order to create healthier human species. Third, an increasing concern of health risk may reinforce managerial-economics led policies, such as the expansion of private health insurance, or the expansion of private health care services that are assumed to be more efficient and of better quality than the public ones. This consequently further reinforces managerial domination in the name of "risk management."

Rethinking Work: Work-centered vs. Work-life Balance

The deterioration of public health is also closely linked with an "over-work culture," which has led to poor physical and psychological health of the masses. Hong Kong is a notoriously 'over-worked society." In eras of booming economy before the mid-1990s, it was believed that labor flexibility and a hardworking labor force were the keys to Hong Kong's economic success. Ironically, the economic downturn since 1997 and the shrinking of the economy did not reduce the amount of work, but exacerbated this "over-working culture" since employees had to work even harder to maintain their competitiveness and to avoid redundancy.

Within this "over-working culture," most workers continue to work as long as possible even though they might be ill. For example, while it is customary for an employee in many developed countries to take sick leave if he/she has contracted influenza, in order to avoid infecting others, an employee in Hong Kong is regarded as hardworking if he continues to work under this condition. The risk of infecting others has seldom been a concern. In fact, medical professionals have pointed out that one of the reasons for the rapid spread of SARS at the Prince of Wales Hospital in Hong Kong in early March was that some medical workers continued to work despite having symptoms (Tomilinson and Cockram, 2003). Sometimes, the employees have no choice but to continue to work even when they are ill, because most employers are unhappy and unwilling to grant sick leave. Some employees, especially low-income manual workers, are paid on a daily or hourly basis, meaning having to give up their salary if they take sick leave.

Bowring (1999) has argued that job scarcity could be a "potential blessing" to reflect on the "work-center" or over-working life pattern in modern society. Logically, modernization and the development of technology could reduce labor and liberate human beings from work (Gorz, 1995; 1999), which could contribute to a reform in the traditional industrial wage-based society. Fitzpatrick (2002) calls attention to emancipate social time as an alternative ethics to paid employment, while Pillinger (2000) argues for a redefinition of work, the promotion of job-sharing, and a general reduction of working hours. However, these debates are essentially nonexistent in Hong Kong, evidenced by a traditional ideology of work, which evolved from an industrial-productivist model. Overtime work, work on holidays and extreme long working hours are common in Hong Kong. Individual health, family life, social and leisure activities are all sacrificed for work (Chiu and Ng, 1999; Chan and Chan, 2002). Balanced work life policies, as implemented in many Western societies (Duncan, 2002; Lewis and Lewis, 1996), especially the Nordic countries (Etherington, 1998), are largely absent in Hong Kong.

This deteriorating working condition and increasing employment risk do not only affect the health of the individual employees, but also this causalization of work and overemphasis on economic competitiveness have led to deteriorating environmental hygiene. The post-SARS Clean Hong Kong Campaign and the promotion of health education have failed to address this problem, while other 'reviving' campaigns are mainly concerned with economic growth, rather than healthy lifestyles.

According to the notion of risk society, the SARS crisis in 2003 could be regarded as a classic example of an unintended consequence of an overconsumed, overproduced, and over-worked society in late modernity. However, the HKSAR Government remains oblivious to these social changes. In adopting a managerial-economic led strategy, the HKSAR Government is overly dependent on medical technology and managerial control, which we argues has contributed to an exacerbation of the problem. Unaware of the unequal distribution of risk, remedial actions by the government failed to target disadvantaged groups who were the hardest hit. Even worse, "individualization" strategies increased the burden of some disadvantaged groups, while diverting public attention from more fundamental problems in social structure and social practice. The solution of the problem lies with a critical rethinking of social development in various aspects, such as health and work, and in revealing the unintended consequences of existing policies.

This managerial-economic led approach to policy making is not unique to Hong Kong, although Hong Kong may be a more extreme example due to its long history of dominant laissez-faire capitalism. This has become the prevailing strategy in most economically developed countries over the last decade, irrespective of a conservative or a labor/democratic government. This approach is concerned with economic growth more than the quality of life, which is not only ineffective in tackling health crises and social risks, like the SARS pandemic, but also lagging behind changing social needs and lifestyles in a new stage of modernity. We call for a more thorough reflection on policy making which is not only limited to technical and managerial improvements of social services in responding to a global health crisis, but also aims at a more comprehensive social development and reconstructing a healthier society.

REFERENCES

Adam, B; Beck, U., and Van Loon, J. (2000). *The Risk Society and Beyond: Critical Issues for Social Theory*. London: Sage Publications.

Beck, U. (1992). *Risk Society: Toward a New Modernity*. London: Sage Publications.

———. (1999). *World Risk Society*. Cambridge: Polity Press.

Beck, U., Giddens, A., and Lash, S. (1994). *Reflexive Modernization: Politics, Tradition and Aesthetics in the Modern Social Order*. Stanford: Stanford University Press.

Beck-Gernsheim, E. (2000). "Health and Responsibility: From Social Change to Technological Change and Vice Versa." In Adam, B.; Beck, U. and Van Loon, J. (eds.) *The Risk Society and Beyond: Critical Issues for Social Theory*. London: Sage Publications, pp. 122–135.

Bowring, F. (1999). "Job Scarcity: The Perverted Form of a Potential Blessing." *Sociology*, 33(1), pp. 69–84.

Carter, J. (1998). "Postmodernity and Welfare: When Worlds Collide." *Social Policy and Administration*, 32(2), pp. 101–15.

Census and Statistics Department. (2003a). *Result of Weekly Consultation on Effect of SARS on Business*. Hong Kong SAR Government website, accessed at July 16, 2003, www.info.gov.hk/censtatd/eng/nterest/sars/sars_index.html.

Census and Statistics Department (2003b), *Statistics on Labour Force, Unemployment and Under Employment*. Hong Kong SAR Government website, accessed at July 2, 2003, www.info.gov.hk/censtatd/eng/hkstat/fas/labour/ghs/labour1_html.

Chan, K. W. and Chan, Y. C. (2002). *Family-friendly Work Environment: A Research Report*. Hong Kong: Centre for Social Policy Studies, the Hong Kong Polytechnic University, and The Harmony House, in Chinese.

Chiu, W. and Ng, C. (1999). "Women-friendly HRM and organizational commitment: a study among women and men of organizations in Hong Kong." *Journal of Occupational and Organizational Psychology*, 72(4): 485–502.

Clarke, J., Gewirtz, S., and McLaughlin, E. (ed.) (2000). *New Managerialism New Welfare?* London, Thousand Oaks, and New Delhi: The Open University in association with Sage Publication.

Culpitt, I. (1999). *Social Policy and Risk*. London, Thousand Oaks, and New Delhi: Sage Publications.

Davies, S. (1999). "Empowerment and Health: A Community Development Approach to Health Promotion." Chapter 8 in Purdy, M. and Banks, D. (ed.), *Health and Exclusion: Policy and Practice in Health Provision*. London: Routledge, 136–157.

Dominelli, L. and Hoogvelt, A. (1996). "Globalization and the Technocratization of Social Work." *Critical Social Policy*, 16: 45–62.
Doyal, L. (1979). *The Political Economy of Health*. London: Pluto Press.
Drakeford, M. (2000). *Privatization and Social Policy*. London and New York: Longman.
Duncan, S. (2002). "Policy Discourse on 'Reconciling Work and Life' in the EU." *Social Policy and Society*, 1(4): 306–314.
Edwards, R. and Glover, J. (ed.) (2001). *Risk and Citizenship: Key Issues in Welfare*. London and New York: Routledge.
Elliott, A. (2002). "Beck's Sociology of Risk: A Critical Assessment. *Sociology*, 36(2): 293–315.
Etherington, D. (1998). "From Welfare to Work in Denmark: an Alternative to Free Market Policies?" *Policy & Politics*, 26(2):147–162.
Fitzpatrick, T. (2002). "In Search of a Welfare Democracy." *Social Policy and Society*, 1, 1: 11–20.
Gauld, R. and Gould, D. (2002). *The Hong Kong Health Sector: Development and Change*. Hong Kong: The Chinese University Press.
Gorz, A. (1995). *Path to Paradise: on the Liberation from Work*. London: Pluto Press.
Gorz, A. (1999). *Reclaiming Work*. Cambridge: Polity Press.
Hewitt, M. (1994). "Social Policy and the Question of Postmodernism." Chapter 3 in Page, R. and Baldock, J. (ed.) *Social Policy Review: 6*. London: Social Policy Association.
Hier, S. P. (2003). "Risk and Panic in Late Modernity: Implications of the Converging Sites of Social Anxiety." *British Journal of Sociology*, 54(1): 3–20.
Hong Kong Government. (1985). *The Delivery of Medical Services in Hospitals*. Hong Kong: Government Printer.
Hong Kong Government. (1990). *Health for all the Way Ahead: Report of the Working Party on Primary Health Care*. Hong Kong: Government Printer.
Hong Kong SAR Government. (2000). *Life Long Investment in Health: Consultation Document on Health Care Reform*. Hong Kong: HKSAR Government.
Hong Kong SAR Government. (2003a). *Health, Welfare & Food Bureau—SARS Bulletin, 17 June 2003*. Hong Kong SAR Government website, accessed on July 2, 2003, www.info.gov.hk/dh/diseases/ap/eng/bullentin0617e.pdf.
Hong Kong SAR Government. (2003b). *Health, Welfare & Food Bureau—SARS Bulletin, 5 June 2003*. Hong Kong Government website, accessed on July 2, 2003, www.info.gov.hk/dh/diseases/ap/eng/bullentin0605e.pdf.
Hong Kong SAR Government. (2003c). *Outbreak of Severe Acutre Respiratory Syndrome (SARS) at Amoy Gardens, Kowloon Bay, Hong Kong—Main Findings of the Investigation*. Hong Kong: The Hong Kong SAR Government, Department of Health. On the government website: www.info.gov.hk, as at April 17, 2003.
Illich, I. (1976). *Limits to Medicine: Medical Nemesis: Expropriation of Health*. London: Penguin Books, 1990 reprint.
Kemshall, H. (2002). *Risk, Social Policy and Welfare*. Buckingham and Philadelphia: Open University Press.

Levitas, R. (1998). *The Inclusive Society? Social Exclusion and New Labour*. Hampshire: Macmillan.

Lewis, S. and Lewis, J. (ed.) (1996). *The Work-Family Challenge: Rethinking Employment*. London: Sage Publication.

Lund, B. (2002). *Understanding State Welfare: Social Justice or Social Exclusion?* London, Thousand Oaks, and New Delhi: Sage Publications.

Manning, N. and Shaw, I. (ed.) (2000). *New Risks, New Welfare: Signposts for Social Policy*. Oxford: Blackwell Publishing.

Mooney, G. (2001). "New Labour and Managerialism: Privatizing the Welfare State?" Chapter 11 in Lavalette, M. and Pratt, A. (ed.) *Social Policy: A Conceptual and Theoretical Introduction*. London: Sage Publication, 2nd edition, 193–212.

Navarro, V. (1986). *Crisis, Health and Medicine: a Social Critique*. London: Tavistock Publication.

Oxford Economic Forecasting. (2003). *Impact of SARS on the travel and tourism industry 15th May 2003*, and *Update of SARS: Further analysis of implications for GDP growth and assessment of impact 15th May 2003*, on the Oxford Economic Forecasting website, accessed on July 1, 2003, www.oef.com.

Penna, S. and O'Brien, M. (1996). "Postmodernism and Social Policy: A Small Step Forward?" *Journal of Social Policy*. 25(1): 39–61.

Pillinger, J. (2000). "Redefining Work and Welfare in Europe: New Perspective on Work, Welfare and Time." Chapter 21 in Lewis, G., Gewirtz, S., and Clarke, J. (ed.) *Rethinking Social Policy*, London: The Open University and Sage Publications, 323–337.

Purdy, M. (1999). "The Health of Which Nation? Health, Social Regulation and the New Consensus." Chapter 4 in Purdy, M. and Banks, D. (ed.) *Health and Exclusion: Policy and Practice in Health Provision*. London: Routledge, 62–77.

Ring, P. (2003). "'Risk' and UK Pension Reform." *Social Policy and Administration*, 37(1): 65–28.

Taylor-Gooby, P. (1997). "In Defence of Second-best Theory: State, Class and Capital in Social Policy." *Journal of Social Policy*, 26(2): 171–192.

Tomilinson, B. and Cockram, C. (2003). "SARS: Experience at Prince of Wales Hospital." Hong Kong, *The Lancet*, 361 (May 3):1486–87.

Turner, B. S. (1995). *Medical Power and Social Knowledge*. London: Sage Publication, 2nd edition.

Turner, B. S. (2001). "Risks, Rights and Regulation: An Overview." *Health, Risk and Society*. (3)1: 9–18.

Wilkinson, R. G. (1996). *Unhealthy Societies: The Afflictions of Inequality*. London: Routledge.

Women's Commission. (2003). *Women's Commission appeals to Women in Hong Kong to support one another to combat atypical pneumonia*, Hong Kong SAR Government, Women's Commission website, accessed on July 6, 2003, www.women.gov.hk/eng/issue/issue.html.

Wong, C. W. (1999). *The Political Economy of Health Care Development and Reforms in Hong Kong*. Aldershot: Ashgate.

World Health Organization (WHO). (2003a). *Cumulative Number of Reported Probable Cases of SARS, from 1 November 2002 to 24 June 2003.* WHO announcement as at June 24, 2003, on website: www.who.int/csr/sars/country/2003_06_24/en.

World Health Organization (WHO). (2003b). *World Health Organization changes Hong Kong, Guangdong travel recommendations.* WHO announcement as at May 23, 2003, on website: www.who.int/mediacentre/releases/2003/proha4/en.

World Health Organization (WHO). (2003c). *Update 86—Hong Kong removed from list of areas with local transmission.* WHO announcement as at June 23, 2003, on website: www.who.int/csr/don/2003_06_23/en.

World Health Organization. (2003d). *Environmental Health Team Reports on Amoy Gardens*, Geneva: World Health Organization, Regional Office for the Western Pacific, on the Hong Kong SAR Government website, www.info.gov.hk as at May 16, 2003.

10

Between Idealism and Realism

The Evolution of Full Employment Policy in China

Ho Lup Fung

The making and development of public and social policies is an interacting process between idealism and realism. Idealism provides not simply the values and ideologies that guide policy decisions, but also involves the demand on, and also the attempt of, the state in using ideal plans to master the course of changes. Idealism is an attempt to go beyond limits, as it tries to unite the strength of a complicated society to overcome restraints imposed by reality. Realism, however, involves a gradualist, incremental, and piecemeal reformist tendency as the state and its people accept their own incompleteness in mastering the complexity of social changes. It is a reaction to social problems, and it is characterized by the practical problem-solving approach. Lindblom points out that the difference between the idealists and realists is that the former want to use a rational-comprehensive approach while the latter adopt a disjointed incrementalist one to "make (slight) advancement" in policy changes.[1] The policy process is characterized by the interaction between rational-comprehensive idealism and problem-solving realism, in the forms of negotiation, conciliation, or conflict.

History is full of images, and our understanding of the socialist regime in China is also clouded with shorthand images. There is a popular perception that socialist China has moved from one ideological extremity to another in its employment policies. It is believed that, before the economic reform, the Chinese socialist regime was committed to the ideals of labor decommodification by devising full employment and employment protection policies resulting in the formation of the iron rice bowl. It is also believed that, after the economic reform, the iron rice bowl was smashed under the advent of the labor market, and it looked as if raw capitalism had begun to take over the socialist quest, and the fate of laborers, especially low-income earners, was to face a pessimistic future under harsh competition of the market.

It is the aim of this chapter to argue that this simplified understanding is a misleading one. Ideological interpretations can give us an abridged understanding, yet it is not sufficient to analyze the complexity of policy changes. As George and Wilding[2] contend, the force of ideology looks pale and dull as it moves from the minds of the theoreticians into the hands of cabinet ministers who confront social demands and resource restraints on a day-to-day basis. Social policies are practical measures that meet the tangible but complicated needs of the people, thus policy makers can hardly govern with a simple internally consistent logic, as they have to adjust their ideological quests with pragmatic adaptations and compromises to pressures from the socioeconomic reality. Ideological quests only constitute one of the many variables in the making of social policies, and the policy process is paved with the interplay of idealism and realism, with numerous deviations and contradictions coexisting within the domineering ideology. The quest for rational, comprehensive, and long-term utopian plans coexist with the realistic trial-and-error testing, experimental and incremental policy process in the policy making process.

With the above contention as a background assumption in the policy making process, this chapter attempts to analyze the changes of employment policies in the Chinese socialist regime to provide a dynamic understanding of the interplay of ideology and reality, or idealism and realism, in the shaping and design of employment policies in China. It does not attempt to create analytic models. Rather, it tries to analyze how the regime learns from the historical lessons of policy changes, and how it continues to adjust to the new problems arising from the political and economic changes. It aims at making a dialectic understanding about the coexistence of idealism and realism in a policy regime, and tries to understand how they interact in the making of employment policies. The chapter is based on an analysis of ordinances, regulations, and government notices, and provides a historical account of the full employment policies from 1949 to 1997. About 193 legislative documents on employment, as well as 101 general ordinances in the said period, were reviewed.

BEFORE THE ECONOMIC REFORM: CONFLICTS AND CONCILIATION BETWEEN SOCIALIST IDEALS AND REALITY, 1949–1978

Discreet Idealism: The Early Period of Full Employment, 1949–1957

When the socialist regime took power in 1949, it was endowed with an underdeveloped industrial economy and its labor force. Modern industrial productivity only constituted a small fraction of the economy, and the industrial labor force was marginal to the total working population. In 1949, the urban industrial labor force was estimated roughly to be 3 million, and it constituted only 2.2 percent of the total population of 540 million. In 1949, the Peoples' Republic was endowed with only 300,000 relatively well-trained technicians in the whole workforce of 200 million.[3] Under such industrial backward conditions, an economic ideal—rapid industrialization with full employment policy—was made to ensure labor decommodification under a planned economy. As the planned economy was in gradual formation in the early 1950s, policies were initiated to handle two major problems of unemployment: structural unemployment and organizational inefficiency of the enterprises. As a result, two important documents, the *Measures Concerning the Treatment of Unemployment* and *Decisions on the Problems of Unemployment* were issued in 1952, and they finally germinated into a comprehensive employment policy beyond passive and piecemeal provisions against unemployment.

Unemployment due to industrial shift was to be treated in a positive way. In preventing such unemployment type, the regime tried to retain workers in their enterprises as it encouraged all types of "sunset industry enterprises" to transfer their capital, together with their workers, to new industrial plants. The Communist regime was to provide subsidies for enterprises to adjust to new industrial demands, and enterprises were to be responsible to retrain unfit workers for skills improvement. Under the guidance of the planned economy, unemployment was prevented as bankrupting employers were advised to improve organizational resources and management rather than dismissing workers to save cost.[4] The optimistic idealism generated a primitive Scandinavian model of active labor market policy, in which the regime regulated industrial shift with overall manpower policies in a comprehensive way. The only difference, perhaps, was on the different levels of technological and managerial sophistication in the matching and allocation of workers to their jobs.

However, rapid industrialization created unexpected consequences as the regime began to open up employment by granting jobs to everyone who could work. In order to attract higher quality workers, educated workers were particularly welcomed, and jobs were allocated to them even when they were sick and retired. Domestic work of housewives was also considered as economically unproductive, and housewives were mobilized to join the labor force. Educated women were given privileges to take up half-day jobs or part-time jobs, and they were given extra living supplements to take care of their family members. Even domestic helpers were allocated to jobs in urban commune factories to work for the new economy.[5] Such generous expansionary policy led to damaging results. From 1957 to 1958, in just one year, the size of the female urban labor force expanded from 3 million to 8 million. Furthermore, labor recruitment based on welfare principles was also proposed for rural labor, minority racial groups, the disabled, the sick, and even vagabonds, so that welfare dependency could be reduced to make way for more self-reliant productive workfare. Consequently, the participation rate of the urban labor force rose to 41.5 percent in 1957, a proportion higher than other countries at similar levels of development.

As the urban labor force leaped from 8 million in 1949 to 15.8 million in 1952, the Chinese socialist regime was alarmed by the growing labor force and it promptly made a realistic turn. A committee was formed in 1953 to halt over-recruitment, and it proposed "employment recruitment and allocation shall be abided by the interest of production, and unsuitable people shall not be recruited to factories and enterprises, while suitable employment shall be given priority."[6] The crisis of mal-recruitment blunted the idealistic attempt of providing universal and nonselective employment for the labor force.

Idealism was further blunted by financial considerations and economic reality. In the second Five Years Plan in 1956, it was estimated by premier Zhou Enlai that, even after all the necessary arrangements, the industrial capacity of urban China was unable to absorb the new recruits, and there were 2 million excessive from-school-to-work students waiting for employment. Although a full employment policy was paramount in the socialist quest, the socialist regime had to provide jobs outside the urban sector to control the oversized urban labor force. Zhou ordered the 75,000 rural production teams to each absorb 5 workers, thereby offering more than 3 million jobs to the young entrants.[7] Although full employment policy was still upheld, there were slight deviations from the original intentions of using rapid urban industrial growth as the source of employment.

The two realistic measures were merely slight deviations from the original policy intention, and they were still acceptable to the idealists. However, the third realistic turn—reintroduction of the pre-1949 contractual employment system—was considered offensive to the idea of full employment. In 1956, a study delegation was sent to the USSR to study its labor contract system, and it proposed that there were to be two layers in the urban labor force, with the core layer filled with permanent jobs and the outer layer temporary and contract jobs. The core was composed of technicians and managerial staff, while the outer layer consisted mostly of manual labor. Furthermore, enterprises were allowed to dismiss workers, while workers were free to choose jobs. The existing workforce was to be employed in permanent posts, while new recruits were to be employed in contract posts. The proposal was an innovative attempt to create flexibility in the job structure, yet it contradicted the core value of the socialist ideal, and such "realistic" measures led to furious reactions questioning the commitments of the regime in employment protection. Facing such reactions, the Chinese regime made a tactful turn and delayed the implementation of such policy measures through experimentation, and only two experimental projects in the provinces of Hebei and Sichuan were carried out.[8] Had the proposal been effectively carried out during that time, the iron rice bowl would have been dismantled at the early period of the regime.

It could be observed that, in the early periods of the regime, the interplay between idealism and realism could be described as "discreet idealism," that is, the implementation of socialist ideals with sensitivity to social complexity. The regime felt that it had the obligations, and also the capacity, to provide employment protection to its labor force. It was optimistic about the planned economy; thus the rational comprehensive model of policy making was used to carry out its employment policy. However, it was also responsive to the limitations imposed by industrialization and economic backwardness, and policy deviations were made to prevent the ironing of the iron rice bowl. The socialist regime was not, as we believed, a rigid structure that adhered strongly to the socialist quest and neglected social and economic costs involved in the full employment policy. The proposal of the reintroduction of labor contracts was ideological suicidal, yet the socialist regime was willing to file such a proposal to test social reactions. The socialist regime was not a uniformed regime without variations, deviations, and even contradictory policy alternatives.

The Clash Between Idealism and Realism in the Revolutionary Period, 1958–1978

The interplay of idealism and realism is an interesting phenomenon. Idealism is concerned with open expressions about visions, collective moral commitment, and popular appeal to the quest for a good society. It depends on the articulation of hopes and aspirations to transcend the limitations of reality. However, realism is characteristically inarticulate, unwilling to translate itself into formulae or maxims, loath to state its purpose or declare its views.[9] Realism is a reaction to unrealistic demands, yet it cannot become a systematic political doctrine since it is reactive rather than proactive. Without an articulated value discourse, it is subject to challenges raised by the idealists, and it is only under such challenges that realists become self-conscious of their strength in the policy making process. When idealism is raised to the extreme, realism can also be consolidated into a self-conscious counter-ideology to mend the wounds of overexpectations and disillusionment.

The Great Leap Forward, launched by Mao, was an extreme idealism attempting to test the limits of reality by using political mobilization and collectivization to achieve rapid industrialization. As a result, a primitive full employment policy was enforced through the formation of rural and urban communes, inviting the whole workforce, rural and urban, to participate in the national industrialization program. However, such idealism led to avalanche damages on the rural economy, and workers voted with their feet to seek employment protection in the urban economy. In 1958, in less than three months, there was an increase of 3 million workers flowing from the rural areas to the urban areas looking for jobs and economic security in the cities. Crises in the urban economy and the rural economy called for a halt of idealism, and Mao rapidly faded into the backstage of the political arena. The "all should work" full employment policy was under harsh scrutiny.

To remedy the crisis, the realists, represented by premier Zhou Enlai and Financial Secretary Chen Yun, began to impose strict control on entry into the urban labor market.[10] Rigid plans were exercised to control labor mobility, and approval from central authorities was needed even for the transfer of one single worker; furthermore, there were also strict control over undisciplined workers, enterprises, and local authorities. However, these measures were mild and ineffective and an additional 25 million unemployed workers entered the urban labor market from 1958 to 1960, virtually doubling the total workforce in a short period of time. The urban economy was seriously affected, and living standards of the urban workers dropped at least 30 percent.[11]

Full employment and employment protection policies were discarded. In reassessing the industrial capacity of the economy, the realists decided to limit the supply of jobs in the urban area, and emergency measures were used to send labor to the rural area. Millions of workers were sent to the rural area and were given a small piece of land to till. As a compensation measure preventing economic hardship and political unrest, asset distribution was carried out and basic tools for subsistence production were provided to alleviate the problems of livelihood maintenance. Under such strict enforcement, the total urban workforce was reduced by 8.72 million in 1961, and an additional figure of 10 million in 1962. Nearly 20 million jobs were reduced in three years' time, and full employment policy ceased to exist. In 1958, the urban labor force constituted 16.6 percent of the total labor force in China; and in 1965, it was reduced to 6.4 percent.

Further, entry into the labor force was also tightened. In 1962, the Ministry of Education announced that there was to be a close down of 400 out of the 845 tertiary colleges and universities, and 120,000 students were deprived of access to tertiary education. Furthermore, there was also a cutback of 1,459 out of 2,724 vocational training bodies, and 320,000 students were again not able to obtain training for better jobs.[12] In 1964, all the 320,000 students were sent to the rural areas to work. The "rustication policy" of sending young people to the rural area was thus made, and from the mid-1960s to the mid-1970s, nearly all graduates from secondary education, about 17 million of them, were sent to the countryside.[13]

Other than controlling labor entry, exit policies were also needed, and the realists determined to use contractual policies to keep the size of the labor force under control. The regime began to speed up the use of contract jobs, temporary jobs, and rotation jobs for such a purpose. At first, the regime was still uncertain about the ideological implications of this policy measure, so it was stipulated that it was to be carried out in a modest manner.[14] Yet, in the later period, it was reported in 1965 that about thirty occupations joined the experiment, including mining, forestry, chemical industry, postal services, textile, commercial, construction, water work and electricity, geological investigation, transportation and railway etc. There were about 2,500 experimental units, and about 580,000 contract jobs were created.

The previous conciliatory "discreet idealism" was replaced by an interaction of extreme idealism and realism from 1958 to 1966. Hopes and aspirations in the previous stage were substituted by the urge for patience, perseverance, and tolerance to the hardships of life.[15] Visions for development were refocused to the raising of individual strength, and the socialist values of social solidarity were supplemented by the call for self-reliance and frugality.[16] In historical retrospect, it should be noted that though the realists were in control over the economy, they did not raise their realism to a counteractive ideology against idealism. They still accepted the overall direction of socialism, though disagreeing on the speed and intensity of development. To them, the damage control measures of individual effort and self-reliance, wage rewards and economic incentives, and extensive deployment of the urban labor force were only transitory deviations from the socialist quest. Such docile hesitation of the realists, however, provided ample space for the idealists to maneuver. To the idealists, the measures implied a return to an oppressive regime that was not concerned with the livelihood of the people.

During the Cultural Revolution, idealism was pushed to another extreme as the revolutionaries began to unify a pluralistic society under one ideal, and ideological deviations and contradictions in public and social policies were not welcomed. The major political battlefield on employment policy was on the labor contract, and they condemned contract jobs as oppressive tools that were anti-socialist and anti-labor. To the revolutionaries, the most important policy tool to prevent unemployment was the state's willpower to industrialize, and they defended employment security as the socialist core value, demanding the abolition of contract jobs, temporary and part-time jobs.[17] The realists, though failing in the ideological argument, insisted on the importance of contractual policy, and did not yield to such demands. It was stipulated that all part-time work, contract work, rotation work, contract-out work systems were to be kept as they were.[18]

As the Cultural Revolution continued, the revolutionaries successfully dismantled the state apparatus. The administration and normal operations were seriously disrupted, and legislative control was virtually paralyzed and dysfunctional. Individual enterprises, yielding to political pressures, began to convert temporary posts, contract posts, and part-time posts to full-time permanent jobs. Although the regime continued to demand for the reinstallation of contract jobs in the employment structure, the instructions were deliberately ignored. At the end of the Cultural Revolution, in 1976, almost all of the 6.5 million temporary workers, contract workers and apprenticeship were firmly converted to permanent posts under the anarchical political condition.[19] Before 1971, the proportion of temporary workers, in the labor force was maintained at 12–14 percent. At the end of the Cultural Revolution in 1976, it dropped to less than 6 percent. Other than the battlefield on contract employment, the revolutionaries also demanded the state to strengthen its paces of rapid industrialization, thus insisting that the state should have a stronger role in employment recruitment. From 1970 to 1971, the original plan of the increase of urban labor force was 3.06 million, yet it turned out to be 9.83 million, which was three times more than expected. From 1972 to 1974, another 12 million rural workers were recruited to serve the urban economy.

The Cultural Revolution (1966 to 1976) was another clash between idealism and realism, and it resulted in another damaging consequence to the employment conditions and structure in China. Unfettered recruitment and entrenched employment protection led to the consolidation of the iron rice bowl, and the demand for full employment was a heavy burden to the socialist regime. The underdeveloped urban economy was not able to accommodate the huge demand for jobs, and idealism had to be curbed. The realists also realized that they should not continue to be conciliatory and perform the role of damage-controller. They had to open themselves to new ideas in employment policies and go beyond the traditional socialist idea of full employment.

ECONOMIC REFORM: HOPES AND FRUSTRATIONS IN THE LABOR MARKET, 1978–1997

Extreme idealism in the Cultural Revolution created an aftermath of cautious realism, as was clearly noted by Deng's famous slogans like "practice as the only criterion of validating truth," "it does not matter whether it is black cat or white cat, so long as it catches the mice," and "grope with the stones while crossing the river." Realism and pragmatism were raised to an ideological height against empty slogans and orthodox socialism. Since the Cultural Revolution had led an expansionary labor force with inflexible employment structure, the realists recognized that certain market mechanisms had to be established so as to control market entry and facilitate exit. Yet they also knew that market uncertainty and insecurity were in serious contradiction to the socialist ideal; it was not realistic to use drastic measures to open up the labor market. Such dilemma led to the slow but gradual launching of the labor market so as to create least resistance and defenses. It was cautioned that the iron rice bowl was not to be smashed, but melted down in a gradual manner.[20]

Cautious realism was shown in the three stages of market reform. In the first stage between 1978 and 1986, the regime was still cautious about the possible damaging effects of the market, and the "smaller plans, plus supplementary market" idea was proposed. The role of the state to maintain employment protection was emphasized. In 1984, the labor ideology of decommodification was still upheld, as it was stated in an important document: "in the socialist conditions of our country, labor power is not a commodity, so as state enterprises in land, mines, banks and railways."[21] The iron rice bowl was still under protection. The second stage was initiated in 1987, as the regime decided to push for further market reform under the name of "primary stage of socialism," and reforms in state enterprises were made to reduce dependency between the enterprise and the state, and also workers and their enterprises. The Bankruptcy Ordinance was passed in 1988, and the 1992 Enterprise Ordinance gave more power in employment decisions as well as dismissal decisions. The third stage was announced in the 14th Party Congress in 1992, coining a new term "socialist market economy" as the state rolled back its functions from the planned economy to directive planning. Enterprises were given full autonomy in employment recruitment, allocation and dismissal, and workers had to face challenges of employment insecurity and uncertainty under a competitive market economy.

Cautious realism was also shown by the use of two major employment strategies—the introduction of positive hopes as well as punitive measures on the misfits. The first strategy involved the opening up of employment opportunities in non-state sectors, and it was treated with high priority and was carried out without strong resistance. The second one was characterized by imposing disciplinary and punitive actions on workers through the making of contract posts or dismissing redundant workers from unwanted posts, and its implementation was filled with caution so as to minimize political and social grievances.

Making Markets Work: Creating Opportunities and Hopes in Employment

In the economic reform, the socialist regime tried to go beyond traditional socialist conceptions on employment and opened up every possible avenue for the provision of jobs. The state sector was still maintained, yet other sectors—the collectively owned sector and the individual sectors—were also used to take up the mission of job creation. Job opportunities were opened in non-state sectors to absorb the growing employment demand, and more autonomous enterprises were formed relatively independently of the state.[22] Consequently, a "three-tier integration" employment policy was endorsed in 1981.

The first tier was the regular employment in the state-owned sector. In the process of economic reform, the state sector still remained as an important part of the economy, and it continued to serve as a stabilizing factor against the vagaries of the labor market. Employment in this sector continued to expand, and from 1978 to 1997, the number of workers increased from 74.5 million to 110.44 million, and it still constituted 64.9 percent of total urban employment. In order to control unfettered recruitment, an open and performance-based recruitment system was set up, giving the enterprises more power in the recruitment exercise. Dismissal of workers was treated with extreme care, and conducted in a gradual and discreet way to minimize possible damages, both to the enterprises and the workers concerned. Dismissal was merely confined to undisciplined workers and enterprises had few powers of dismissal due to economic reasons. It was only from the mid-1990s onwards, when the regime decided to further embark on the road of market socialism, that more bold attempts were made to press for market considerations in dismissal affairs. The problems of labor hoarding and overmanning, though recognized as a heavy burden on the state owned enterprises (SOEs), were still treated with caution, and rapid slimming and reengineering was not considered politically appropriate and economically feasible until 1997.

The second tier, the collectively owned sector, was the major system for employment at the early stage of economic reform. The term "collectively owned sector," however, was an ill-defined category embracing virtually all types of enterprises relevant to the socialist ideal yet outside the planned economy. Before the economic reform, it existed in the form of contracting-out units owned by local authorities, workers cooperatives, small street-level service units, and jointly-owned small-scale economic units.[23] The sector existed at the outer margin of the state sector, and enterprises had to meet the production quota assigned by the state, though they were allowed to retain a certain proportion of profits on their own. The provision of employment in this sector did not violate orthodox socialist dogmas, as it only acted as a supplement to the state sector.

In the early stages of the economic reform, the state encouraged large SOEs to hive off some of their production and service activities to smaller and semi-autonomous, labor-intensive, collectively owned enterprises (COEs). Crèches, restaurants, hairdressing, bathrooms and many other services were hived off to the street level, away from the state enterprises, and workers were to be organized into independent and self-sufficient economic units and operated according to commercial purposes. The regime was responsible to provide the logistics of loans, tax allowances, land, urban facilities, resources, and cheaper raw materials. Thus, this tier operated as a kind of subsidized employment sector under the patronage of the state sector with greater flexibility in labor recruitment and allocation, wage levels, and commodity pricing. The role of the state was to guide this sector to build up the labor intensive tertiary industries, create channels of mobility, as well as the national allocation of industrial manpower. Without ideological and political resistance, the growth of employment in the sector was substantial, with the climax reaching about one quarter of the total urban labor force in the mid-1980s. The initial employment takeoff was successful; within six years from 1978 to 1984, the labor force increased from 20.4 million to 32 million. Though employment in the sector was oversatiated from the mid-1980s onward, it still served as an effective avenue of job creation to protect workers from unemployment. Employment in this sector generated opportunities and hopes in the process of change, and it escaped ideological challenges from traditional socialists. Within the sector, enterprises were still considered as public functionaries, and workers were not considered a commodity under an exploitative labor market. It served as a buffer for the regime to balance socialist responsibility with a changing employment structure susceptible to the fluctuations of the market.

Another tier, the individual sector, however, was subject to ideological challenges, and the regime took great pains to revitalize employment in this sector. The sector consisted of the self-employed working in small business, and workers in the service sector like doctors, nurses, and private tutors with higher personal qualifications and capabilities in making a living. In this sector, employees could be recruited and dismissed freely by the employers.[24] Before the economic reform, the individual sector was considered the seedbed of capitalism because employers worked for their own profits rather than the public interest. The regime, recognizing the ideological contradiction, tried to justify its existence by defining the self-employed and shop owners as members of the working class. Further, it accepted that the employment relationship involved only "a little bit of exploitation," and it was still acceptable.[25] Since the individual sector was a complete deviation from the traditional decommodification principle, the socialist regime was embarrassed in facing the ideological taboo. Therefore in some instructions and legislation, the point of "non-exploitative individual economy" was stressed so that the capitalist element in this economic sector was restricted, at least in ideological terms.[26]

Employment in this sector continued to grow as regional authorities were to arrange or provide shops and places as well as raw materials for individual enterprises, and the commodity prices in this sector were also under control of the state. In the first six years of the reform (1978–1984), employment in the sector was still bound by the ideological straitjackets of socialism. Yet, with the relaxation of price control in 1984, employment in the sector grew rapidly. Before 1985, it constituted less than 1 percent of the total urban labor force. By 1985, employment in this sector reached 4 million, which was 3.5 percent of the urban labor force. By 1995, it had expanded enormously and employed more than 20 million workers, constituting 12 percent of the total urban labor force. This tier of employment—small, flexible, and with high turnover rate—became the hopes and aspirations for job opportunities for the poorly educated and low skilled labor.

Other than these three sectors, the regime also opened up the private sector and invited foreign investment. In the early stages of the economic reform, the opening of these sectors was confined to certain cities for easy control.[27] In the later stages, restrictions were gradually relaxed. The provision of employment in the private sector witnessed a quantum leap, with 0.37 million workers in 1984 and 8.9 million in 1995. A most remarkable increase occurred in 1992–1993 in which the total number of workers in this sector virtually doubled after the push for more marketization in 1992 by Deng (see table 10.1).

Cautious realism in employment policy was still under ideological questioning. In the early stages of the economic reform, social debates on ownership of production were launched, and there were queries on the possible capitalist development of the non-state sectors. Traditional socialists were worried about the problems of exploitation in the employment relationship, especially over the problems of lower-income groups in the contracting-out projects. The 1989 Tiananmen Incident further provided fuel for the idealists to questions of "bourgeoisie liberation" on policies of privatization, marketization, and the shareholder economy. People began to question the significance of the economic reform, whether it would bring in social harmony or social conflicts, and whether capitalism was revived under the growing social inequality. The realists were unable to answer these questions, and they tactfully evaded such arguments and took on a pragmatic and problem-solving approach on unemployment rather than analyzing the socioeconomic context.[28]

Table 10.1. Urban Employment Conditions of China in Terms of Ownership Structure

Year	Total Labor Force	Urban Labor Force	State Sector	Collective Sector	Other Sectors e.g. Joint Business, Foreign Investment	Private Sector	Individual Sector
1978	401,520	95,140	74,510	20,480	—	—	150
1980	423,610	105,250	80,190	24,250	—	—	810
1981	437,250	110,530	83,720	25,680	—	—	1,130
1982	452,950	114,280	86,300	26,510	—	—	1,470
1983	464,360	117,460	87,710	27,440	—	—	2,310
1984	481,970	122,290	86,370	32,160	—	—	3,390
1985	498,730	128,080	89,900	33,240	—	—	4,500
1986	512,820	132,930	93,330	34,210	560	—	4,830
1987	527,830	137,830	96,540	34,880	720	—	5,690
1988	543,340	142,670	99,840	35,270	970	—	6,590
1989	553,290	143,900	101,080	35,020	1,320	—	6,480
1990	646,800	166,160	103,460	35,490	1,640	570	6,140
1991	655,900	169,770	106,640	36,280	2,160	680	6,920
1992	663,800	172,410	10,8890	36,210	1,970	980	7,400
1993	672,400	175,890	10,9200	33,930	5,360	1,860	9,300
1994	680,900	184,130	11,2140	32,850	7,590	3,320	12,250
1995	689,100	190,930	11,2610	31,470	9,700	4,850	15,600
1996	688,500	198,150	112,440	30,160	9,610	6,200	17,090
1997	696,000	202,070	110,440	28,830	11,100	7,500	19,190

Source: Statistical Survey of China, various years. Since 1990, the categorized employed population was calculated under the estimates of the National Census, and the sum of parts do not equal to the total number.

The gradual opening up of the labor market under the "ideology" of cautious realism was successful in creating opportunities and hopes for workers to leave their iron rice bowls. From 1978 to 1997, the labor market was not fully opened up to the test of market competition. The state was still the major sector in the provision of jobs, though its relative size was reduced from 78 percent to 55 percent. Employment in the collective sector was also relatively secure, since the chief buyer of their services was from the state sector which was less susceptible to market fluctuations. The gradual opening up of the labor market in individual and private sectors was fruitful, though the regime was confronted with ideological challenges and criticisms from adherents to socialist ideals. With all these measures, the labor market was formed incrementally on a piecemeal basis. A mixture of direct state intervention, state-sponsored, and private labor market coexisted in China, and as new employment opportunities were expanding, the strong demand for employment protection was gradually weakened. In the arena of promoting employment opportunities, the socialist idealism gradually faded into the background, and realism reigned.

Pains in the Labor Market: Insecurity and Frustrations of Unemployment

Though hopes in the labor market were created by the provision of opportunities, frustrations and insecurity were also awakened by the punitive measures of the market. As early as in the early 1980s, the regime had already decided to create exit for the labor force through two major attempts: 1) a time-limited labor contract system to ensure labor mobility; 2) dismissal policies to ensure labor discipline and allow room for reengineering. These attempts created a sense of insecurity and frustration among workers in the state sector.

From 1983 onward, the regime began to launch a nationwide project to stimulate experimentation in labor contracts.[29] Yet it was met with suspicions, especially from old workers who claimed that they "risked their lives to struggle for a new society, yet they were now living in fear and anxiety over job and wage insecurity."[30] Attempting to minimize resistance, the regime confined labor contracts to new recruits, and the permanent posts were still protected under the tenure system.[31] With such conciliation, labor contracts were being accepted. By the end of 1985, 29 provinces and cities had joined the experimentation, and the number of contract workers virtually tripled from 760,000 in 1984 to 2.04 million in 1985. In 1990, there were 12.23 million contract-posts and they constituted 12 percent of total employment. By 1995, the employment contract system was extended to 55 percent of the urban labor force. In the period of 1986 to 1995, about 80 percent of new jobs were employed as contract posts.

Though the regime made promises on employment security, the contract system led to widespread fear and anxiety. In a survey of the reform period in 1987, the Hong Kong periodical *Ming Pao Monthly* noted that worries about employment security was ranked higher than increased individual income. Workers questioned the existence of the "golden rice bowls" held by their bosses while their humble rice bowls were smashed, and social discussions began to focus on the deficiencies of the management system in state owned enterprises. Although there were further legislative measures attempting to protect workers from employment insecurity, reality offered another picture. Howard noted that, ". . . there were complaints of discriminatory pay despite being allocated the most difficult, dirty, and dangerous jobs. There were accounts of breaches of contract and of workers being denied promotions after serving apprenticeships with minimal remuneration. There were reports of workers being excluded from membership in the trade union and the workers' congress in many units. There were reports of workers being fired when they became ill or injured."[32]

In the socialist ideal, work was sacrosanct and rewarding, therefore dismissal was only confined to undisciplined workers while the economic and financial aspects of dismissal were not to be taken in account. In 1983, as the regime began to upgrade productivity and efficiency of SOEs, dismissal policies became a policy agenda for consideration.[33] However, the regime realized that dismissal policies had to be carried out in a very cautious manner. Workers resisted dismissal because dismissal power was susceptible to misuse, and malpractice in management was often cited as the reason for defense. Without independent tribunals, workers were subject to the personal biases of employers. As a result, in 1983, enterprises were only granted with power to dismiss disobedient workers rather than workers who were unable to meet performance standards.[34] In 1987, it was even announced that "(the intention of dismissal policy) is to raise the level of understanding, unify thoughts, enhance the idea of labor discipline, and to raise the self consciousness of implementing the regulation. The enterprises shall uphold education as the major principle in dealing with disobedient workers, and they shall treat punishment as only supplementary measures ... enterprises dismissing workers have to be alert to the consequences and prevent the rise of conflicts."[35] Tighter measures were introduced in 1994 on dismissal policies by instructing enterprises to take cautious action against drastic reorganization, and also protect vulnerable workers due to enterprise reshuffle.[36] It was only when enterprises were granted with more autonomy at the later stage of economic reform that the power of dismissal was relaxed, and employers were free to dismiss workers due to economic reasons.

There were negative as well as punitive aspects of the free labor market— contracts and dismissal—and they created frustrations, anxieties, and anger. The realists were alarmed at the possible massive damages inflicted on the labor force, and they tried to exert damage control in the process of the economic reform. Cautious realism was exercised, as was clearly evident in the employment policies for *xiagang* (off-post) workers who were laid off due to the reengineering of the SOEs in the 1990s. In the reengineering process of the SOEs, the state tried to maintain the social responsibilities of the State enterprises by passing a regulation to accommodate the employment demands of redundant workers. The regulation stipulated that, though the enterprises were granted with full autonomy in recruitment and dismissal, they had to retain the *xiagang* (off-post) workers with nominal positions and provide special allowances and housing to alleviate them from poverty.[37] The *xiagang* workers had to report regularly to the enterprises that were obliged to arrange employment opportunities for them. The nominal employment relationship existed in different forms. Some enterprises provided "productive accommodation" by strengthening their own productivity to absorb labor redundancy. Some provided "expansive accommodation" in creating new service industries to provide employment opportunities, and a lot of enterprises provided "livelihood accommodation" with extended long leave, providing early pension, an internal waiting list of re-employment, housing, and retraining provisions to retain the massive exit. The state-owned enterprises, in their downsizing process, were urged to provide safety nets as well as new employment opportunities for their redundant workers. Some sort of rice bowl had to be offered to the unemployed to prevent the rise of massive poverty as well as social tensions that might lead to political unrest. Another damage control measure was the use of labor supply policy to match labor to new jobs. At the end of 1993, a "Re-employment Engineering Project" was initiated to provide more re-entry opportunities for urban "off-posted" workers. The focus was to support the long-term unemployed to re-enter the labor force through unemployment registration, employment guidance, job matching, information dissemination, re-employment training as well as workfare programs.[38]

The pains inflicted by the labor market were not simply confined to the problem of employment insecurity and unemployment. The labor market was filled with misuse of power and unethical behavior of the employers, and the state had to act in the interest of the working class through legal litigation. In 1994, the overall delay of wage payment amounted to 335.698 million yuans, and the livelihood of 500,000 workers were affected. Over 9,000 enterprises demanded overtime work without pay, and over 5,000 enterprises refused to contribute to social security payments. Furthermore, employers demanded workers to work while postponing the signing of contracts, and the state had to re-enforce the signing of approximately 2.7 million contracts. The negative aspects of the labor market were revealed, and they raised the awareness of the working class to struggle for the defense of their basic rights, and court cases of labor negotiation increased from 8,200 in 1992 to 12,400 in 1993, a 51.6 percent increase in one year.[39]

This chapter attempts to analyze the interplay between idealism and realism in the formation and development of employment policies in China between 1949 and 1997. The findings revealed that the socialist regime was not blinded to economic reality, and it tried to make conciliations between ideals and reality. Cautious idealism was exercised in the early 1950s, as the socialist regime was already making policy deviations to control the expansionary labor force, and also making labor contract policies to slim the iron of the iron rice bowls. However, such cautions and deviations were uncompromising to the idealists, and it led to extreme idealism in the Great Leap Forward and Cultural Revolution, further aggravating the problem of an expanded labor force. Such extreme idealism gradually uplifted the Chinese realism into an ideological height surpassing the attractiveness of the socialist ideals in the economic reform era. However, in the economic reform, a cautious realistic policy tendency was also made. The road to the labor market was not conducted under drastic shock therapies, but was carefully experimented and negotiated by the parties concerned. The findings of this chapter also help us to understand that, behind the façade of ideological stereotype, idealism and realism coexisted even in an authoritative regime. Ideological analysis is necessary, yet insufficient to understand the complexity of the formation and development of social policies. In the undulating terrain of the socioeconomic context, the regime sometimes has to make a detour to avoid blockages and impasse, and consequently, deviate from or even contradict its original intentions. The historical evidence of the employment policies in China also revealed the need for a conciliatory system for the idealists and realists to work together to maintain its original policy direction with flexibility and pragmatism. Unfettered ideological extremity led to overwhelming rather than conciliatory tendencies, and the historical lessons that can be learned from the case of China is the creation of a political system that can accommodate the coexistence of idealism and realism in the policy making process, so that they can supplement one another in advancing, and also in making correct, policy changes.

NOTES

1. Lindblom, C. (1977). *Politics and Markets: The World's Political Economic Systems*. New York: Basic Books, pp. 314.

2. George, Vic and Paul Wilding. (1993). *Welfare and Ideology*. New York: Harvester Wheatsheaf, pp.1–15.

3. Rawski, T. G. (1979). *Economic Growth and Employment in China*. London: Oxford University Press.

4. Administration Council, "Measures concerning the Treatment of Unemployment." June 17, 1950.

5. Administration Council, "Decision on the Problems of Unemployment" June 25, 1950.

6. Yuan L. K. (1992). *Economic History of Chinese Labor*. Beijing: Beijing Academy of Economic Publisher, pp.100–12.

7. Chinese Communist Party Central Committee (CCPCC), "Dispatch of Comrade Zhou Enlai's Report on Wages and Labor Insurance and Welfare at the 3rd Plenum in the 8th Party Congress." October 24, 1957.

8. Hsia J. J. et al., (1991). *Information Handbook of Labor Administration and Management*. Beijing: China Labor Publisher, pp.47–59.

9. Scruton, Roger. (2001). *The Meaning of Conservatism*. Hampshire: Palgrave.

10. Chinese Communist Party Central Committee (CCPCC), "Opinion Concerning Problems of Job Allocation and Additional Workers." Discussion paper tabled in the Chengdu Meeting of the Chinese Communist Party Central Committee, March 1958.

11. Wu, S. G. and Liu, S. N. (1985). *Brief Economic History of Socialist China, 1949–1983*. Harbin: Heilongjiang Peoples' Publisher, pp.224–39.

12. Economic and Finance Group (CCPCC). (1999). *50 Years' of Development of the Chinese Economy*. Peoples' Press and CCPCC Party Academy Press, pp.175.

13. CCPCC Approved of the State Council's "Report of the Working Meeting concerning the Nation-wide Rustication of Educated Youth," August, 1973.

14. "Temporary Regulations Concerning the Use of Temporary Workers in SOEs." State Council, October, 1962.

15. "CCPCC's Approval of the Report from the All-China Federation of Trade Unions Concerning the Reorganization and Consolidation of Urban Peoples' Communes," September 18, 1960.

16. "CCPCC's Approval of the ACFTU's Report Concerning the Demands of Frugality on Union Expenditure and Labor Insurance Funds in 1961," January 25, 1961.

17. People's Daily, "Hold High the Proletarian Revolutionary Banner of Criticism and Repudiation," April 8, 1967, quoted from K. H. Fan (1968) *The Chinese Cultural Revolution: Selected Documents*. New York: Grove Press.

18. CCPCC, State Council, Central Military Committee, and Central Cultural Revolution Committee, "Notice Concerning Further Attack on Anti-revolutionary Economism and Speculative Activities," January, 1968.

19. Chiu, T. H. (1991). *Economic History of the Peoples' Republic of China: 1967–1984*. Henan: Henan Peoples' Publisher, pp. 267.

20. Fung, Ho Lup. (2001). "The Making and Melting of the 'Iron Rice Bowl' in China, 1949 to 1995." In *Social Policy & Administration*, 35(3), July 2001, pp. 258–73.

21. CCPCC, "Decisions of the Central Committee on Reform of the Economic Structure," 1984.

22. CCPCC and the State Council, "Certain Decisions on Opening Up Channels, Activate the Economy and Solve the Employment Problems in the Urban and Village Areas," 1981.

23. Odgaard, O. (1992). "Entrepreneurs and Elite Formation in Rural China." *Australian Journal of Chinese Affairs*, 28: pp. 89–108.

24. State Council, "Regulations Concerning Certain Policies on Non-agricultural Individual Economy in the Urban Areas." July 7, 1981.

25. Propaganda Department and six ministries of the CCPCC, "Report Seeking Approval on the Problems of Demarcating Labor from Their Original Commercial Statuses." October 29, 1979.

26. State Council, "Regulations Concerning Certain Policies on Non-agricultural Individual Economy in the Urban Areas." July 7, 1981.

27. State Council, "Regulations on Labor Management in Joint Venture Enterprises with Overseas Investment." July 26, 1980.

28. Ma, L. Z. and Lin, J. J. (1998). *Confrontation: Description of the Three Thought Liberations of Contemporary China*. Beijing: Today's China Press, pp. 227–323.

29. Department of Labor and Personnel, "Notice Concerning the Active Experimentation of Labor Contract System." February 22, 1983.

30. Howard, Pat. (1991). "Rice Bowls and Job Security." *Australian Journal of Chinese Affairs*, 25 (January).

31. Chau, K. C. (1983). "The Inevitable Implementation of the Contract System." *China Labor*, 1.

32. From note 31, Howard, (1991).

33. State Council, "Temporal Ordinance of State-Owned Enterprises." April 1, 1983.

34. Department of Labor and Manpower, "Notice on the Active Experimentation of Labor Contract System." February, 1983.

35. Department of Labor and Personnel, National Economic Committee, Department of Public Order, and the All-China Federation of Labor Union, "Notice Concerning the Problems of Implementing the 'Temporary Regulations on Dismissal of Un-discipline Workers in the SOEs.'" March 3, 1987.

36. Department of Labor, "Regulations on Reduction of Manpower Due to Economic Reasons for Enterprises." November 14, 1994.

37. State Council, "Regulations to Accommodate Redundancy in SOEs." April 26, 1993.

38. State Council, "Supplementary Notice on Problems of Re-employment in Certain Urban SOEs Experimentation." April, 1997.

39. Fung, T. X. (1995). "Conditions and Trends of Workers in China." In Jian Liu et al., (ed.) *The Social Bluebook: Analysis and Forecasts of Social Trends from 1994–1995*. Beijing: China Social Science Press.

11

The Coming Housing Crisis of China

Ya Peng Zhu and James Lee

In the midst of rapid economic transformation of modern China, one of the most pertinent social science questions to ask is what is the impact of economic change on the existing social welfare system. Are Chinese people living better or worse off than before economic reform, particularly in the cities? In the pre-reform period before 1979, China was considered largely a welfare society among low-income countries operating a large scale social program in both the urban and rural areas (Guan, 2000; Liu and Zhang, 1989). In the urban area, the state provided a wide range of social welfare through the work unit system whereby highly subsidized public rental housing was essential to most citizens' livelihood (Gu, 2001a, 2001b; Lu and Perry, 1997). Since the economic reform, the government has striven to build up an economic state where growth has clearly taken priority over social equity (Chen, 2003). This led to fundamental changes in China's welfare philosophy as well as its social arrangements. One example is "societalization" of the welfare system charaterized by the downloading of state welfare responsibility to various stakeholders: namely, the local governments, the work units, and the families (Gu, 2001a, 2001b; Guan, 2000). Social welfare policy takes on board a neoliberal philosohphy aiming at the reduction of state provisions through market substitute, as well as the increase of individual responsibility on one's own welfare (Guan, 2000). In broad terms, economic reform has succeeded in severing workers' former lifetime welfare ties with their work units. The abolition of the old welfare system—one in which the state provides everything—has come to mean a restructuring of domestic consumptions and expenditures. While many middle-income households try desperately to raise their income in order to fit in the new consumption culture, many low-income households are suffering from a much worse off living standard as they found themselves "unfit" within the new system and the new culture. What is troubling, however, is that concomitant with an ever-widening income gap, many low-income urban dwellers now find housing way beyond their affordability (Fang, Zhang, and Fan, 2002). Once the pivot of socialist solidarity, the housing sector has come to be used by both the state and the private sector as the most powerful "growth machine" of urban development. This chapter starts with an overview of the housing problems embedded in the pre-reform housing regime, followed by an exploration of efforts to restructure the housing and a brief assessment on the housing reform prior to 1998. It then focuses on the ongoing housing monetarization reform and its resulting problems: such as urban segregation, urban poverty, widening housing inequality, and enormous affordability problems. The chapter concludes by suggesting that while housing reform in China has improved housing conditions for some, it has at the same time augmented housing inequality and fallen prey to many of the familiar loopholes of modern neoliberal urbanism.

THE HOUSING SYSTEM BEFORE 1979

The housing system in China before the 1979 Housing Reform was characterized by the monopoly of the state and the dominance of public ownership. Since the founding of People's Republic of China (PRC), the Chinese government had taken the sole responsibility of housing its urban citizens either through local governments or work units, which obtained funding from the state budget, built, distributed, and managed public housing. From 1949 to 1978, more than 90 percent of housing investment was funded by the state (Yu, Zhao, and Cao, 1998: 297). While providing decent housing to most urban citizens, the state housing system was plagued with numerous shortcomings. First, there was perennial shortage of housing investment. During the pre-reform period, when the state attached more importance to basic construction, housing, which was considered more as consumption, always received insufficient investment from the state. From 1949 to 1978, the total investment in housing was only 34.3 billion yuan, an average of 1.27 billion per year, which was only 5.8 percent of the basic construction investment and 1.5 percent of GDP in the corresponding period (Yu et al., 1998: 297). Moreover, there was very little housing investment from individuals before the reform. Second, insufficient investment led to housing shortage, which had reached 1 billion m^2 in major cities by the end of 1978. Living space per capita decreased from 4.5 m^2 in 1950 to 3.6 m^2 in 1978 (Yu et al., 1998: 297). Third, housing was administratively distributed through the work units. Public dwellings were allocated to employees mainly through work units and the arrangements were susceptible to abuse and corruptions (Tong and Hays, 1996; Wang and Murie, 1999). Tenure rights were assured unless the tenants chose to move for better flats or changed their jobs. This workplace-based housing system led to widespread inequalities in housing distribution both within and between work units. Fourth, in line with the socialist ideology, housing was viewed as a right and social welfare for the employees. Urban residents paid a minimal rent, which could hardly cover regular maintenance cost (Chen, 1998). For instance, the rent was only 0.13 yuan per m^2, which covered only half of the maintenance cost of such dwellings at the end of 1970s (Yu et al., 1998: 88). As a result, there were, and still are, prevalent many poorly managed and dilapidated public rental housing around Chinese cities.

In short, though the state housing system provided cheap dwellings to urban residents, it also brought about problems such as severe housing shortage, inequality, dilapidation, corruption, and limited choices (Tang, 1996; Wang and Murie, 1999; Zhu, 2000). Moreover, it hindered the mobility of labor force in that employees provided with state housing would tend to stay put unless it was a change for the better (Yu et al., 1998: 304). With the rapid urbanization and population growth, the state housing system went into a deep crisis at the end of 1970s. On the one hand, the government found it very difficult to bear the financial burden of immense housing investment. On the other hand, urban residents were suffering from poor living conditions. The welfare housing distribution system appeared to be unsustainable.

HOUSING REFORM IN 1979–1999: AN INITIAL ASSESSMENT

In response to the above problems, the Chinese government began to restructure its housing system at the end of the 1970s. The major strategies were to commercialize and privatize public housing, establishing a compulsory housing saving scheme (HPF-housing provident fund scheme), an affordable housing scheme for medium-low income households (*Anju* Project) and eventually establish a real estate market. The ultimate aim is to set up a market-oriented housing system and to shift the housing responsibility from the state to a division among the stakeholders: the central government, local governments, work units, and households.

After two decades of efforts since 1979, housing reform did attain considerable achievements. First, the living conditions of urban residents have been ameliorated in terms of both quantity and quality. Living space per capita rose from 3.8 m^2 in 1978 to 8.8 m^2 in 1997 (see Table 11.1). Second, a new housing finance institution—housing provident fund scheme—was established and had accumulated about 80 billion yuan by 1997, playing an increasingly important role in financing both construction and the purchase of housing by citizens (Li, 1997). Third, rent reform made certain progresses. Monthly rent in public housing increased to 0.8–1.8 yuan per m^2 with an average of 1.29 yuan in the thirty-five major cities. Rents in the public sector nearly reached cost level in some cities such as Shenzhen and Daqing, hence providing much needed funding for good maintenance (Li, 1997). Fourth, nearly half of the salable public housing stock had been sold to sitting tenants, shooting up the home ownership to the all time high of 70 percent. Meanwhile housing reform provides much needed impetus to the growing economy. Meanwhile, the *Anju* Project also developed smoothly. In the three years from 1995 to 1997, about 71 million m^2 of low-cost housing was constructed, providing housing for 650,000 low-income households (Li, 1997).

Despite the achievements, problems in the housing field remained. Rent reform proceeded sluggishly in many cities. The average rent in the thirty-five major cities remained low, at only 12 percent of market rent. Rent constituted only 4 percent of household income of a couple in 1997, far below the target proportion of 15 percent by the year 2000 (Li, 1997). Housing Provident Fund Scheme suffered from poor management, limited coverage and low contribution. Most important, welfare housing continued to be distributed through work units, thus engendering a rather unjust dual-track housing market: a public housing market at heavily discounted prices and an open market at competitive prices, targeting different sectors of the population with the same eligibility for housing. In addition, the persistence of the welfare housing system discouraged housing purchase in the private housing market, since there was still a chance of getting cheaper welfare housing from work units, few people would be willing to pay a higher price for a house in the open market. For example, the average rent in the public housing sector in 1997 was 1.2 yuan per month, while the average private house price was 1,700 yuan per m^2, a ratio of 1400 (*Tianjin Youth Daily*, March 12, 1998: 3). This explains why people were unwilling to buy and there was high vacancy of private housing in the market. Furthermore, wage reform proceeded slowly. Housing expenditure remained an insignificant component in the employees' salary and thus do not provide an impetus for people to enter the housing market.

The entry of work units in the housing market generated an exaggerated and misleading housing demand which gave rise to a distorted housing market. Corporate consumption of housing from work units drove up housing prices phenomenally. In 2005, the affordability ratio of house price to household income in Shanghai was approximately ten.[1] Most urban residents could not afford such houses. The higher the house prices, the less chances for or-

Table 11.1. Housing Completed in Urban and Rural Areas and Housing Situations of Urban Residents (1978–1999)

Year	Housing completed in cities and towns in the year (100 million m²)	Housing built by individuals in cities and towns (100 million m²)	Housing completed in rural area (100 million m²)	Per capita usable space in cities and towns (m²)	Per capita living space in cities and towns (m²)
1978	0.38	—	1.00	—	3.60
1980	0.92	—	5.00	—	3.90
1985	1.88	0.63	7.22	—	5.20
1986	1.93	0.72	9.84	8.80	6.00
1987	1.93	0.83	8.84	9.00	6.10
1988	2.03	0.94	8.45	9.30	6.30
1989	1.56	0.78	6.76	9.70	6.60
1990	1.73	0.65	6.91	9.90	6.70
1991	1.93	0.68	7.54	10.30	6.90
1992	2.40	0.86	6.19	10.70	7.10
1993	3.07	0.98	4.81	11.00	7.50
1994	3.57	1.23	6.18	11.40	7.80
1995	3.75	1.33	6.99	11.80	8.10
1996	3.94	1.46	8.28	12.30	8.50
1997	4.05	1.53	8.06	13.00	8.80
1998	4.77	1.82	7.99	13.60	9.30
1999	5.99	2.08	8.34	14.20	9.80

Source: China Statistical Yearbook 2000.

Note: Figures of usable area and living area per capita in cities and towns are from the Ministry of Construction.

dinary wage earners to own and the more they would have to depend on the old work units housing. The role of work units in housing provision was thus strengthened rather than weakened during housing reform.

Ironically, housing reform in some ways also increases housing inequalities. This was largely due to the fact that different categories of employees had unequal access to housing subsidy. A big housing gap exists between employees in the public sector and the private sector. According to a survey conducted in 1995, it was found that the average monthly rent for public housing was 0.71 yuan per m², 10 yuan lower than the average market rent, signifying that those occupying public housing received an annual subsidy of 120 yuan per m² (Wang, 2001). The amount of housing subsidy an employee could get depended on the space of the flat he occupied. The bigger the flat, the more subsidy one gets. With the floor space of 10.80 m² per capita, the annual subsidy to those living in public flats was around 1,296 yuan (Wang, 2001). Employees in the private sector or those in the public sector but not living in public dwellings were deprived of this heavy subsidy. In sum, despite the general improvement of living conditions of a good proportion of urban population in China, housing inequality has become so salient that many scholars have warned that eventually this might give rise to social unrest (Guo, 2000a, 2000b, 2000c; Lai, 1998; Lee, 2000).

LATEST HOUSING REFORM:
HMP AND THE RE-COMMODIFICATION OF HOUSING

In the late 1990s, the Chinese government was facing many thorny policy problems. As a result of the Asian Financial Crisis, China's exports decreased considerably and millions of workers were laid off. To boost domestic demand and to upkeep economic growth, which were crucial for easing the unemployment problem and maintaining social stability, the Chinese government, led by the reformist premier Zhu Rongji, initiated housing monetarization reform in July 1998.

Housing monetarization policy (HMP) refers to the provision of cash subsidies to urban residents in lieu of housing distribution in kind. This is what Davis termed the recommodification of public housing (Davis, 2003). With the cash subsidy or allowance, urban residents are expected to satisfy their housing needs in the open market, assisted by other financial means, including family savings, housing provident fund (HPF) and bank loans. After the implementation of the new initiative, work units are prohibited from building or buying housing for employees and the housing funds previously established to buy or build welfare housing were to be transformed into cash subsidies. Meanwhile, rent reform continues while the sales of public flats are given priority. Moreover, a multi-layer housing provision system will be established, aiming at providing housing to people according to their financial situations. High salary earners are expected to buy private housing; medium- to low-income households are given opportunity to buy low-cost housing; and low-rent social housing is tailored for the lowest income group. It is clear that the Chinese government strives to build up a housing ladder which is commonly found in Western industrial societies. The launching of the housing monetarization reform in 1998 is considered a watershed and a big thrust in China's long housing reform process. This new wave of reform embodies two major goals: to restructure the housing system and to boost the economy. It is expected that the reform will promote the development of the real estate industy, which is considered an engine for economic growth. It is also envisaged that the reform will encourage individuals to enter the housing market and channel individual consumption to property purchase, through which vacant flats in the market will be "digested." What's more, it is hoped that the reform will cure the problem of unfairness in housing distribution (Xie, 1998).

Following directives from the central government, local governments began to terminate housing distribution in the second half of 1998 and to provide cash housing subsidy to eligible employees in the public sector. The tenet of the housing monetarization reform is to change the mode of housing provision from in-kind to in-cash. Two contending approaches were proposed according to coverage, sources of funding and means of distribution: one is the holistic approach proposed by the State Committee of Economic System Reform and the other an incremental approach proposed by the Ministry of Construction (Ji, Du, and Ru, 2001). Both approaches agreed that old employees should be subsidized because their low wages covered little or insufficient components for housing expenditure. However, they took different views in the ways and strategies of providing housing subsidy. Generally speaking, the holistic approach suggested that the whole housing system be restructured including the public housing stock, all state-run work units and their employees. Its rationale is that public employees should be subsidized by the revaluated notional asset of the housing stock which was seen as a component of their historical salaries appropriated by the state in the old wage system. With the provision of the housing subsidy, the purchasing power of employees would be raised and that both the rent and the price for public housing could be elevated to the market level. This approach is featured by recapitalizing and redistributing the entire housing stock and embracing all state-owned work units and public employees into the new housing system.

Advocates of the incremental approach, on the contrary, stressed the difficulties in putting the holistic reform proposals into practice, such as insufficient resources, implementation problems in state enterprises, continuity of the housing policy and possible resentment from beneficiaries of the old housing system (Cao, 1998). They therefore proposed to adopt a more conservative and practical approach by applying different housing systems to different social groups: to continue the preferential sales of public housing, hence not touching the housing benefits of "old" employees who had bought public flats, and to apply the new housing system only to "new" employees who would be provided with a housing allowance to purchase houses or rent in the market. This approach has the advantages such as low cost, minimal social shock and rapid results (see table 11.2).

Debates over these two approaches lasted from 1995 to 1997 with the discussion ended by adopting the incremental approach as a guiding principle (Ji et al., 2001). Apparently, the need for maintaining social stability weighs over and above the concern for social justice, and that prioriy has been given to protect the interest of the existing beneficiaries, that is—people who are already

Table 11.2. Comparison of the Two Housing Reform Approaches

	The Incremental Reform Approach	The Holistic Reform Approach
Coverage of housing	New housing, new system; old housing, old policy	Entire housing stock, including new housing
Coverage of employees	New employees and employees without public housing or with less space than entitled	All employees
Coverage of work unit types	Mainly in the government sectors and public institutions funded by the state budget, enterprises are granted autonomy to work out their housing plans	All kinds of work units, including government sectors, public institutions, state-owned enterprises, and collective-owned enterprises
Philosophy	"Forward looking" and giving priority to efficiency	Redistributing housing benefits and taking social justice into account
Potential resistance from community	Less resistance	More resistance
Resource needed	Needing more state subsidy	Needing much less state subsidy
Property rights structure	Leading to a complicated and ambiguous property rights regime; unfavorable for the setting up of the second-hand housing market	Clear property rights, facilitates the setting up of the second-hand housing market
The role of work units in housing provision	More involvement	Less involvement
Marketization level	Low	High

enjoying good housing benefits as a result of unfair allocation. However, the holistic approach was not totally discarded. It was adopted in Guizhou province with a rather effective outcome despite some implementation problems, largely due to a unique combination of leadership solidarity in the provincial administration and a citizenry who longed for change (Zhu and Guo, 2004; Zhu and Lee, 2004).

THE CONSEQUENCES OF HOUSING REFORM

On the whole, housing monetarization reform proceeds sluggishly since its implementation in July 1998. The termination date of the in-kind housing distribution was postponed several times. It was not until the end of 2002 that all the thirty-one provinces, autonomous regions and municipalities directly managed by the central government, had made out implementation programs of the housing monetarization reform. All thirty-five major cities except Urumqi had worked out specific reform plans; twenty-nine of them had begun to carry out the reform in their jurisdictions. However, by the end of 2002, six major cities (Beijing, Hohhort, Yingchuan, Xining, Urumqi, and Nanchang) had not really carried out the reform. Two-hundred and four prefecture-level cities (93 percent of the total eligible cities to launch the housing subsidy scheme) had made out implementation plans but only 155 cities began to carry them out (Bureau of Real Estate of Ministry of Construction, 2003). As for counties (including county-level cities), more than half (1,031) of the total 2,053 counties should have implemented the reform but only 506 counties had came out with a plan, accounting for 49 percent of the total eligible counties and 25 percent of the total number of counties (Bureau of Real Estate of Ministry of Construction, 2003). Among them only 155 counties had begun to carry out the reform plan. Generally, the implementation went smoother, faster and better in the wealthier Eastern part than the poorer central and western part of the country (Bureau of Real Estate of Ministry of Construction, 2003).

Housing Inequality and Urban Poverty

Housing reform is one of the last acts of the socialist redistributive regime (Wang, 2003). Contrary to the expectation of policy makers, housing monetarization has actually created new inequalities, led to new housing segregation among different social groups, which stems from the institutional arrangement of applying different housing allocation criteria to different social groups. Above all, a huge gap exists between employees in the public and private sector because only public employees can get housing subsidies for purchasing or renting public flats. Employees in the private sector are excluded, and they have to purchase or rent private housing in the market paying not only high prices for "commodity housing" but also more taxes and property insurance cost (Song, George and Cao, 1999).

Distinct housing segregation is also found among employees in the public sector. Homebuyers of public housing are the biggest beneficiaries in the housing reform. They are the ones who had first benefited from low-rent housing before the housing reform. Then as a result of the policy on preferential home sale to sitting tenants, they are able to capitalize tremendously on the resale of their once state-provided home (Zhang, 1998). Housing inequality embedded in the old housing system and housing privatization reform have thus been transformed into immense household wealth disparity especially after the restrictions on resale of purchased public housing were lifted in 2003 (Qi, 2003).

As for current tenants in the public housing sector, they still maintain a privileged position in the housing system despite the gradual "residualization" of the public rental sector. As rent increase is moderate, renters are benefiting from a considerable amount of housing subsidy compared to those in the private sector. For instance, at the end of 2000, the average monthly rent of public housing in the thirty-five major cities was only 1.5 yuan per m^2 (Xie, 2000). Until now this low rent situation has not changed much. It was estimated that the average imputed rent of flats was 5,940 *yuan* per year with the average imputed rent of 139 yuan per m^2. The average annual hidden housing subsidy for public rental housing (the difference between market rent and actual rent paid by the tenant) was 5,873 yuan per household.[2] This reveals that housing reform has not essentially changed the welfare nature of the public housing sector.

With respect to workers in the medium-sized state-owned or collectively-owned enterprises, many of them do not have access to public flats. As such, they neither receive the hidden subsidy from renting a public flat nor benefit from the discounted sale of public flats under the new system (Guo, 2000c).

Distinct housing gaps can also be found between different work units. Work units with more power and housing stock (mainly government departments, financial firms, etc) have more resources to provide housing subsidy to eligible employees; whereas workers in SOEs and COEs have less chances to get their share.[3] This segregation stems not only from the old housing system under which housing investments were unevenly distributed, but also current reform strategies such as allowing work units to keep and dispose of the revenue of sale of public housing.

During the housing reform era, housing inequities continue to get aggravated because work units continue to play an active role in housing provision and housing allocation basing on the hierarchical rank system. Khan et al. (1999) documented a sharp increase in income inequality between 1988 and 1995 as a result of the housing reform. Unequal distribution of housing subsidies are reflected in that some 41 percent of subsidies in 1995 were received by households in the top 10 percent of income earners. Housing policy accounted for 37 percent of overall inequality in the distribution of income in urban areas in 1995. The widening housing inequality is confirmed by a recent survey on 150,000 urban households conducted by the Urban Economic and Social Survey Team of the National Bureau of Statistics. According to the survey, 55.7 percent of the sample households purchased flats with an average house price of 260,000 yuan. Among them, 86.9 percent bought public

Table 11.3. Home Purchase at Different Periods in Cities

Year	% of Households Purchased Property
Before 1990	4.2
1991–1994	19.0
1994–1996	32.5
1997–1999	44.3

Source: Adapted from (Li, 2000)

flats and 9.7 percent purchased private housing. The average prices for public flats and private housing were respectively 19,000 yuan and 79,000 yuan. The majority of homeowners bought their properties after 1991 (see table 11.3), nearly half of the households bought flats in the three years from 1997 to 1999 when the central government was determined to monetarize housing distribution. Clearly, buyers of public flats gain most from the preferential sale of public dwellings given the significant price gap between the public housing sector and the open market.

Housing inequality was evident as shown in table 11.4. Employees in work units with more power of resource redistribution (governmental departments and financial sectors) have bigger flats than enterprise workers. Government officials and cadres are better housed than professionals and employees in general (see table 11.5). Higher rank officials have better living conditions than their lower rank counterparts.

The Affordability Problem

Affordability is another major issue confronting the housing reform. The problem is found in both the public rental sector and the private housing market. In the public rental sector, there are still a large number of renters who cannot afford the rising rent no matter how moderate the increase is. With

Table 11.4. Housing Situation by Occupation

Occupation	Usable Space Per Household (m^2)
Government department and institutions	65
Financial sector	64
Mining sector	44
Industrial sector	45

Source: (Li, 2000)

Table 11.5. Housing Situation by Rank

Rank	Usable Space Per Household (m²)
Department	79
Director	66
Head	62
Senior engineer	59
Engineer	57
Staff	56

Source: (Li, 2000)

rapid privatization reform in the 1990s, most salable public housing has been sold at low prices.[4] Many people, particularly the cadres and implementers of housing reform, have acquired public dwellings and benefited from the sales. Opposition against rent reform has thus been reduced. Meanwhile, the public rental sector has been residualized because the better flats have been sold, leaving only the lower quality dwellings which are mostly occupied by low-income households. They are the ones who are less able to buy or afford rent increase. According to a survey about residents' response to proposed rent increase in public housing in Beijing (from 1.30 to 3.05 yuan per m²), 76.6 percent of respondents were indifferent mainly because they had already bought public housing. The remaining 23.4 percent expressed strong reaction either because their work units were not able to distribute subsidy or because they could not afford to buy a public flat and had to rent private apartments. Rent increase in the private rental market will occur as a result of the interlocking effect between the private and the public housing market. Albeit it is only a small rent adjustment, far away from the market rent of 35 yuan per m², its influence on the tenants in the private sector could be enormous (Dong and Wang, 2000).

Table 11.6. Ratio of House Price to Household Income in Major Cities in 2004

City	Private House Price (Yuan/m²)	Per Capita Household Disposable Income in 2004 (Yuan)	Ratio of House Price of a Flat of 70 m² to Household Income
Shanghai	8627	16683	18.09
Hangzhou	7210	14565	17.32
Beijing	6232	15638	13.94
Shenzhen	6037	27596	7.65
Guangzhou	5660	16884	11.73

Source: Calculated by the author based on figures from http://news.soufun.com/2005-03-24/389844.htm, retrieved last on July 24, 2005.

Housing monetarization reform has somehow successfully driven urban citizens to enter the private housing market. Clearly a real estate boom has been emerging. However, most urban citizens have already found it difficult to afford the high prices of private housing. As indicated in table 11.6, in major cities such as Beijing, Shanghai and Guangzhou, it will take 11 to 18 years for a double-income household to buy a medium-sized flat of 70 m². The ratio of house price to household income is much higher than the international standard of 3–6 found in most Western industrial economies. The housing affordability problem is getting so serious that the government is worried that this will become a source of social unrest (*shi chang bao*, July, 22 2005, p. 7). A series of measures have therefore been taken to cool down the overheated real estate market and depress the housing price, although their effectiveness remains to be seen.

HOUSING SHORTAGE AND HOUSING POLICIES TO REMEDY

It appears that the Chinese government has noticed the various problems associated with the housing reform and the importance of keeping up social justice in housing allocation. In an effort to assist the medium-low income households to obtain affordable housing, the *Anju* (Comfortable Housing) Project was launched in 1995. It planned to provide 25 million m² of affordable housing for the medium- and low-income households in cities each year from 1995 to 2000. The *Anju* Project was merged with the Economic and Appropriate Housing (*jing ji shi yong fang*) scheme in 1998. The new program is also targeted at helping medium-low income households to be homeowners but with an extended scope of coverage. This scheme has become a major part of housing policy and plays a critical role in stabilizing house price in the market. However, both the *Anju* Project and Economic and Appropriate Housing scheme encounter problems, such as insufficient resources, limited provision and coverage, developers' abuse of the policy, no strict means-test for purchases better off benefiting from schemes, and so on (Cui and Peng, 2003). The provision of Economic and Appropriate Housing has decreased considerably in recent years while the private housing price is still roaring. For instance, in 2004, the average private house price was 2714 yuan per m², increased by 14.4 percent compared to 2003, while the percentage of the affordable housing of the total housing investment has decreased from 6.13 percent to 4.61 percent. In the 5 years from 2000 to 2004, the percentage of investment of the Economic and Appropriate Housing of the total housing investment had reduced by 6 percent (Economic Daily, April 7 2005).

The *lian zu fang* (social rental housing) scheme has been positioned as an important component in the multi-layer housing provision system since the launching of housing monetarization reform in 1998 and targeted mainly at the urban poor. It is quite different from the welfare public rental housing in that it is targeted at providing decent dwellings to the low-income households in cities who cannot afford to buy either commercial houses at market price or Economic and Appropriate Housing (*jing ji shi yong fang*) at government-designated prices. Rent for *lian zu fang* is administratively set much lower than the public rental housing. It is a residual system for officially recognized urban poor (Wang, 2000, 2004). *Lian zu fang* includes public dwellings controlled by either local housing bureaus or work units that are vacated or newly built by local governments. The scheme as a housing security system for low-income urban residents is still in a stage of experimentation and it is suffering from unstable resources, support, and limited coverage. By the end of 2002, only half of the thirty-five major cities had worked out the relevant regulations and plans for the implementation of the scheme (Office of State Committee of Planning and Ministry of Construction, April 10 2001). The beneficiaries are confined to households in "double difficuties," that is households with extreme financial difficulty and housing problem. As a result, its role in solving housing problems of the urban poor is very limited. The slow development of social rental housing hinders the establishment of a housing ladder system (Office of State Committee of Planning and Ministry of Construction, April 10, 2001).

Due to poor implementation and limited housing provision, it is quite obvious that the Economic and Appropriate Housing scheme and the *lian zu fang* scheme are far from being able to eradicate the housing problems of the medium-income households and the urban poor. There are also a great number of households belonging to the "sandwich" class. They are not "poor" enough to be eligible to the social rental housing but not "rich" enough to buy a flat of Economic and Appropriate Housing even though they were given the opportunity. For instance, in Guangzhou there are about 50,000 households which have been registered and officially recognized as the lowest income households, accounting for 0.03 percent of the population in the city whereas the number belonging to the sandwich class is estimated to be no less than 20,000 households (Zhu and Chen, 2005). It is estimated that 20 percent of China's urban population needs assistance from the government (Zhu and Chen, 2005).

The housing problem is further aggravated by the insufficient institutional arrangement for the non-officially recognized urban poor, for example the peasant workers or the "floating population" (Lau, 1997; Wang, 2000, 2004). According to the 2000 census, there were about 121 million of "floating population," the majority of whom are peasant workers (around

99 million).[5] Despite their contribution to China's economy, they are not officially recognized as the urban poor, and henceforth not entitled to any kind of social welfare (Wang, 2000, 2004). Their housing problems have not been on the government agenda at all. Clearly, China could not achieve a sustainable development and build up a "harmonious society" without addressing this issue since the exclusion of such a large group of people amounts to a potiential political risk.

CONCLUSION: THE COMING HOUSING CRISIS AND ITS POSSIBLE SOLUTION

The Chinese housing system has undergone significant changes. Housing reforms of more than two decades have successfully redivided housing responsibilities among the three main stakeholders: the government, work units, and urban citizens. With the dismantling of the in-kind housing provision system, urban residents are forced to enter the private housing market. Housing reform provides more choices and improves living conditions for a majority of urban citizens but there remains a great number of people who cannot afford a minimally decent place to live since house prices skyrocketed in the private sector.

Housing reform and the HMP in particular have redistributed the housing benefits among different social groups and shifted the distributive structure. Under the given political setting, compromise to former beneficiaries under the old housing system and poor implementation of the reform largely accounted for the widening housing inequality and segregation among urban inhabitants. The gap in housing benefits among urban citizens has gradually been transformed into great disparity in household wealth. Those who have access to public flats gain a lot more benefits from the new reform initiative while those who don't have suffered. In fact, workers who have no access to public flats are doubly deprived by both the socialist institutions and the market mechanism, along with housing marketization and privatization. Social welfare that was available or provided to them under the socialist regime has shrunk as a result of housing and economic reforms. With the gradual disappearance of the so-called "mini welfare state," many poor workers are suffering from the market transition as the social welfare system that comes together with Western market economies is not in place in China now. In fact, the reform has brought about greater housing disparity among different social groups. Housing inequality has been in a way *fossilized* and further aggravated along with the housing monetarizaton reform and especially after the opening up of the secondary housing market for the privatized public flats.

While acknowledging the government's efforts in resolving the medium- to low-income households' housing problems, our examination reveals that economic efficiency has clearly been given priority over social justice during the decision-making process. The current public housing system consisting of the Economic and Appropriate Housing scheme and the *lian zu fang* scheme has proved to be insufficient due to poor implementation and limited coverage. A great number of citizens, including the peasant workers, cannot solve their housing problems through the existing institutions, and they are also excluded from the private housing market because of their limited financial capability. It appears a housing crisis is imminent if the state continues to allow the spirit of neoliberalism to plague its public housing policy unabatedly.

Wider implications for social policy in transitional China can also be inferred from the current housing reform practice. Many urban citizens in China, especially those workers in poorly-performed SOEs are exploited and deprived of by both pre-reform insitutitions and marketization and privitization reforms. Under the rhetorics of the reform, they are losing their social status and social welfare quietly. The exclusion of a great number of citizens including the "floating population" means a big risk that may upset social stability and political legitimacy in the long run. The Chinese government is still facing a big challenge of struggling among eonomic efficiency, social stability, and social equality in making and implementing social policy. In order to achieve sustainable development and build up a "harmonious society" the social welfare system has to be revamped to supplement the highly predictable failure of a market-based economy.

NOTES

1. Use the ratio between the average annual household income of 40000 yuan in 2005 (double earners) and the average commercial house price of a 80m² condominium flat in Shanghai of 5000 yuan per m², to estimate the affordability ratio (400,000/40,000). home.wangjianshuo.com/ and english.people.com.cn/200306/06/eng20030606_117783.shtml.

2. According to a survey conducted by China Academy of Social Science in 1999, unpublished.

3. According to fieldwork conducted in Guiyang in 2002, 2003, and 2004 in Beijing.

4. By March 2000, about 75 percent of salable public housing in the major thirty-five cities had been sold off with an average price ranging from 680 yuan to 1700 yuan per m². (Xie, 2000).

5. Please visit www.cin.gov.cn/cxjs/ml/050307.doc. Last retrieved on May 29, 2005.

REFERENCES

Bureau of Real Estate of Ministry of Construction. (2003). *zhu fang huo bi hua ji lian zu zhu fang zhi dou (Housing Monetarization and the Social Rental Housing System)* (Internal document). Beijing: Bureau of Real Estate of Ministry of Construction.

Cao, J. (1998). *lun zhu fang huo bi hua* ("On Monetary Distribution of Housing"). *Housing and Real Estate*, 44(11), pp. 4–9.

Chen, A. (1998). "China's Urban Housing Market Development: Problems and Prospects." *Journal of Contemporary China*, 7(17), pp. 43–60.

Chen, S. (2003). "The Context of Social Policy Reform in China: Theoretical, Comparative, and Historical Perspective." In C. Jones Finer (ed.) *Social Policy Reform in China: Views from Home and Abroad* (pp. 23–36). Aldershot, Hants; Burlington, VT: Ashgate.

Cui, Y., and Peng, L. (2003). jing ji shi yong fang shui jing ji? shui shi yong? ("Who benefit from the j*ing ji shi yong fang* scheme?"). *jing ji ri bao (Economic Daily)*, p. 5.

Davis, D. (2003). "From Welfare Benefit to Capitalized Asset: The Re-commodification of Residential Space in Urban China." In R. Forrest and J. Lee (eds.) *Housing and Social Change: East-West Perspectives*. London; New York: Routledge, pp. 183–198.

Dong, M., and Wang, X. (2000). Gongfang zujin jiang dafu tisheng, wei mai gongfang zhe fanying qianglie ("Rent in Public House to be Raised Considerably, Those Not Buying Public Housing Much Concerned"). *Jingji Cankao Bao*, Feb. 29, p. 7.

Fang, C., Zhang, X., and Fan, S. (2002). "Emergence of Urban Poverty and Inequality in China: Evidence from Household Survey." *China Economic Review*, 13(4), pp. 430–43.

Gu, E. X. (2001a). "Beyond the Property Rights Approach: Welfare Policy and the Reform of State-owned Enterprises in China." *Development and Change*, 32, pp. 129–50.

——— . (2001b). "Dismantling the Chinese Mini-welfare State? Marketization and the Politics of Institutional Transformation, 1979–1999." *Communist and Post-Communist Studies*, 34(1), pp. 91–111.

Guan, X. (2000). "China's Social Policy: Reform and Development in the Context of Marketization and Globalization." *Social Policy and Administration*, 34(1), pp. 115–30.

Guo, S. (2000a). Guan yu zhu fang huo bi hua de ji ge wen ti ("On Some Issues About Housing Monetarization Reform"). In S. Guo (ed.) *Guizhou zhu fang fen pei huo bi hua gai ge (Housing Reform of Monetarisation Distribution in Guizhou)*. Beijing: Zhongguo caizheng jingji chubanshe (China Finance and Economy Press), pp. 3–17.

——— . (2000b). *guan yu zhu fang zhi du gai ge de jian yi* ("Suggestions on Housing Reform). In S. Guo (ed.) *Guizhou zhu fang fen pei huo bi hua gai ge (Housing Reform of Monetarisation Distribution in Guizhou)*. Beijing: *Zhongguo caizheng jingji chubanshe* (China Finance and Economy Press), pp. 458–65.

———. (2000c). *Guizhou zhu fang fen pei huo bi hua gai ge (Housing Monetarisation Reform in Guizhou)*. Beijing: Zhong guo cai zheng jing ji chu ban she (China Finance and Economy Press).

Ji, W., Du, D., and Ru, Q. (2001). *wu jing lian zong lun jing ji re dian (2)* ("Wu Jinglian Talk About Hot Economic Issues"). *zhong guo jing ji shi bao (China Economic Times)*, March 10.

Khan, A. R., Griffin, K., and Riskin, C. (1999). "Income Distribution in Urban China During the Period of Economic Reform and Globalization." *American Economic Review*, 89, pp. 296–300.

Lai, O.-K. (1998). "Governance and the Housing Question in a Transitional Economy: The Political Economy of Housing Policy in China Reconsidered." *Habitat International*, 22(3), pp. 231–43.

Lau, K.-Y. (1997). *Housing Inequality and Segregation: An Exploratory Study on Housing Privatization in Shenzhen City of the People's Republic of China* (Working Paper). Hong Kong: Department of Public and Social Administration, City University of Hong Kong.

Lee, J. (2000). "From Welfare Housing to Home Ownership: The Dilemma of China's Housing Reform." *Housing Studies*, 15(1), pp. 61–76.

Li, T. (1997). zai fang gai gong zuo zuo tan hui shang de jiang hua (Speech on the discussion meeting of housing reform). *Housing and Real Estate, 1998*, pp. 9–15.

Li, X. (2000). *fang gai qu de shi zhi xin jing zhan zheng ce you dai jin yi bu wan shan* ("Housing Reform Makes Substantial Development While the Policy Needs Further Improvement"). *jing ji jie (Economic Circle)*(5), pp. 25–8.

Liu, R., and Zhang, X. (1989). "China: A Welfare State with Low Income." *China: Development and Reform*, 6.

Lu, X., and Perry, E. J. (1997). *Danwei: The Changing Chinese Workplace in Historical and Comparative Perspective*. Armonk: M. E. Sharpe.

Office of State Committee of Planning, and Ministry of Construction. (2001). *guan yu 2000 nian quan guo gong you zhu fang zu jin gai ge qing kuai de tong bao (Announcement of national rent reform in the public housing sector in 2000) (Document of Office of State Committee of Planning No. 370 [April 10, 2001])*. Retrieved August 10, 2004, from www.cin.gov.cn/fdc/file/2001062601.htm.

Qi, Z. (2003). zhong guo guo wu yuan zhong zhi yao qiu gu li ju min huang gou zhu fang ("China's State Council Urged Urban Residents to Change their Flats"). *jing ji ri bao*, September 1.

Song, S., George S.-F, C., and Cao, R. (1999). "Real Estate Tax in Urban China." *Contemporary Economic Policy*, 17(4), pp. 540–51.

Tong, Z. Y., and Hays, R. A. (1996). "The Transformation of the Urban Housing System in China." *Urban Affairs Review*, 31(5), pp. 625–58.

Wang, F. (2003). "Housing Improvement and Distribution in Urban China: Initial Evidence from China's 2000 Census." *The China Journal*, 3(2), pp. 121–43.

Wang, L. (2001). "Urban Housing Welfare and Income Distribution." In C. Riskin, R. Zhao and S. Li (eds.) *China's retreat from Equality: Income Distribution and Economic Transition*. New York: M. E. Sharpe, pp. 167–83.

Wang, Y. (2000). "Housing Reform and Its Impacts on the Urban Poor in China." *Housing Studies*, 15(6), pp. 845–64.
Wang, Y. (2004). *Urban Poverty, Housing and Social Change in China*. London: Routledge.
Wang, Y., and Murie, A. (1999). *Housing Policy and Practice in China*. New York: St. Martin's Press.
Xie, J. (1998). *jin yi bu shen hua cheng zhen zhu fang zhi du gai ge cu jin guo min jing ji de zeng zhang* (Further Deepening of Urban Housing Reform and Promoting National Economic Growth). *China Real Estate*, 10(214), pp. 8–12, 21.
Xie, R. (2000). *zhong guo fang gai ge de ru he* ("How Far Has China's Housing Reform Gone?"). *jing ji ri bao (Economic Daily)*, May 22, p. 5.
Yu, S., Zhao, J., and Cao, J. (1998). *fang di chan zhu fang gai ge yun zuo quan shu (Encyclopedia of the Real Estate and Housing Reform)*. Beijing: *zhong guo jian cai chu ban she* (China Construction Material Press).
Zhang, Z. (1998). *jia kuai zhu fang huo bi fen pei ji zhi zhu huan, pei yu zhu fang jian she xin de jing ji zeng zhang dian* ("Speed Up the Transformation of the Mechanism of Monetary Distribution and Build Up a New Economic Growth Pole of Housing Construction"). *China Real Estate*, 209(5), pp. 4–10.
Zhu, H., and Chen, M. (2005). "*Guangzhou lian zu xin zheng: bian 'bu zhuan tou' wei 'bu ren tou'*" ("New Social Rental Housing Policy in Guangzhou: Changing from 'Subsidizing Bricks' to 'Subsidizing Target Groups'"). *"Nang fang zhou mo" (Southern Weekend News)*, April 28, 2005.
Zhu, J. (2000). "The Changing Mode of Housing Provision in Transitional China." *Urban Affairs Review*, 35(4), pp. 502–19.
Zhu, Y., and Guo, W. (2004). "Inter-governmental Relations and Policy Implementation: A Case Study of Guiyang Housing Monetarization Reform." *Hong Kong Journal of Social Sciences*, 28 (Autum/Winter), pp. 35–57.
Zhu, Y., and Lee, J. (2004). "Redistributive Justice and Housing Benefits in China: The Guiyang Model." *Journal of Societal and Social Policy*, 3, pp. 47–62.

12

Concluding Observations

Is There a Crisis of Welfare in East Asia?

Kam-wah Chan

After reviewing existing facets of welfare systems in various East Asian contexts, this chapter intends to pull together the various themes that illuminate the so-called "East Asian welfare model." Our major concern here is not to falsify the existence of such a model, although some chapters in this book might implicate such tendency. Nonetheless, there is a growing literature about the "East Asian welfare model" (Goodman et al., 1998; Ramesh 2000; Holiday and Wilding, 2003; Gough, 2004; Walker and Wong, 2005), notwithstanding the fact that most of these studies largely concentrate on describing the possibility of such a model while lacking critical analyses of the problems of East Asian welfare. Our concern is that in building explanations for this model, or in identifying the trajectory of East Asian welfare development we run the risk of contributing to legitimizing social inequalities and social injustice inherent in this model. Fundamentally, we see the issue of social welfare in East Asia as one which involves both ideological and institutional issues. The economic miracle of East Asia hinges on two major policy directions: 1) on the rolling back of state welfare and 2) on subsuming welfare development under economic policy (Midgley and Tang, 2001). James Lee has already suggested in the beginning chapter why such subordination is essentially problematic. As suggested by Fitzpatrick (2005), this is indeed a form of modern conservatism characterized by the establishment's craving for "ordered freedom" and "individualism." Business and capitalist interests dominate the whole public and social space with views such as "there is no other alternative," "government doesn't work," "trade unions are unnecessary," "regulations are destructive," "the welfare state is pernicious," "no big deal for inequality as long as economy in good health" (Fitzpatrick, 2005: 6).

The "ordered freedom" supported by free market liberals therefore involves a hostility to anything more than the minimal state and to any system of distributive welfare. Our major concern in this book is to point out that a large part of the rhetoric underpinning the "East Asian welfare model" is about legitimizing this form of conservatism. The hegemonic nature of this debate has ascended the superiority of economic policy to such an extent that social policy either must be complementary to economic development or else it is necessarily detrimental and must be stalled at all cost. Social inequality as a consequence of uneven power in the market is seen as what Kristol (1995) and others have argued are a reflection of natural inequalities so that any attempt to interfere with them, for example, through a welfare state, is an unnatural attempt to portray the wealth-creators as villains and the unproductive as victims. This form of productivism, as James Lee argues in chapter 1, has fundamentally skewed the original meaning of what developmentalism has set out to achieve—the integration of the economic and social system in a manner that provides citizens with choices and the greatest degree of equality possible. This is the first of the two crises we have sought to expound in this book—*the ideological crisis*. The second crisis is more concerned with institutional change whether existing sociopolitical environment provides those facilitating factors (or rules) that make welfare institutions responsive to those who really need them and which we will coin *the institutional crisis* here. Neoliberalism and neoconservatism have somehow successfully hijacked the strength of traditional families and community ties and repackaged them as productivism par excellence. But first of all I will explain more on the first crisis.

EAST ASIAN WELFARE MODEL REVISITED

Broadly, there are two dominant explanations of the "successes" of the East Asian welfare model. The first is a cultural explanation that emphasizes the role of "oriental culture" or Confucianism (Jones, 1993) as the major architectural framework of East Asian societies. These societies are portrayed as consisting of coherent families with strong mutual support between family members; a harmonious society built on cooperation between different ethnic groups, race, gender, and class. This effectively maintains positive social cohesion and hence effectively reduces government's role and thus expenditures on social welfare. The second explanation focuses on the overall political economy, which suggests that the "productivist welfare model" in these countries helps to cultivate work ethics, promote workfare, maintain a pool of hard working and flexible labor, uphold laissez-faire capitalism, and construct a highly competitive economy (Holiday, 2000). To a certain extent, these two approaches may help to explain some of the characteristics of welfare systems in the region, especially those high-growth places such as Japan, Hong Kong, Taiwan, Singapore, and South Korea. However, it is problematic to talk of an "East Asian welfare model" for such a diverse area or scale (Goodman et al., 1998). For example, it is doubtful whether huge metropolises such as Singapore, Hong Kong, and Tokyo can be simply regarded as Confucius for the fact that they all have relatively strong family ties. Japan and Singapore are far from a laissez-faire capitalist state, not to mention Mainland China still claims to be socialist. An overarching model for East Asia is likely to be unsuccessful since it is almost impractical to distill a general cultural framework to understand microfamilial or community behaviors pertaining to welfare.

However, while academics are still seeking to find a holistic explanation of East Asian welfare, the main thrust of this book is to show that welfare systems in East Asia are facing crises just as their counterparts in the West, albeit the nature of the crisis may vary across different countries and at different historical conjunctures. Overemphasis on the "success" of the Confucius welfare state or productivist welfare state have unfortunately led to the oversight of social inequalities in these societies as structural unemployment is still a serious problem in many metropolises in the Asian-Pacific region. The most disadvantaged: such as unskilled workers, new immigrants, and ethnic minorities are among the hardest hit. Aging population and age discrimination have been threatening Japan, Taiwan, South Korea, and Hong Kong as Ko, Oh, and Ogawa suggest in chapter 3, while the existing welfare provision for old people is unlikely to provide them the means to maintain a decent life. Many elderly people are being forced to make a living beyond sixty-five.

To many, the productivist strategy seems to work before the Asian Financial Crisis, partly the result of general rapid growth in the region in the last two decades and partly the result of a global shift of capital to the East. As Beng Huat Chua points out in chapter 2, the Singapore government is successful in maintaining a low level of welfare expenditure in the past because of a combination of various social conditions: rapid industrialization, rising economy, and a relatively young population. However, after the Asian Financial Crisis in the late 1990s, most East Asian metropolises are no longer able to enjoy sustained growth. Many of them began to face similar urban problems encountered by people in the West, such as persistent and rising unemployment, aging population, and family breakdowns. Partly due to the rapidly expanding economy before the mid-1990s, the lack of a fully developed democratic political system, and the lack of a forceful democratic movement, women's movement, anti-racist movement, and anti-ageist movement, these problems are largely hidden. To a certain extent, the dramatic economic downturn of Asian countries in 1997 has shattered the dream of this "East Asian miracle" (Campos and Root, 1996). The belief that this "East Asian welfare model" could sustain a competitive and continuously growing economy has come under severe challenge. In many East Asian countries, the declining economy is unable to support even the existing welfare provision, even though this is already considered meager when compared to many welfare states in the West. There is increasing evidence that welfare development in many East Asian countries is facing crises of a sort not entirely different from the West. It is all about unemployment, underemployment, urban poverty, socio-spatial segregation. The economic crisis in Asia in 1997 and its aftermath didn't seem to provide a good lesson for governance. There is increasing emphasis by countries on the enhancement of productivity, promotion of workfare, marketization of social services, promoting individual and family responsibility, and improving competitiveness of the working population.

Concomitant with the emphasis on economic growth is the incorporation of the *New Public Management* (Clarke et al., 2000) ethos with the government machinery in the late 1990s when the concepts of "efficiency," "value for money," and "quality assurance" dominated welfare agenda. To a large extent, the Asian Financial Crisis was triggered by an obsession with an "expansionist" and "productivist" ethos in East Asian countries. Ironically, however, the solution to the economic crisis in many East Asian countries is the further reinforcement of this productivist ethos. In general, the arguments for an East Asian welfare model can be summarized into five major, interrelated theses. First, the promotion of "workfare," work ethnic, and competitiveness of workers in the labor market and hence the reduction of dependency on welfare. Second, supported by the philosophy of New Public Management, managerial "welfare reform" is argued as equivalent or leading to improvement in "efficiency" and "quality" of social services. However, evidence in our respective chapters and elsewhere seriously doubt the validity of such claims. The new welfare regime has in fact undermined the delivery of existing social services. Third, it is argued that the East Asian welfare model hinges on a strong family system in which family members support each other in times of trouble and this then reduces the demand for social welfare. Fourth, while social conflicts such as class, gender, and racial differences are important issues in Western capitalist welfare states these are relatively inconspicuous in East Asian countries. It is argued that social harmony and stability are both virtues aspired by East Asian societies and one of the secrets of its success.

Fifth, the idea that major "success" in East Asia is the result of unfettered emphasis on growth and "productivity," and that is the only way out for sustainable advancement in social welfare. These five elements, to a great degree, succeeded in legitimizing an economic-led welfare policy in many East Asian countries and also justified welfare cutbacks.

Rethinking Workfare and Competitiveness

One of the most important elements of the "East Asian welfare model" is its emphasis on welfare services that promote work ethics. Welfare is seen as something moving away from welfare dependency. This conception of "workfare" becomes popular in policy making with the emergence of Third Way politics in the UK in the mid-1990s (Giddens, 1998). It is argued that neither the traditional Left nor the New Right can solve the social ills of modern society. The Left, with its overemphasis on social welfare and security, has led to inflated welfare expenditures and hence impedes growth. Overprovision of welfare fails to target resources on the most needy, and hence leads to inefficiency and injustice. The New Right, on the other hand, emphasizes welfare cuts and the expansion of private sector, and therefore leads to a deterioration of life qualities of the poor and the needy. The Third Way, as it claims, tries to strike a balance between them. The emphasis is on "positive welfare" where people are encouraged to earn a living through work, rather than through receiving welfare. Examples are the retraining program for the unemployed and young people to enhance their competitiveness, subsidizing job-seeking activities and penalizing those failing to show adequate effort to find jobs. This global trend of "Third Way" politics has affected many Asian countries, of which Taiwan is a typical example. Lin and Chou suggest President Chen Shui-bian of Taiwan has explicitly adopted a "New Middle Way" which is modeled after the British Third Way thinking which places emphasis on investment in education, vocational training, and lifelong education.

It is sometimes ironic that "workfare" is being regarded as a key to the success of East Asian countries. In fact the most competitive East Asian metropolises, like Tokyo and Hong Kong, are notorious for an over-worked culture. As Chan and Leung point out in chapter 9, the over-worked, over-stretching culture in Hong Kong is partly responsible for the adverse impact of SARS. The competitiveness of many East Asian countries is thus for a long time hinged on flexible labor, or more precisely, cheap labor who accepts long working hours and low pay. State welfare provision in many East Asian countries was minimal before the 1990s and could hardly be termed a "workfare model" as compared to many social democratic states in Northern Europe.

This minimal provision was made possible because many East Asian countries are enjoying rapid economic growth through neoliberalization, partly based on export-led industries such as clothing and textile (like Hong Kong), footwear (like Malaysia), and assembly of electrical appliances and computers (like Taiwan and South Korea). In the 1990s, some developed economies such as Hong Kong and Singapore have gradually developed into financial centers of the region. Economic restructuring has led to unemployment problems similar to many post-industrial economies in the West. This process does not simply affect capitalist metropolises such as Tokyo, Singapore, and Hong Kong, but also Mainland China who still claims to be socialist. As spelled out succinctly by Ho Lup Fung in chapter 10, Mainland China is struggling hard to face the unemployment crisis in the past decade. This is further exacerbated by the Asian Financial Crisis in the mid-1990s. "Welfare to work," which emphasizes "self-reliance" and "work ethic," became a popular strategy in East Asia to get out of the crisis. A typical example is Singapore as suggested Beng Huat Chua in chapter 2, where even for highly planned government like Singapore, unemployment was also a major issue after the Asian Financial Crisis. Workfare in this manner is simply a replication of a widely-used welfare retrenchment strategy in the West, and not at all an East Asian policy innovation. The most important question here is not who invented this "welfare to work" approach, but does this strategy help to solve the welfare problems in Asia? Most East Asian countries are facing some degree of economic restructuring as a result of globalization, particularly in terms of labor restructuration. The most vulnerable groups are hence the manual workers. It is difficult for them to take up new skills in the highly competitive, service-based and knowledge-based society. Although some employees may benefit from retraining program, they are usually the more competitive ones. Those less competitive will be marginalized in a labor market that put increasing emphasis on credentials, qualifications, and creativity. A group of middle-class workers with a higher education or higher qualification is appropriating a higher proportion of social resources, while the manual workers are getting paid less and have to endure longer working hours. In chapter 5, Lin and Chou point out that the adoption of the Third Way strategy in Taiwan has led to greater polarization in Taiwan and worsened inequalities, laying the seeds of social discontent, as reflected in the anti-government demonstrations in the latter part of 2006.

Rethinking Efficiency and Quality

For a long time, East Asian states have maintained a low level of social welfare provision made possible by rising income and a dependence on family mutual support. It is only in the 1990s that East Asian countries have begun to improve their social welfare in response to popular demand. South Korea and Taiwan are two examples. They share similarities in reaping the benefits of decades of increasing industrial output and yet at the same time facing the challenges posted by years of organized labor and politics demanding for macro changes in social welfare. After the Asian Financial Crisis, most East Asian states had to face a tightening welfare budget. Contracting out, commodification, privatization, and marketization of social services have become common practices in a bid to tide over the difficult period. In Japan, as expounded by Tang in chapter 4, after the economic recession in the early 1990s, the government also tried to marketize and residualize social housing, which led to deteriorating social issues such as homelessness, lone-parent problem and inadequate housing for the elderly. In chapter 8, Sam Yu again points out that Hong Kong government was trying to fully utilize market principles in social security and health care policy in welfare reform in recent year. This governance strategy has been widely practices throughout East Asia after the Asian Financial Crisis, not to mention the dramatic economic changes in Mainland China. Market principle is introduced into state policy in the hope of improving efficiency and quality of services, which has directly or indirectly worsened the unemployment problem in Mainland China in the past decade. Similarly, the housing reform in Mainland China that relied heavily on using the private housing market has in fact deepened housing inequalities and worsened housing affordability as explained by Zhu and Lee in chapter 11. Sam Yu argues that there is a basic contradiction between social welfare principle and market principle, which cannot be resolved easily in the East Asian welfare model. This marketization strategy inevitably affects the quality and quantity of social services that are needed even more badly during economic recession. To rationalize this cut, many East Asian countries are using excuses such as "streamlining," "efficient" utilization of social resources, services targeting, "choice," and "quality improvement." The "managerialist ethos" coupled with the marketization social services is in fact similar to the retrenchment of welfare state in West. Of course, the scale of retrenchment in Asia may be much less acute than those in some Western welfare states, but the spirit of letting the market reign remains.

It is too simplistic to assume that marketization coupled with managerialism could help to save money and improve quality (Clarke et al., 2000). Although some public expenditure on social services may be saved, this is at the expense of lowering the quality of services. A higher proportion of the expenditure has gone to support managerial staff instead of providing direct services. Social service professionals such as social workers, doctors, and nurses are spending more time on administrative duties rather than providing direct services. Grievances from social services recipients and social services professionals are escalating. As Chan and Leung suggest in chapter 9, the incompetence of the government in handling and managing the SARS crisis in 2003 is the whole problem associated with the inherent problem of "efficiency" and "quality" of the so-called scientific management of health services, which was aggravated by the over-worked nature of Hong Kong people that impairs the population's resilience to infectious diseases.

Rethinking "Family"

"Family support" is often times an overblown concept in the rhetoric of social welfare for East Asia. It is argued that the success of an Asia welfare model is based on close kinship network and strong family mutual support, to the effect that people could solve their problems without much dependence on social welfare provisions. Some scholars even go as far as to name this a "Confucius welfare state" (Jones, 1993). While it is true that kinship ties in some East Asian societies are known to be strong, this is often not the case. There are great variations among different countries at different historical junctures. Family structure and family relationship in East Asia is a changing entity. Half a century ago, most parts of East Asia were largely agrarian societies where extended families and close kinship ties were prevalent. Rapid economic growth and urbanization in the last four decades have come to transform the basic social fabrics as the fundamental unit of East Asian societies—the family—has changed overtime. For example, family breakdowns are common when young people from poor families in the rural areas flock to find jobs in large cities—a social phenomenon better known as the "blind flows" in Mainland China where cities are filled with illegal migrants from rural areas looking for jobs in bustling cities. Many domestic workers from Thailand, Indonesia, and the Philippines broke up with their families for a long period in order to work in Hong Kong, Singapore, and Taiwan. In addition, the changing concept of marriage has also led to rising divorce rate, increasing number of lone parent families, and delaying the age of first marriage. The declining birthrate has led to a higher dependency ratio and the problem of aging society. The breakdown of extended family system has increased the burden of the carers within the family, to the extent that the capability of the family in caring for its dependent members—the elderly, the children, the sick, or the disabled—is diminishing. That is one reason why several authors in this book point to the situation of an aging population in the region. The insensitivity to family and population change, and the lack of adequate social security by many East Asian states has exacerbated urban poverty and inequality. As Raymond Ngan points out in chapter 6, while on one the hand many East Asian governments emphasize the importance of the family rhetorically; on the other, there is perennially inadequate support for the family. Singapore seems to be an exception where the state's housing policy is largely "pro-family." However, it is mainly because housing policy in Singapore serves a significant role in political control, not family support as such (Chua, 1997). The lack of supportive social services seems to assume that the families will take care of themselves autonomously. Moreover, the assumption that family can take good care of their members actually results in underinvestment in developmental services for children and young people, underdevelopment of retirement protection for older people, and underprovision of education, housing, and health services at large. In a nutshell, rapid social changes in East Asian countries have transformed traditional family pattern and relationship, consequently diminishing its capability in taking care of its own members.

Rethinking "Social Harmony"

The notion of a "Confucius welfare state" also implies that oriental societies are essentially harmonious among different sectors of the society. Social harmony is seen as the foundation of prosperity. Conflicts between different classes, gender, age groups, races, and ethnicities are fundamentally undesirable and hence socially divisive. While class, gender, age, and racial inequalities are conspicuous in Western welfare states, these issues seem relatively unimportant or inconspicuous in the East Asian context. This is of course a socially-constructed myth rather than the reality. Social division along class, gender, race, and age lines do exist in East Asia. It is not less, or more serious than the West. Raymond Ngan and others, in chapter 7, points out that age discrimination in the labor market significantly affects the opportunities of older workers in Hong Kong. This seems ironic in a "Confucius" society that claims to respect the elders and cherish social harmony. In chapter 9, in addition, Chan and Leung showed that health risk is not equally distributed among different social groups. It in fact concentrates on the most disadvantaged, such as manual workers, women, and old people. The gap between the rich and the poor is growing, not diminishing, in most East Asian countries. This is much worse than welfare states in Western societies. Patriarchal culture still to a great extent dominates in most East Asian societies. Women's movements in many Asian metropolitans are just in the infant stage as compared to the long history of women's movements in the West. Rapid economic growth may help to set women free on one hand, but the social changes that break down traditional family ties may increase their burden again on family care. Race and ethnic inequality is also serious in many East Asian countries even though this is largely invisible. For example in Singapore the conflicts between the Chinese, the Indian, and the Malaysian ethnic groups are always an issue of great concern for the government. In Mainland China, the migrant workers moving from rural to urban areas are vulnerable to ethnic discrimination. Similar situations occur in Taiwan where minorities from tribal societies in the mountain area are forced to migrate to the city to find jobs when their land is lost through urbanization and economic expansion. Those cosmopolitan cities such as Tokyo and Hong Kong are not much better. Although claimed to be international cities, they are in lack of culture-sensitive policy to the extent that new arrivals and low-income migrant worker are perennially disadvantaged. These conflicts exist, but remain largely invisible in the past decades. First, as compared to Western societies, East Asian people do not have a strong tradition of individual rights. Democratic movements and other social movements are largely underdeveloped. It is not surprising to see that anti-racist and anti-sexist movements, which are based on the conception of individual liberty, are less developed in East Asian societies. Second, without a democratic tradition, the state in East Asian countries tends to adopt a more high-handed or top-down strategy when conflict rises. This is a typical strategy to suppress social unrests in countries like Mainland China, Singapore, and Korea. Third, the balance of power between the ruling class and the disadvantaged groups are more skewed than that in Western countries. The media, social policies and social services are in a general lack of cultural and gender sensitivity. The "success" of an East Asian welfare model is not built on a truly "harmonious society," but on the success of suppressing the disadvantaged and silencing their voices. In other words, Asian countries were generally quite successful in "harmonizing social inequalities" in past decades. Despite all such strategy, it does not necessarily work. Increasing globalization and economic growth have stimulated demand for democracy and social equality. The widening gap between the rich and the poor, between men and women, and between different ethnic groups are destabilizing factors emerging in many East Asian countries. The only solution to the problem seems to be paying more attention to social policy and restoring social equalities. Dressing up Asia as a harmonious society does not help to solve the problem, but only adds to its current and future social costs.

Rethinking "Productivity"

Another important argument is that the economic success of East Asian countries hinges on a "productivist welfare model" (Holiday, 2000). Briefly, this implies that most welfare policies are production-oriented or economic-led. Social services are provided to backup economic growth. For example, in

Beng Huat Chua's chapter 2, it is argued that social housing in Singapore serves as an anchor for economic development, and similarly, the Japanese government is using housing policy to fuel economic growth. Although many social policy analysts participated in the discussion of an economic-led social policy in Asia, are,in fact, quite uncritical of capitalism as most failed to deconstruct the myth underpinning "productivity" or "economic growth." This limited the critique of the "productivist welfare model" run the risk of further." Neoliberalists would push this argument further to advocate that all welfare services should be economically efficient, contributing to economic growth and discouraging welfare dependency. Laissez-faire economy and a minimal interventionist model is portrayed as the key to success. The cases of Hong Kong and the Special Economic Zones in South China serve as examples of this argument.

To challenge the "productivist model," it is important to deconstruct the discourse of "productivity." What is productive? What is unproductive? By being "productive," what we usually mean concerns a certain kind of output. However, in policy studies, it is always problematic to decide what is or isn't productive. According to traditional economics or what has come to be termed as "GDPism," a worker taking up a full time job is regarded as productive economically, while a mother taking care of her children at home is unproductive. A cook working in the restaurant is productive, while a homemaker cooking at home is unproductive. Discussion in previous chapters has pointed out that speculation in housing has led to a bubble economy that eventually ended up in recession. This happened to Japan in the early 1990s as suggested by Connie Tang's chapter and other East Asian countries such as Hong Kong and Thailand in the late 1990s. Ironically, speculative activities in the financial market or the housing market could be regarded as productive, while all other work outside the labor market such as voluntary work and housework are regarded as unproductive. This is reflected in the classical debate on underclass, welfare dependency, and lone parents. Lone parents on social security are labeled as "welfare dependent" and are being seen as unproductive even though they have to take care of their young children. It has long been argued that classical economics tends to marginalize work outside the capitalist production system. Those working outside the formal labor market are regarded as unproductive. Work performed by low-pay workers are labeled as "unskillful" or "less productive," thereby rationalizing their low remuneration. Consequently, the work of the disadvantaged such as women, new immigrants, ethnic minorities, older workers, young people, and manual workers, are marginalized as less productive. Ngan and others' survey study in chapter 7 suggests that older workers in Hong Kong are often stereotyped as "less productive" or even "lazy," which helps to rationalize the exclusion of older workers from the labor market. Many workers of the disadvantaged groups are forced to work long hours in low-pay jobs, or even no-pay jobs for many women and homemakers. Yet, they are regarded as unproductive. The success of a "productivist welfare model" is largely based on the exploitation of workers at the margin, or underrecognition of their economic contribution.

From another point of view, this "productive welfare model" could be counterproductive. Since it is largely based on marketization, and cut-back, of social service growth, this model may bring about economic growth in the short term. Nonetheless, it creates serious social and economic consequences in the long run. For example, the economic boom before the mid-1990s seems to benefit many East Asian countries. However, the bubble economy that burst in 1997 has brought more problems than many East Asian governments could cope with. This "productivist model" is thus inherently risky. It depends on whether the production system is structurally and economically sound. For example, the age discrimination of older workers in Hong Kong is a form of social construction of the welfare dependency of older workers. On the one hand this wastes valuable human resources of older workers, while on the other hand, it impairs the health and life quality of older people and consequently increases the demand on social services. Another example is the quest for massive production of food which led to epidemic diseases such as SARS, bird flu, and mad cow disease. The unintended consequence of this "productivist model" is sometimes counterproductive. We are not unproductive, rather, we are overproducing and overconsuming, to the extent we are using up scarce resources of the future generations. The emphasis of a productivist approach in welfare is engendering future inequalities, social exclusion, and possibly a welfare crisis.

REINSTATING "SOCIAL" IN SOCIAL POLICY

At the beginning of this book, James Lee distinguished "productivism" from "developmentalism," and challenged the notion of "productivist welfare model" in which economic development and social development are treated as two separate entities. He argued for a "developmental" approach in social welfare as proposed by Midgley (1995) where greater emphasis is placed on the positive integration of economic policy and social policy. The various chapters in this book reveal the limitations of adopting the productivist approach, as well as the oversimplified use of the Confucius concept in analyzing welfare in East Asian societies. Social policies based on the belief of productivism and Confucianism tend to subsume social development under economic development rather than integrating them. There is a fundamental difference in ideology here. An integrative social policy is fundamentally social democratic, seeking a way out to bring capitalist economies under some form of collective control, using statist reforms that are more ambitious and interventionist in nature. However, a subordinate social policy fundamentally reflects a conservative ideology, seeking some kind of "ordered freedom" in social arrangement. Most of the time, such an arrangement is bound to be neoliberal in orientation. Evidences have shown that this strategy or arrangement is ineffective in dealing with thorny social issues such as rapidly aggravating social inequalities, unemployment, and family breakdowns. This concluding chapter highlights the argument that the construction of a successful "East Asian welfare model" is hinged upon a rather fragile and fluid "productivist" concept, wherein associated concepts such as "workfare," "competitiveness," "efficiency," "quality," "social harmony," and "family responsibility" are all supposedly blended to form a new pattern of social development which eventually excludes the new immigrants, the unemployed, and the aged. Though able to capture short-term growth, this mode of development cannot help to forge a balanced and sustainable social policy in the long run. The obsession with "productivity" in East Asian countries reminds us of the discussion of "first modernization" in risk society theory (Beck, 1992), wherein the pursuit of efficiency and high productivity by high growth economies is producing unintended consequences and risks that are beyond normal state capacity to cope both for the current and future generations. In the past decade, the major strategy in policy making in many East Asian countries was seeking to individualize these social risks through the construction of a "productivist ethos" (Beck, 2000). What we try to argue in this book is that the East Asian welfare crisis, if there is one coming, lies not simply in the redistribution of resources and opportunities. It is a crisis of ideology, a crisis of a mind-set that believes in something that doesn't exist, a mythological state that suggests that there is always an East Asian way out! The chapters of this volume fall short of a practical solution, but our hope is that appreciating the true nature of the issue is an important step forward to resolving our future welfare crisis.

REFERENCES

Beck, Ulrich. (1992). *Risk Society: Towards a New Modernity*. London: Sage Publication.

———. (2000). *The Brave New World of Work*. Cambridge and Oxford: Polity Press.

Campos, Jose Edgardo and Root, Hilton L. (1996). *The Key to the Asian Miracle: Making Shared Growth Credible*. Washington DC: The Brookings Institute.

Chua, Beng-Huat. (1997). *Political Legitimacy and Housing: Stakeholding in Singapore*. London and New York: Routledge.

Clarke, John; Gewirtz, Sharon, and McLaughlin, Eugene. (2000). *New Managerialism New Welfare?* London, Thousand Oaks, and New Delhi: Sage Publication and Open University, pp. 1–26.

Fitzpatrick, T. (2005). *New Theories of Welfare*. London: Palgrave.

Giddens, Anthony. (1998). *The Third Way: The Renewal of Social Democracy*. UK: Polity Press.

Goodman, Roger; White, Gordon, and Kwon, Huck-ju, (1998). *The East Asian Welfare Model: Welfare Orientalism and the State*. London and New York: Routledge.

Gough, Ian. (2004). "East Asia: The Limits of Productivist Regimes." In Gough, Ian and Wood, Geof (eds.) *Insecurity and Welfare Regimes in Asia, Africa, and Latin America: Social Policy in Development Contexts*. Cambridge: Cambridge University Press, pp.169–201.

Holiday, Ian. (2000). "Productivist Welfare Capitalism: Social Policy in East Asia." *Political Studies*, 48, pp. 706–23.

Holiday, Ian and Wilding, Paul. (2003). "Welfare Capitalism in the Tiger Economics of East and Southeast Asia." In Holiday, Ian and Wilding, Paul (eds.) *Welfare Capitalism in East Asia: Social Policy in the Tiger Economies*. London and New York: Palgrave Macmillan, pp.1–17.

Jones, Catherine. (1993). "The Pacific Challenge: Confucius Welfare States." In Jones, C. (ed.) *New Perspectives on the Welfare State in Europe*. London: Routledge, pp.198–217.

Kristol, I. (1995). *Neoconservatism: The Autobiography of an Idea*. New York: Free Press.

Midgley, James. (1995). *Social Development*. London: Sage.

Midgley, James and Tang, Kwong-leung. (2001). "Social Policy, Economic Growth and Developmental Welfare." *International Journal of Social Welfare*, 10(4), pp. 244–52.

Ramesh, M. (2000). *Welfare Capitalism in Southeast Asia: Social Security, Health, and Education Policies*. New York: Palgrave.

Walker, Alan and Wong, Chack-kie. (2005). *East Asian Welfare Regimes in Transition: From Confucianism to Globalization*. Bristol: The Policy Press.

Index

abortion, 63, 64, 66
AFL Cannery Workers Union, 117, 120nn9–10
Africa, 21, 78n11
L'Agnese va a morire (Viganò), 41, 49nn18–19, 77n7
agricultural labor, 4, 26–27n4, 35–36, 37, 47n5. *See also* mondine
Albania, 21
Alberti, Margherita Di Fazio, 56
Alle risaiole, 46
American Federation of Labor Cannery Workers Union, 117, 120nn9–10
Le amiche, 1–2
"Among Women Alone" (Pavese), 1
Andiamo a spasso (Viarengo), 78n14
antifascism, 16, 38
Antonioni, Michelangelo, 1–2
Arbizzani, Luigi, 38
Are Italians White? (Guglielmo and Salerno), 88
Argentina, 21
Aristarco, Guido, 45
Asia, 78n11
assimilation: and detachment from past alliances, 113, 114, 117; in *The Godfather,* 82; in *Household Saints,* 98, 99–100, 101, 102–104; of Italian American immigrants, 88, 105n9, 105n11, 111; in *Tarantella,* 94, 97; in *Westward the Women,* 115
Australia, 21

Baker, Aaron, 98, 99, 100, 105
Bakhtin, Mikhail, 17–18, 30n23, 30n25
Barbieri, Remigio, 48n10
Baron, Ava, 5, 6
"Bella ciao," 40, 49n17
Birnbaum, Lucia Chiavola, 9, 38, 78n10
Bitter Rice, 39, 45–46, 50n27
Blood Brothers, 87
Bolivia, 21, 68
Bona, Mary Jo, 83
Bono, Paolo, 66
Bortolotti, Franca Pieroni, 48n7
Bossi, Umberto, 78n13
Bound by Distance (Verdicchio), 19, 21
Braidotti, Rosi, 22, 32n31
Brazil, 21
A Bronx Tale, 87

California: cannery workers in, 110, 111, 112–13, 116–17; immigrants from northern Italy in, 120n7; immigrants relocation to, for

agricultural employment, 116. *See also* San Diego
Calvino, Italo, 44, 49n24, 50n28
Canada, 21
Candelora, Giorgio, 26–27n4
Cannery and Agricultural Workers Industrial Union, 117
cannery workers, 110–11, 112–13, 116–17
Cape Verde, 21
capitalism, 4, 13–14, 57
Capra, Frank, 115
Carlini, Giuliano, 54, 69–70, 73, 74, 79n16
Casalinghe di riserva (Turrini), 67
Castellani, Giuliana, 21
Centro Italiano femminile, 78n10
Cgil (Italian General Confederation of Labor), 33–34, 47n1, 79n16
Chase, David, 89
China, 21
Chohra, Nassera, 78n14
Christian Democratic Party (DC), 78n10
Cialente, Fausta, 39
Clark, Donald Martin, 31n29
Clark, Martin, 30–31n26
class: effect on acceptance of immigrants, 4; privileging of, over race in labor histories, 4, 8; relationship to language, 17–18, 30n23
Codrignani, Giancarla, 65
Cohen, Miriam, 26–27n4, 85
Colombi, Marchesa, 39, 45, 46, 48n14, 50n28
common sense: as the basis for cultural identity, 16; emphasis of, in *Household Saints,* 98, 99, 101; folklore *versus,* 29n18; good sense *versus,* 15, 109; role in creating a counter-hegemony, 16, 105n6, 109. *See also* folklore
Confetti for Gino (Madalena), 120n3
Cookbook of Happiness (Petronius), 51, 54, 57–60, 77n4
Coppola, Francis Ford, 82, 89–94, 106n14, 106n17, 106–7n22

Cornelisen, Ann, 48n8
Coro delle mondine, 34, 39–40, 46
counter-hegemony: common sense and, 16, 105n6, 109; definition of, 29n15; everyday experiences and, 14, 16, 26, 109, 119, 125; folklore and, 16, 46, 54–55, 119; language and, 17–18, 30n23; organic intellectuals and, 119; subalterns and, 17, 19, 30n23, 54–55, 60, 119, 125
Crisantino, Amelia, 54, 69–73, 79n16
cryptoethnic, as a term, 104n2
culture. *See* counter-hegemony; international popular culture; national popular culture

Daffini, Giovanna, 49n17
Davis, John A., 27n4
De Grazia, Victoria, 38
de Lauretis, Teresa, 10, 11, 83
de Michiel, Helen, 82–83, 94–98, 103–104, 106–107n22
Demme, Jonathan, 89, 107n23
DePalma, Brian, 89
De Santis, Giuseppe, 39, 45–46, 50n27
De Sica, Vittorio, 60
di Leonardo, Micaela, 84
Diotima Community, 51
Dirt in the Face (Carlini), 54, 69–71, 73, 74, 79n16
Di Scala, Spencer M., 20, 26–27n4
discrimination. *See* racism
Distributive, Processing, and Office Workers of America, 117
domestic labor: absence of, from labor histories, 4; as gendered labor, 4, 56, 57; low monetary and symbolic value give to, 53; as one of few types of employment open to women immigrants, 21, 25, 68, 75. *See also* unwaged domestic labor
domestic workers: immigrant women as, and the entrance of middle-class Italian-born women into professional careers, 76; influence on the creation of culture, 16, 52–55, 75; isolation

of, 51–52; lack of private space allotted to, 62; low value given to the labor of, 74; marginalization of, within publications, 68; migration and, 57; occupation of private and public space, 54, 57–58, 59–60, 74–75; use of creative representations as acts of liberation, 52; women of color as, 25, 32n33, 67–68
Le donne di casa Gramsci (Paulesu), 11

Egypt, 21
emigration from Italy, 20, 24, 30–31n26, 104n4, 120n7
Empire (Hardt and Negri), 26n3
Eritrea, 21
Ethiopia, 21
ethnicity, role of, 4, 7, 111, 113–114, 119
Ets, Marie Hall, 104n5
everyday experiences: in *Household Saints*, 82; role in the creation of a counter-hegemony, 14, 15, 26, 110, 119, 125; in *Tarantella*, 82, 95, 96, 97, 98
Ewen, Elizabeth, 7
extracomunitari, 21, 31n28, 78n12. *See also* immigrants

fascism, labor protests against, 16, 38
Fatalità (Negri), 39
female rice workers. *See* mondine
Filipino American cannery workers, 116
folklore, 16, 29n18, 46, 54, 119, 124–125. *See also* common sense
food in Italian American cinema, 81, 92–93, 95, 96, 106n15
Fordism, 13, 14, 53
Forgacs, David, 29n20
The Fortunate Pilgrim (Puzo), 93
Forty Days, Forty Nights (Lajolo), 39
France, 5
Fraser, Nancy, 59
From Wiseguys to Wise Men (Gardaphè), 104n3

gangster films: absence of women's labor in, 82, 91, 92–93; gangsters as Italian American in, 106n16; male bonding in, 106n17; representation of gangsters as cooks in, 81, 82–83, 91–92; rhetoric of nostalgia and, 81–82, 87, 88–89, 93–94
Gardaphè, Fred L., 93, 104n3
Gardiner, Michael, 30n23
Gedaf, Irene, 32n31
Ghana, 21, 68
Gilbert, Sandra Mortola, 81
Ginzburg, Natalia, 50n28, 60
Girlfriends, 1–2
Giuseppe De Santis (Vitti), 45
Gluck, Sherna Berger, 6
The Godfather, 82, 89–94, 106n14, 106n17, 106–107n22
Goodfellas, 81, 91–92, 93, 106n15
good sense, 15, 86, 99, 109
Gramsci, Antonio: as co-founder of the Italian Communist Party and *L'Unità*, 8; on common sense, 15, 105n6, 109; correspondence with his wife and sister-in-law, 10–11, 13; on the creation of a counter-hegemony (*see* counter-hegemony); on the creation of a national popular culture (*see* national popular culture); death of, 9; desire for a new kind of masculine and feminine character, 12–14; discussion of Fordism, 13, 14, 53; education of, 8; on everyday experiences, 14, 15, 110, 119, 124–125; on film, 105n7; on folklore, 16, 46, 54–55, 119, 125; on good sense, 15, 109; imprisonment of, 8–9, 10; influence of the Gramsci sisters on, 11; involvement in the Italian Socialist Party, 8; on language, 17, 18, 30n23; *Letters from Prison,* 9; on national popular, 17, 30n22; omission of female migrant labor from alliance-making process, 10; on organic intellectuals, 17, 19, 109, 119, 124–125; *Prison*

Notebooks, 9, 12, 13; on sexuality in the production of capital and culture, 10, 52; *The Southern Question,* 9, 21–22, 109, 124; on subalterns (*see* subalterns); use of the term "war of position," 29n20; view of women, 11–12
Gramsci and Italy's Passive Revolution (Davis), 26–27n4
Gramsci Notwithstanding, 11
Green, Nancy L., 83
Greenberg, Jaclyn, 116–117
Gualandi, Irea, 37, 38, 41, 47n1, 47n6
Guglielmo, Jennifer, 88, 114
Guglielmo, Thomas A., 105n11
Gutman, Herbert, 7

Habermas, Jurgen, 59
Hall, Stuart, 29n20
Hardt, Michael, 26n3
hegemony. *See* counter-hegemony
Holub, Renate, 10, 11, 14, 18
homosexuality, 28–29n14
Ho trovato l'occidente (Crisantino), 54, 69–73, 79n16
Household Saints, 83, 98–104, 107n24, 107n25
Huston, John, 89
How Fascism Ruled Women (De Grazia), 38
Hutcheon, Linda, 104n2

If Eight Hours Seem Too Few (Zappi), 35
immigrants: acceptance of, 3–4; exclusion and isolation of, 70, 74–75; racism against, 24, 70–73, 75–76; as workers in California's agricultural industry, 113, 116–117, 120n7. *See also* immigrant women; Italian American immigrants; Italian American women
immigrant women: autobiographical narratives of, 68–69; as cannery workers, 110–111, 112–113, 119; creation of an international popular culture, 73–74, 76; lack of cross-immigrant alliances between, 71, 73; racism against, 24, 71–73, 75–76; rearticulation of racist discourse of the dominant culture, 71–72; types of employment open to, 21, 25, 68, 75. *See also* domestic workers; Italian American women
Immigrant Women in the Land of Dollars (Ewen), 7
immigration to Italy, 21, 31n28, 31–32n29, 68, 78n11
In risaia (Colombi), 39, 46, 48n14
international popular culture, 19, 55, 73–74, 76, 98
In the Rice Field (book: Colombi), 39, 46, 48n14
In the Rice Fields (pamphlet), 46
I promessi sposi (Manzoni), 56
Iran, 21
Italianamerican, 106n15
Italian American immigrants: cinematic representations of, and the rhetoric of nostalgia, 83–89; and whiteness (*see* assimilation: of Italian American immigrants). *See also* Italian American women
Italian American women: assimilation into mainstream, dominant culture, 105n9; as cannery workers, 112–113; changing roles of, 87–88, 105n9; cinematic portrayal of, as outside of labor, 82, 85, 86, 89, 94; in *Household Saints,* 82–83, 98–104; lack of historical information about labor contributions of, 83–84; in *Tarantella,* 82–83, 94–98, 107. *See also* Italian American immigrants
Italian General Confederation of Labor (Cgil), 33–34, 47n1, 79n16
Italian rice workers. *See* mondine
Italian Socialist Party (PSI): formation of, 35; membership, 8; women's leagues organized by, 36, 48n7
Italian Communist Party (PCI): 43, 45; Gramsci's help in formation of, 8;

position on abortion, 64, 66; representation of, in *Una storia di ragazze,* 66

Italy: constitution of, 2; emigration from, 20–21, 24, 30–31n26, 104n4, 120n7; entrance of middle-class Italian-born women into professional careers, 75–76; exclusion and isolation of immigrants to, from middle-class identity, 69–70, 74–75; immigration to, 20–21, 31n28, 31–32n29, 68, 78n11; internal migration in, 20–21, 24, 31n27, 35–36, 38, 78n13; legalization of abortion, 63; marginal status of women in the dominant culture of, 68; as outside the borders of the first world, 3, 26n3; as predominantly peasant-based at the end of World War II, 26n3; racism against immigrants in, 24, 70–73, 75–76; racism against southern Italians by northern Italians, 21, 24, 78n13; women's right to vote in, 5, 49n22, 78n10. *See also* domestic labor; domestic workers; mondine

I've Discovered the West (Crisantino), 54, 69–73, 79n16

Japanese American cannery workers, 113, 117
Jewish immigrant women, 7

Kemp, Sandra, 66
Krieger, Bob, 24, 32n32
Kroha, Lucienne, 46, 50n28

labor histories: absence of women from, 4–8, 112–114; exclusion of agricultural labor from, 4, 26–27n4, 35–36, 37, 47n5; lack of discussion about domestic labor in, 4; lack of recognition of the roles of race and ethnicity by, 4, 6, 7, 114; marginal status of cannery workers within, 110–111; revisionist approaches to, 4–5

labor protests, 9–10, 16, 28n10, 33, 35, 36–37
Lajolo, Davide, 39, 45
Lakhous, Amara, 78–79n14
Landy, Marcia, 10, 13–16, 55
Latino cannery workers, 111, 112, 114–115
Leaving Little Italy (Gardaphè), 93
Le mondine (Viganò), 41, 48n13
LeRoy, Mervyn, 106n16
Letters from Prison (Gramsci), 9
Liberazione delle donne (Birnbaum), 38
Little Caesar, 106n16
Lollobrigida, Gina, 23
Loren, Sophia, 23
Lowe, Lisa, 16, 68

Mac, 87
Madalena, Lorenzo, 120n3
"Mafioso" (Gilbert), 81
magical realism, 102
MAID in the U.S.A (Romero), 25
Mangano, Silvana, 23, 45
Mangione, Jerre, 84, 87–88
Manzoni, Alessandro, 56
Margotti, Maria: death of, 33–34, 41, 44–45, 47n1, 47n4; as a historical figure, 40, 43–45, 46
marionettes, 95–96
Martinez, Thomas, 110, 111, 112, 113, 114–115, 119
marxism, 4, 8
Mazza, Maria, 24, 25
Mechling, Jay, 116
Meluschi, Antonio, 41, 42–43
Mendez, Denny, 24, 25, 32n32
Mexican American cannery workers, 111, 112, 114–115
Middle East, 78n11
migration. *See* emigration from Italy; immigration to Italy
Mirigliani, Enzo, 24
Miss Italia pageant of 1996, 23, 25
mobster films. *See* gangster films

Modern Italy (Clark), 30–31n26
Modotti, Tina, 15, 26, 123–124, 125
Mohanty, Chandra Talpade, 7, 27n6
Mondariso, 40
mondine: creative and critical texts about, 39, 41–42, 45, 46; definition of, 47n2; diversity among, 36, 37; formation of a counter-hegemonic national popular culture, 34–35, 39–40, 44–45, 47; lack of coverage in labor histories about, 34–35, 36, 47n5; organized group protests of, 10, 28n10, 33, 35, 36–38; paintings and photographs of, 39, 48n13; as seasonal migrants, 35–36, 38; symbolic link to all underrepresented people, 34, 43–44, 46; tradition of singing, 16, 34, 39–40. *See also* Margotti, Maria
Le mondine (Viganò), 41, 39–43, 48n13
Montanari, Otello, 35–36, 37
Morocco, 21
Morreale, Ben, 84, 87–88
motherhood, unwed, 15, 61, 64–65, 66, 77–78n9
Murphy, Timothy S., 19
Mussolini, Benito, 8, 9, 28–29n14, 38

national popular, 17, 30n22
national popular culture: dependency on language, 17–19, 30n23; establishment of a, in *Tarantella,* 83, 95, 96, 98; participation of the mondine in the formation of, 34, 39–40, 44–45, 47; potential of domestic workers to create a, 53, 54–55, 73–74; production of, by subaltern classes, 9, 15, 16–17, 52, 86, 119; representations of the operations of, in *Household Saints,* 83, 103; use of visual representations to create, 110, 114–115
Negri, Ada, 39, 48n12
Negri, Antonio, 26n3
Noce, Teresa, 38

Noi donne, 39, 41, 61, 77n6, 77n9, 78n10
Nomadic Subjects (Braidotti), 22
nomadism, 22–23, 32n31
Nonostante Gramsci, 11
nostalgia, rhetoric of, 83–89, 91, 93, 94, 97

oral narratives, 22, 68–69, 73–74, 76
organic intellectuals: in *Household Saints,* 82–83; role in the development of an alternative national popular culture, 17, 19, 109, 119, 124–125; in *Tarantella,* 82–83, 95, 96, 97

Palazzi, Maura, 56, 76
Parati, Graziella, 78–79n14
Paterlini, Marco, 35, 47n6
Paulesu, Mimma, 11
Pavese, Cesare, 1
Petronius, 51, 54
Philippines, 21
photographs: as a political tool, 123, 124, 125; use of, to create a national popular culture, 109, 113–114
Picarazzi, Teresa, 22, 70, 79n17
Pileggi, Nicholas, 91, 104n1
Portuguese American cannery workers, 113, 117
Prison Notebooks (Gramsci), 9, 12, 13
private spaces and public spaces: domestic workers inhabitation of, 54, 57–58, 59–60, 74–75; *Household Saints'* critique of, 98, 99–100; relationship between, 15, 94, 124
PSI. See Italian Socialist Party (PSI)
Pucci, Idanna, 104n5
Puzo, Mario, 89, 94

Quaderni dal carcere (Gramsci), 9, 12, 13
Quando saremo a Reggio Emilia (Paterlini), 35, 47n6
Quaranta giorni, quaranta notti (Lajolo), 39
Quasi, Annarella, 48n10

race: effect on acceptance of immigrants, 3–4; effect on internal migration within postwar Italy, 3; lack of recognition of the role of, by labor histories, 4–8, 109–110
racism: against immigrants in Italy, 24, 70–73, 75–76; rearticulation of dominant culture's discourse of, by minority classes, 71–72; against southern Italians by northern Italians, 20, 24, 78n13
Ready-to-Wear and Ready-to-Work (Green), 83
Red Week, 10, 28n10
Reich, Jacqueline, 86, 103
rhetoric of nostalgia, 82–89, 91, 93, 94, 97
Riccettario della felicità (Petronius), 51, 54, 58–59, 77n4
Riccò, Gianfranco, 35–36, 37
rice workers. *See* mondine
Riso amaro, 39, 45–46, 50n27
Rivolta femminile group, 9
Roediger, David R., 8, 28n9, 114, 118, 119
Romania, 21
Romero, Mary, 25, 54, 62
Rosa, the Life of an Italian Immigrant (Ets), 104n5
Rosie the Riveter Revisited (Gluck), 6

Salerno, Salvatore, 88
San Diego, 111–112, 114. *See also* California
Sarti, Raffaela, 56
Sasson, Anne Showstack, 10, 14–15, 29n20
Sautman, Francesca Canadé, 86–87, 92
Savoca, Nancy, 83, 98–104, 107nn23–25
Scansance, Vasco, 49n17
Schucht, Julia, 10–12
Schucht, Tatiana, 10–11
Scontro di civiltà per un ascensore a piazza Vittorio (Lakhous), 78–79n14

Scorsese, Catherine, 106n15
Scorsese, Martin, 82, 89, 91, 93, 106n15
Scott, Joan, 1, 2–3, 4, 6
Senegal, 21
sexuality, role of, 4, 9, 13-14, 53, 55
single motherhood, 15, 63–66, 77–78n9
Socialismo e questione femminile (Bortolotti), 48n7
Soja, Edward, 93, 106n18
The Sopranos, 89
The Southern Question (Gramsci), 9, 21–22, 109, 124
speech genres, 17–18, 30n24
Sraffa, Piero, 10
Sri Lanka, 21
Stam, Robert, 84–85
Starr, Kevin, 118
States of Grace (Clark), 31n29
stereotypes of Italian Americans, 82, 86–87, 88, 89, 94, 96, 97
Storia dell'Italia moderna (Candelora), 26–27n4
Una storia di ragazze (Viganò), 15, 54, 60–66
La Storia (Mangione and Morreale), 84
Le storiche, 6–7
A Story About Girls (Viganò), 15, 54, 60–66
subalterns: ability to create a counter-hegemony, 17, 19, 30n23, 53, 59–60, 118–119, 124–125; alliances between, 26, 41, 110; definition of, 9; relationship between organic intellectuals and, 124–125; role in developing a national popular culture, 9, 14–17, 52, 83, 118–119

Tarantella, 82–83, 94–98, 103–104, 106–107n22
La terra in faccia (Carlini), 54, 69–70, 73, 74, 79n16
testimonials of immigrant women, 22, 68–69, 73–74, 76
thirdspace, 93, 106n18

Ti ho sposato per allegria (Ginzburg), 60
Tommasi, Wanda, 51–53, 76n1
Tra cronaca, storia, e testimonianza (Gualandi), 47n6
"Tra donne sole" (Pavese), 1
The Trials of Maria Barbella (Pucci), 104n5
True Love, 107n23
Tunisia, 21
Turrini, Olda, 67–68

UDI (Unione donne italiane), 66, 78n10
Ukraine, 21, 68
Umberto D, 60
"Under Western Eyes" (Mohanty), 7, 27n6
Unione donne italiane (UDI), 66, 78n10
unions, 117–118, 120nn9–10
L'Unità, 8, 39, 41
United States: domestic labor in, 25; immigration to, from Italy, 20–21, 31n28, 104n4, 120n7. *See also* California; Italian American immigrants; Italian American women; San Diego
unwaged domestic labor: in *Household Saints,* 98; in *Tarantella,* 94, 95
unwed motherhood, 15, 61, 64–65, 66, 77–78n9

Verdicchio, Pasquale, 19, 21–22, 112, 123, 124
"Viaggio in risaia" (Cialente), 39
Viarengo, Maria, 78n14
Viganò, Renata: *L'Agnese va a morire,* 41, 49nn18–19, 77n7; creation of Margotti as a historical figure, 40, 43–44; linking of the mondine to all underrepresented people, 44–46; *Le mondine,* 39–43, 48n13; personal history and political activism of, 41–45, 61, 77n5; on single motherhood, 77–78n9; *Una storia di ragazze,* 15, 54, 60–66; writing of, as part of a national popular culture, 35, 46–47

Vitti, Antonio, 45
Vitullo, Julian, 98, 99, 100, 105
Volevo diventare bianca (Chohra), 78n14
"Voyage in the Rice Fields" (Cialente), 39

Wages of Whiteness (Roediger), 8, 114
war of position, 29n20
Wellman, William, 110, 115–116
Weston, Edward, 123
Westward the Women, 110, 115–116
White on Arrival (Guglielmo), 105n11
wiseguy. *See* gangster films
Wiseguy (Pileggi), 91, 104n1
women: absence of, from labor histories, 4–6, 7, 119; of color as domestic workers, 24–25, 32n33, 67–68; Gramsci's description of a new type of, 13; immigration to Italy, 21; independence of wives of migrating men, 36, 48n8; labor as a mode of expression and independence for, 1–2; limitations on involvement of, in labor protests, 36–37; marginal status of, in dominant Italian culture, 69; right to vote, 5, 49n22, 78n10; role in the formation of culture as subalterns, 9. *See also* domestic workers; immigrant women; Italian American women; mondine
The Women of Gramsci's Home (Paulesu), 11
women rice workers. *See* mondine
The Women Rice Workers (Viganò), 39–43, 48n13
The Women Writer in Late-Nineteenth Century Italy, 46
Work Engendered (Baron), 5
working classes. *See* subalterns
Workshop to Office (Cohen), 26–27n4, 85
World War II, 5, 38, 40–41, 43–44

Zappi, Elda Gentili, 10, 35, 36, 37, 47n6

About the Contributors

Kam-wah Chan is Associate Professor at the Hong Kong Polytechnic University. He specializes in the teaching and research of social policy, with particular emphasis on gender and ethnic minority issues. His representative publication includes *Social Construction of Gender Inequality in the Housing System* (Ashgate 1997)

Jacky Chau-Kiu Cheung is Associate Professor at the City University of Hong Kong. He has written works on civic participation, community integration, quality of life, organizational commitment, success and reputation, delinquency, youth development, academic achievement, and service effectiveness. His current research addresses issues of distress, acculturation and adaptation, social capital and cohesion, and intergenerational relationship.

Wen-Chi Grace Chou is Associate Professor of labor and gender studies at National Chung-Cheng University. Her research interests include comparative employment policy for ageing, young, and women people, as well as gender equality at work. Her recent publications include *Women in Asian Management* (2006 Routledge); *Labour in a Global World: The Case of White Goods* (2005 Palgrave).

Ho Lup Fung is formerly Associate Professor at the Chinese University of Hong Kong. He specializes in community development, China social policy, and Hong Kong politics. His recent publication includes 'The right of abode issue: a test case of One Country and Two Systems' in Wong, Y. (ed) *One Country, Two Systems in Crisis* (2004 Lexington)

Ping Kong Kam is Associate Professor at the City University of Hong Kong. He specializes in social work teaching and research. He publishes widely in social policy, community development, and macro social work practice. He co-edited four books: *Community Work: Theory and Practice* (1994 Chinese University Press), *Skills in Community Work*, (1997 CUHK Press), *Analysis of Housing Policy in Hong Kong*, (1997 Joint-Publishing), *Hold on to your faith* (2006 CityU Press).

James Lee is Associate Professor at the City University of Hong Kong. He specializes in teaching and research in comparative housing and social policy. He is a founder of the Asian Pacific Network of Housing Research. His more recent publications includes: *Housing, Home Ownership and Social Change in Hong Kong* (1999 Ashgate) and *Housing and Social Change: East West Perspectives* (2003 Routledge).

Lai Ching Leung is Associate Professor at the City University of Hong Kong. Her research interests are in gender studies, social policy and social work. She is the author of *Lone Mothers, Social Security and the Family in Hong Kong* (Ashgate, 1998) and the first editor of *Gender and Social Work* (Chinese University Press, 2006). Her recent publication: 'Reflective practices: challenges to social work education in Hong Kong' *Social Work Education* (2007).

Wan I. Lin is Professor of Social Work at the National Taiwan University. He publishes widely on Taiwan social policy, housing policy, family policy, and social administration. His publications include'Labor Movement and Taiwan's Belated Welfare State' *Journal of International and Comparative Social Welfare*, 7 (1&2), 31-44; and'The Structural Determinants of Welfare Efforts in Taiwan.' *International Social Work*, 34(2),171-190.

Raymond Man Hung Ngan is Associate Professor at the City University of Hong Kong. He concentrates his research in social security, pension reform and long term care. His work has appeared in international journals: *Social Development Issues, International Journal of Social Welfare, Social Security & Guangdong Social Insurance Bulletin.*

Tetsuo Ogawa is Associate Professor of Public Policy, Chiba University, Japan. He concentrates his research on ageing under such international agencies as UN. His recent publications include 'Inter-generational Equity and Social Solidarity: Japan's Search for an Integrated Policy on Ageing.' in Maltby, T. (eds), *Ageing Matters: European Policy Lessons from the East.*

Kyeung Mi Oh is the Executive Coordinator for the WHO Collaborating Center at the School of Nursing, George Mason University. She did research in health information needs of Korean immigrants for cancer prevention Her recent publication includes 'Implications of Population Ageing in East Asia-An Analysis of Social Protection and Social Policy Reforms in Japan, Korea and Taiwan' (2004).

Connie P. Y. Tang is a Research Fellow at the Oxford Institute for Sustainable Development at the Oxford Brookes University. She previously worked as a housing researcher in Center for Housing Research at the University St Andrew, Scotland. She also specializes in Japan housing policy

Ya Peng Zhu is Associate Professor of the School of Government, Zhongshan University, China. He specializes in China's housing reform and monetarization policy since 1979. His recent publication includes *Housing Policy and Housing Reform in China* (2007)

Chyong Fang Ko is Research Fellow at the Academia Sinica, Taiwan. She specializes in sociology and applied demography. Her recent research include: 'The subjective well-being and self-rated health of the elderly in EU'; 'Attitudes toward geriatric care and family formation' and 'Globalization and the agglomeration of foreign firms in Taipei'.

Sam Wai-Kam Yu is Assistant Professor at the Hong Kong Baptist University. He teaches Social Research and Social Policy. His research interests include: social exclusion, the historical approach towards social welfare and comparative social security. His recent publications include 'Pension Reforms in Urban China and Hong Kong' published in *Ageing and Society*.